D0843177

THE GLOBAL PHARMACEUTICAL INDUSTRY

THE GLOBAL PHARMACEUTICAL INDUSTRY

ECONOMIC STRUCTURE, GOVERNMENT REGULATION, AND HISTORY

HANK LASKEY

Library of Congress Control Number: 2017917072
ISBN: Hardcover   978-1-5434-6349-1
               Softcover   978-1-5434-6350-7
               eBook   978-1-5434-6351-4

Print information available on the last page.

Rev. date: 11/08/2019

To order additional copies of this book, contact:
Xlibris
1-888-795-4274
www.Xlibris.com
Orders@Xlibris.com
712177

TABLE OF CONTENTS

ABOUT THE AUTHOR

Hank A. Laskey, Ph.D., retired as Assistant Dean of the Silberman College of Business and Academic Director of the MBA program in Pharmaceutical-Chemical Studies at Fairleigh Dickinson University in Teaneck, New Jersey, in 2003. He has also held faculty positions at Bloomsburg University, Clemson University, Dekalb College, Florida International University, the University of Georgia, and Western Michigan University. He has been a Visiting Professor at INCAE (Instituto Centroamericano De Administracion De Empresas) in Alajuela, Costa Rica, and Kaunus University of Technology in Panevezys, Lithuania. He has presented lectures and seminars at the University of Quebec at Montreal, Canada, and Queensland University of Technology in Brisbane, Australia, among others.

Dr. Laskey has taught specialized courses for Bayer, Johnson & Johnson, Motorola, and Schering-Plough. He has served as a consultant to Pfizer, Upjohn, and Whitehall Laboratories, as well as the World Trade Center, and the United States Agency for International Development (USAID). Prior to his career in academia, Dr. Laskey held positions in the Office of Applied Technology of the Container Division of the Joseph Schlitz Brewing Co., in the Synthetic Fabrics Division of J.P. Stevens & Co., and at the Hunt-Wesson Foods Savannah Refinery.

During his 30+ years as an educator, Dr. Laskey has published research articles on topics related to brand management, international business, and advertising effectiveness in such journals as the *Journal of Global Marketing, Journal of Advertising, Journal of Advertising Research, International Journal of Bank Marketing, International Journal of Advertising, Journal of Promotion Management, Academia, International Review of Retail, Distribution, and Consumer Research, Benefits Quarterly, Journal of Insurance Issues and Practices, Journal of Segmentation in Marketing, Journal of Applied Business Research, Journal of Travel Research, Journal of Business and Industrial Marketing, Journal of Hospitality and Leisure Marketing*, and the *Journal of Marketing Channels.*

Dr. Laskey holds a Bachelor of Science degree in Chemistry and a Master of Science degree in Management (Operations Research) from Clemson University, where he was a J. E. Sirrine Foundation fellow. He holds a Ph.D. degree in Marketing from the University of Georgia, with concentrations in both Social Psychology, and Risk Management and Insurance (Pensions and Benefits). Dr. Laskey has been happily married to Dr. Rachel E. Laskey for more than 40 years. They have had two beautiful children, Chris and Jenny, and a wonderful grandson, Erik.

PROLOGUE

A "global" anything, such as the global pharmaceutical industry, involves by definition a multiplicity of perspectives, points of view, and belief systems. Alternative belief systems sometimes employ different concepts and different terminologies to argue different interpretations of events. This reality has implications for industry structure, foreign direct investment, regime and institutional stability, regulatory compliance, political and corporate governance systems.

A book that combines the study of business and the conventional "disciplines" of business such as marketing, production-operations, personnel management, cost accounting, corporate finance, and so forth—as they apply in a global or international, business context—with the study of medicine, science, and technology, together with the details and broad implications of this very specialized area of scientific endeavor in a worldwide context, is a difficult and complex undertaking. The level of sophistication that has developed in each of these areas and others can make their individual study a challenge, and expertise in any one of them can command the highest of salaries in the global marketplace.

This book concerns not only what is still referred to as "bench chemistry," i.e., the micro-world of scientific inquiry, but also the macro-world of large-scale (some would say enormous-scale) chemical engineering projects, combined petrochemical, process chemical, and biochemical operations, including biotechnology, and integrated, world-class production facilities, together with their related distribution and marketing organizations. The book not only concerns medicine (pharmaceuticals or drugs) and the treatment of disease at the very personal level of the individual human being, but also at the level of national and international policy, national health care systems, and various world health care organizations. Furthermore, the book covers the evolution over many decades, even centuries, of corporate organizations, institutions, national economies, and diverse markets in many different countries of the world.

REFLECTIONS

In the process of embarking upon an all-encompassing work such as this, I sometimes felt like Andrew Shonfield, when in 1965 he wrote his classic text on modern capitalism (*Modern Capitalism: The Changing Balance of Public and Private Power*) and questioned what had led him to consider writing such a work in the first place. As it did to him, I too have been struck by the realization that to take on such a project and comprehensively describe its subject matter would require more knowledge of a detailed and varied character than any single person is likely to accumulate. Yet, also like him, I frequently have been left with "a faint, though unmistakable, sense of dissatisfaction" (Shonfield 1965, p. xvii) with the only other alternative being to collect a number of experts from around the world and obtain from each a section on their own respective, individual and specialized areas of expertise.

PRIOR WORKS

There have been a number of important texts compiled on multiple, complex dimensions of the chemical and pharmaceutical industries in this alternative, collaborative manner. In particular, Professor Ralph Landau, who has been associated with both Harvard and Stanford universities and received the coveted Perkin Medal for his contributions to the chemical industry in 1973, has edited insightful texts with a number of co-authors on the importance of the chemical industry to long-term economic growth (1988), and on the nature and importance of pharmaceutical innovation (1999). While these and other such works contain a great deal of valuable information and analysis, they do not comport with Andrew Shonfield's or my own preferences as readers for the "unitary, though partial, vision of a grand scheme by a single pair of eyes." Generally, single-author works and grand schemes have appealed to me personally more than compiled and edited multi-author manuscripts. It is certain, however, that along with many other such authors, Professor Landau understood the nature of the problem himself, as his own words in the following quotation so aptly demonstrate:

> *Since joining the community of professional economists, I have been able to commit myself to attending conferences, workshops, and seminars; to writing papers; and to co-editing books. I became convinced that a book that would bring together academic economic inquiry and real world experience would be of great value for scholars and practitioners alike.*
>
> *It quickly became clear to me, some years ago, that no one person had the expertise and background*

necessary to write the sort of book I had in mind, a volume that would combine an insider's knowledge of economics, the chemical industry, business history, social history, issues such as finance and the environment - and moreover address these topics in a way that would do justice to the experiences of the United States, Britain, Germany, and Japan over the last 150 years. But fortunately the editors were able to form a team with collective capabilities to take on this project. (Arora, Landau, and Rosenberg 1998, p. viii)

Certainly many more years of painstaking research and analysis would be required for a single-authorship than for any such multi-authored work. Nevertheless, the text on the worldwide chemical and pharmaceutical industries by Kurt Lanz (1978), ex-chairman of German chemical and pharmaceutical giant Hoechst AG (now part of Aventis); the compiled history of strategic and organizational changes at the British giant, Imperial Chemical Industries (ICI), by Professor Andrew M. Pettigrew (1985); the history of the international chemical industry, written in French by renowned industry executive Fred Aftalion and meticulously translated into English by O. T. Benfey (1991); the text on chemicals and allied products (plus several related industry groups, including SIC codes 26, 28, 29 and 30), by Professor Philip J. Chenier (1992), and the formidable text on multinational pharmaceutical companies and their practices by Professor Bert Spilker (1994), all served as inspirations that I might be able to do a decent job of it myself. Each of these books presents a consistency of perspective and method of expression that I much prefer, as did Shonfield.

The Context of Political Economics

In the overall scheme of things, one single-authored text on the pharmaceutical industry stands out among the rest in terms of its well-researched, frank, and authoritative discussion of what remains in my view the most sensitive of all issues facing this and other industries. The book, *The Pharmaceutical Industry and Dependency in the Third World,* by Duke University professor Gary Gereffi, published in 1983, is a masterpiece of ideological synthesis applied to the pharmaceutical industry that is without equal. Although Gereffi's book focuses on steroid hormones produced from the roots of a Mexican plant called Barbasco, it does so in a context thoughtfully constructed between the ideals of capitalism and Marxism (the two great conflicting ideologies of the twentieth century). Furthermore, Gereffi's conceptualization of the transnational corporation and commodity chains broke new ground in the literature on the worldwide pharmaceutical industry. If one looks very carefully at some of the most recent literature by European and other foreign scholars, it is possible to detect the outlines of Gereffi in their thinking, yet few have given him the credit he so richly deserves.

In truth, Gereffi drew heavily on previous works by predominantly Latin American scholars; and the common thread among many of these is a largely Marxist-socialist perspective. Furthermore, while the fire of Marxist ideologues around the world has been tempered somewhat by the overwhelming success of capitalism in what posterity must surely view as the great battle of the twentieth century, the true believer has not yet given up the ghost. Thus, works like Gereffi's are particularly important because of the bridge they provide between these two encampments. In fact, such works may be viewed as touchstones in a 360° perspective on the structure and dynamics of international capitalism and its regulation, particularly with respect to the pharmaceutical industry.

The realm of international political economy is fraught with dangers of many kinds. Nowhere will you find more idealistic actors or a more stressful, tense, and nerve-racking dialogue than in this global arena of money and power. In the modern era, no society is isolated from the effects of unequal capital accumulation and the arguments that are advanced by various centers of influence on virtually any subject can usually be reduced to the realities of an unequal distribution of wealth. Such is the economic view of social dynamics and their governance. The focus of economic thought here centers on the mechanisms, or dynamics, by which such conditions arise in the first place and how they tend to perpetuate themselves over extended periods of time. Finally, methods by which change might occur are debated in terms that frequently obscure their underlying economic motivations.

Concepts of Wealth, Power, and Governing Dynamics

It is important in the study of any industry to realize that at least since the time of Scotland's Adam Smith (i.e., the *Wealth of Nations* published in 1776), wealth is conceived not simply as money or possessions, nor the ability to produce money income by any means; rather it is conceived as the ability to consume goods and services. Indeed, it is the consumption itself that defines wealth. Thus, if I pay three dollars for a single tablet of the analgesic drug *Glucophage*, a diabetes medication, and you pay two dollars for a single tablet of the exact same medication, we are each equally wealthy in this unit of consumption, even though I paid three dollars and you paid only two.

How crucial a concept is this? It is, herein, never a question of the money. It is only a question of what the money will buy. To say that a person "has a lot of money" is a fairly meaningless statement in terms of assessing his or her actual wealth, for if you and I each have only 100 dollars, and I use mine to purchase 20 tablets of a particular allergy medication, but you are able to buy 25 tablets of the exact same medication, then (as in the above example) you are wealthier than I, even though we each had just 100 dollars. The "idea" of money as something other than wealth is absolutely essential to understanding the forces that impel industries, and indeed societies along their various trajectories.[1]

Gary Gereffi's book also broke new ground within the literature on pharmaceutical business by delineating his treatise from the "Eurocentric" or "metropolitan" emphasis that continues to dominate discussions on the structure and dynamics of the pharmaceutical industry today. With unusual objectivity, Gereffi describes, rather than criticizes, the generally elitist ideology that accounts for the

---

[1] I once observed a man, a man from Kiev, in 1993, board a public bus in Istanbul, Turkey, with a suitcase containing what certainly appeared to be one million American dollars. He was en route to purchase sawmill equipment from a manufacturer located near our common destination. He had no qualms about showing me, or the others on the bus, the contents of the suitcase. His only concern seemed to be with the probability that he might actually be able to purchase the equipment with the money and return with it to Kiev. It seemed uncanny to me how little value he seemed to place on the contents of his baggage. He referred to it in terms more related to scraps of paper, or Hollywood-style "propaganda," Disneyland-induced fantasy, and similar terms with which he associated Western ideals in general, than anything resembling *real* purchasing power. He evidently had no idea how *many* sawmills his money could have bought elsewhere, or believed that it would be utterly impossible to return with them to Kiev (consumption).

rather stark contrast between the success of a few Western nations and Japan and the extreme backwardness that characterizes most of the rest of the world. His discovery of a useful, alternative point of view and intriguing account of this stark contrast, which he also describes with unusual candor and objectivity, was delayed by the translation into English of important Latin American theorists (e.g., H. Cardoso, and Enzo Faletto) until the late 1970s.

The commonly held view among many within the pharmaceutical industry for decades has been that the primary impetus for rapid industrial development in the United States, portions of western Europe, and Japan consisted of endogenous cultural factors, value-orientations, religious ideologies, and related institutional transformations. Gereffi's alternative analysis is based, in part, on the concept that world industry, in general, has consisted of a functional division of labor into "central" and "peripheral" economic regions. Countries of the "center" develop dynamically as an autonomous function of their own internal characteristics and are the main beneficiaries of globalization and enhanced global trade. Countries of the "periphery" develop as a less autonomous response to the requirements of the center's expansion.

Finally, at the present time, a rather remarkable body of theory, developed primarily by French scholars, and known as Régulation Theory, has at least the superficial appearance of what is referred to in science as a *general theory*, in this case: a *general theory of capitalism*. Much of this literature has only recently been translated into English. We will, therefore, consider its central laws in the context of both Marxist and neoclassical economics, as well as those ideas advanced by other schools of economic thought. Throughout the text, economics and the law will be dominant themes. Social institutions, business, scientific, and other "associations" of a supranational kind will be discussed in terms of their influence on the structure and dynamics of the modern pharmaceutical industry. The concept of the "quasi-organization" will be employed in this context, and with the so-called "obligations of membership" described in terms of modalities and logics of both self-interest and common-interest, which may supersede extant concepts of law, but not the most fundamental principles of valuation and exchange from among the various schools of economic thought.

The Roots of Socio-Economic and Political Systems

The famous American geographer, Ellen Churchill Semple, once wrote that man is first a product of the earth's surface, which directs the formation of both his religious beliefs and his economic pursuits. These in turn sow the seeds of his law, which is designed to encapsulate and protect its source, as well as to organize and structure the larger society that soon encroaches upon a bountiful geography. Today, the study of economic geography is more concerned with the relationships between population centers and industry than the location of mineral deposits or fertile soils, yet the linkage espoused by Semple concerning the natural resources of an economy, it's religious beliefs, and it's system of laws, industry and social structure is as intriguing today as it was when she first returned with it from Germany at the end of the nineteenth century.[2] As late as 1983,

---

[2] In the 1890's, the young and somewhat outlandish Ellen Semple desired so terribly to study under the renowned Professor Friedrich Ratzel at the University of Leipzig (an institution completely dominated by men and which allowed enrollment of only male students), that she traveled to Germany, learned the German language on her own, and then (apparently with Ratzel's permission) she actually sat in a small room adjoining his lecture hall with

Gereffi pointed out the importance of the plantation enclave and the mining enclave as two distinct subtypes of foreign-controlled export economies in the *dependency theory* approach to understanding the modern, global industrial society. If nothing else, *dependency theory* is a sharp, almost biting alternative to the "ahistorical" (absent history) and "apolitical" (absent politics) assumptions of *modernization theory* that arose in the wake of World War II and was advocated for a time by the United Nations.[3]

---

the door slightly ajar and took copious notes of virtually everything the man had to say. She returned with these to the United States and published a number of influential scientific papers and books on the pervasive influences of geography in a unique but also engrossing literary style. Thereafter, she was invited to join the faculty at the University of Chicago, which had established America's first Department of Geography in 1903. She has been characterized as a fascinating lecturer, and was a seminal exponent of the theory of Environmental Determinism in America (although some people considered her a racist). Semple also taught at Oxford University, UCLA, the University of Colorado, Clark University, Western Kentucky University, and Wellesley College. She was elected president of the Association of American Geographers and received a number of prestigious awards for leadership and contributions to science. She remains one of the most fascinating women in the history of science. She died in Florida in 1932.

[3] It is best to **read** Gereffi (1983) on this treatise because his focus is somewhat different; however, it seems relevant and important to mention his reference on page 9, footnote 10, to Alejandro Portes (1980), who pointed out an unexpected yet significant contribution of *Modernization Theory*, which, with its focus on cultural factors (religious ideologies, cultural values, etc.) as determinants of social change, liberated students of industrialization and the global industrial society from earlier ideas that the inequality between nations and their relative levels of industrialization were due primarily to immutable racial differences. Gereffi elaborates subsequently (in footnote 11) that *Modernization Theory* not only assumes early industrialization occurred as a result of endogenous cultural transformations, but also as a result of endogenous institutional transformations.

The Economics of Property Rights

Ellen Semple's harshest critics have always called her ideas simplistic, but does that make them any less real? Today there is a vast literature predicated on similar ideas, referred to generally as the economic theory of property rights. It forms the theoretical basis of what is known as "supply-side" economics.

Researchers have applied concepts from the economic theory of property rights to explain phenomena as diverse as the boundaries of tribal hunting grounds in pre-colonial America, the valuation of mineral lands in the American west, the rise and fall of populations in natural fisheries, the productivity and exiting behaviors of employees and managers under various incentive plans, the world price of petroleum, chemical intermediates, fine and specialty chemicals, and the pricing of prescription pharmaceuticals as well as the retention of key scientists and the numbers of patents issued to particular pharmaceutical companies over time.

The fundamental idea is rather simple when divorced from the notion of geologic formations and religious beliefs. If a person or group of persons holds an enforceable interest or ownership in something of perceived or real value, tangible or intangible, they will do whatever is within their power to maintain and enhance its value over time. Furthermore, during periods of rapidly increasing or decreasing valuations, there will be a flurry of exchange transactions, judicial and legislative activities, all with the object of influencing the ownership of these values.

PHILOSOPHY AND LANGUAGE

Cross-national and cross-cultural studies are plagued by a number of special problems. Of particular importance is the fact that all authors impart a particular philosophical orientation to their works, which, though frequently subtle, can usually be detected with some effort. Such underlying philosophies are not insurmountable, however. Once their particular sense of the cause and nature of things has been discerned, the reader is enabled to better understand the work and evaluate the writer's most fundamental ideas, as well as to construct his own argument and form a personal opinion. Then, the reader's opinion could possibly present new and different ideas on the subject matter, or add depth and perspective to a previously held point of view, which may or may not be shared by the author. I believe these are important to the development of new knowledge, innovation, and the development or application of new or emerging technologies, particularly in the pharmaceutical industry.

As emphasized earlier, it has generally been easier for me to perceive the underlying philosophical orientation in a single authorship than in a compendium of diverse contributions by more than one author. Knowledge of an author's particular system of beliefs can be very important to effective discourse within the realm of economic thought, political economics, social interaction and interpersonal or group influence, as well as market interventions by government agencies or similar actions by other institutions such as the financial system, or industry associations, and other forms of corporate governance. As these subjects are all relevant to any meaningful discussion of the structure and regulation of the pharmaceutical industry, their associated major philosophical orientations should also be understood.

Sometimes it is useful to consider generally more obscure, but nevertheless insightful, foreign philosophies (when they are well translated), such as the French Régulation Theory, particularly when their ideas provide interesting and different perspectives that might be helpful in explaining unanticipated or unexpected, important, but otherwise incomprehensible market or global industry dynamics.

Often foreign publications can be properly understood only when translated by significant experts in the subject matter. Those who are experts in more than one language (to the extent that they can readily detect subtle nuances in meaning), and also experts in a particular field of study (to the extent that they can detect subtle theoretical or conceptual differences), tend to specialize by country or region and particular schools of thought. They also are inclined to translate certain works by particular authors influenced by their own philosophical interest in the particular interpretation, perspective, or argument presented by that author. Thus, it has been common in the past for certain foreign authors to be seen (incorrectly) as voicing a consensus body of thought, quite representative of that time in that part of the world, simply because these are the only authors who have been well translated and distributed abroad by their aficionados.

Different schools of thought or philosophical orientations tend to predominate at various times in different parts of the world. This can make the study of historical works, theories and explanations by foreign scholars particularly difficult during periods of transition, novelty, or genuine reconfiguration and innovation in political, social, economic or industrial structures, even when they are well interpreted in translation. It can require an almost excruciating attention to detail and both the denotative and connotative meanings of words, together with their associated cultures, histories, etc.; all must be considered in order to truly understand an author's intended meaning.

Thus, language <u>and</u> philosophy are at least two major problems associated with any scholarly work on an international or global industry such as the worldwide pharmaceutical industry. These two problems, among others, can become acute when studying foreign works on the social context of exchange transactions, economic relationships, economic history, government or state intervention, and industry or related social dynamics.

SCOPE OF THE INDUSTRY

The pharmaceutical industry is huge and worldwide and envelops thousands of companies and hundreds of thousands, if not millions, of direct and indirect employees. It is one of the most important industries in the world, primarily because it produces thousands of drugs (medicines) that cure disease, and/or alleviate pain and suffering, that plague both man and animals. Historically, it has been one of the world's most profitable industries because a significant premium has always been placed upon new and improved medications. It is reasonable to predict that so long as the industry continues to develop innovative, new, and improved medicines, it can sustain its preeminence among the world's most economically valued industries; however, there are a number of forces at work around the world to reduce the cost of health care and it is possible that these could affect the profitability of the worldwide pharmaceutical industry in the future.

Because of the overall economic and practical importance of the pharmaceutical industry and its highly regulated operating environment, the pharmaceutical industry should be studied from at least two different vantage points. First is the more traditional approach to studying an industry and is largely economics-based and management-oriented. Second is a more political, legal, and regulatory perspective than is typically developed in the analysis of other industries. Both economics and law, independently and in concert, are tantamount to a comprehensive understanding of the evolution, structure, and dynamics of the modern pharmaceutical industry. However, to put it mildly, politics and the law have always had a rather interesting relationship with (1) religion and (2) the relative abundance of natural resources (the guiding principle of economics); so the two approaches (economics-based and legal-regulatory) are far from simple or independent of each other.

DEFINITION OF AN INDUSTRY

Anyone who begins to read a book about an industry, much less a global industry, should have a fairly clear understanding of just what an industry is in the first place. What do we mean by the word "industry" anyhow? How many different kinds of industries are there? What makes them different? How should they be most usefully categorized or classified? How do various industries interact, if they interact at all? (Are industries supposed to interact?) In short, what sense does it make to think about so-called industries? Why should we care? Why don't we begin instead by talking about pharmaceuticals; after all, isn't this a book about the *pharmaceutical* industry?

Suppose we do have a clear idea of what an industry is in the first place, what is so special about the pharmaceutical industry? How do we come up with something called "the pharmaceutical industry" anyhow? Why isn't it called "the drug industry," or "the medicine industry"? Is there such a thing as a "drug" industry that is any different from the "pharmaceutical" industry? What is the difference between a drug and a medicine, between a medicine and a pharmaceutical? How many different kinds of pharmaceutical products are there and how do they interact, or relate to one another on an industrial scale? Is the pharmaceutical industry really just a sub-sector or sub-part of something larger, say the "health care industry," or the "medical industry," "chemical industry," etc.?

It might be simplest to begin by stating that an industry is a system that can be thought of in either a social or an economic context. A "system" is a complex whole of connected things or parts that function together toward a common goal, or a generalized single application, or a group of related applications. So, an industry is, by definition, something that is complex. Some people might say that this is a gross understatement, particularly when it comes to the pharmaceutical industry. Furthermore, an industry is characterized as an integrated whole that consists of many parts. What are the many parts that constitute the pharmaceutical industry? How do they "function" together? What is the common goal, generalized single application, or group of related applications that the many parts of the pharmaceutical industry are working toward? Should industries first be thought of in terms of their constituent parts? Should they be studied from the bottom up, so to speak, or from the top down? What is the best way to study an industry and its parts? Finally, as if this weren't enough, what do we mean when we say that an industry can be thought of in either a social or an economic context? If politicians rather than doctors make the decisions about which drugs require a prescription and which do not, which are legal and which are illegal, etc., why shouldn't we begin our study of this industry, or any other for that matter, from a political perspective?

Obviously these are very serious questions involving very important issues and we will deal with each at some length later. But for now let's get back to the idea or concept of an industry. We have already made the point that an industry is a complex system, yet industries are very specific kinds of systems. Historically, industries have been characterized as being either trade industries or manufacturing industries. Industries consist of many different forms of business enterprise (firms) engaged in commerce—that is, economically or socially oriented work, production, manufacture, fabrication, or buying and selling; i.e., trade. While it is still very important to think about industries in the historical terms of either manufacturing or trade or both, the most modern classification systems are much more detailed and divide the economy into initial categories formally referred to as "divisions." According to the Standard Industry Classification (SIC)[4] code system, used for decades in the United States, trade is broken down into the wholesale and retail trade divisions. Additionally, there are the agriculture division, mining division, construction division, etc., for a total of 10 divisions in the SIC code system of classification (see Table 1). Again, the "division" is the highest level of generality employed.

---

[4] The Standard Industrial Classification system, or SIC system, is a classification system for categorizing the various divisions, or sectors of the U.S. economy. The SIC system has recently been replaced by the North American Industrial Classification System (NAICS), following passage of the North American Free Trade Agreement (NAFTA) among the United States, Canada, and Mexico. The older SIC system is still very useful, however, because of the amount of historical data that has been classified in this way. SIC code 26 is paper and allied products. SIC code 28 is chemicals and allied products. SIC code 29 is petroleum and coal products. SIC code 30 is rubber and miscellaneous plastic products. Under SIC code 28 is SIC code 283, which is Drugs. As another example, SIC code 286 is industrial organic chemicals, where much of the feedstock materials and intermediate compounds for the pharmaceutical industry are produced.

SIC CODES	**TABLE 1 ECONOMIC DIVISIONS** (by SIC Code)
01-09	Agriculture, forestry, and fisheries
10-14	Minerals
15-17	Construction
20-39	Manufacturing
41-49	Transportation, communications, and utilities
50-51	Wholesale trade
52-59	Retail trade
60-67	Financial, insurance, and real estate
70-89	Services
91-92	Scrap, waste, and second-hand merchandise

Most industries are categorized in some way by governments and institutions as either: (1) manufacturing or (2) trade industries—that is, either (1) involved primarily in manufacturing, production, fabrication, etc., or (2) involved primarily in trade, buying and selling, purchasing for resale, marketing, etc. The *U.S. Census of Manufactures*, for example, contains an enormous amount of data on the so-called manufacturing industries, as does the *U.S. Census of Trade* on the so-called trading industries. This is an important point as we begin our study of the pharmaceutical industry because many pharmaceutical companies are engaged in both manufacturing and trade. Others manufacture only synthetic intermediate compounds on a contract basis, for example, and still others are involved only in tableting or the manufacture of capsules or other forms of drug delivery.

The key idea, however, is that the companies comprising an industry are all engaged in related types of work, the sum total of which forms an integrated whole. You will not find petroleum refiners, for example, and tablet manufacturers, in the same industry because they are not closely related types of work in any but the most general and possibly esoteric sense that, for example, some petroleum distillates are *ultimately* used to synthesize medicines of various types, and also their packaging and/or delivery systems. The fact of the matter is that a line of demarcation between industries has to be drawn somewhere, as do the lines between the parts, sectors, and subsectors, etc., of an individual industry. To say that an industry is a "complex" of manufacturing and/or trading companies engaged in related types of work, functioning together toward a generalized single application or group of related applications, leaves a lot of room for differences in just exactly where those lines of demarcation are drawn. The interaction between industries and their component parts is also important, yet there are many types of interaction within the social and economic work-related spheres of influence.

Petroleum distillates are used to synthesize many active pharmaceutical ingredients (APIs) and other components in modern pharmaceutical products, but the production of active ingredients tends to be done by firms that are specialized in that particular aspect of the business, just as tableting companies tend to specialize in tableting and related activities. Petroleum distillers are primarily involved in the production of various types of fuels, and not pharmaceutical ingredients per se. Between the petroleum refiners and the pharmaceutical ingredients manufacturers are another group of industries known in aggregate as "the chemical process industries." It is the interaction of these chemical process industries with the pharmaceutical industry that is most important.

The interaction between the petroleum industry and other "feedstock manufacturers," such as coal-tar distillers, biomass generators, agribusiness firms, etc., with the chemical process industries is also important to our study of the pharmaceutical industry, but not nearly so important as that between the chemical process firms and the drug or pharmaceutical companies per se. It is important to study some of these other industries at some level of detail because of the close interaction between them and the pharmaceutical industry.

On the other side of the spectrum, what about health care providers, are they part of the pharmaceutical industry? What about drug stores and pharmacies? What about physicians themselves? In Japan, for example, physicians not only prescribe medications, but dispense them too. In the United States, physicians frequently give their patients "starter packages" of a prescribed medication, or a free sample, in lieu of or in addition to a prescription to be filled elsewhere. If some drugs or medicines cannot be obtained without a prescription from a physician, then aren't the physicians themselves part of the pharmaceutical industry? They certainly interact with the industry. What about herbalists? Are they part of the pharmaceutical industry? Certainly many medicines are derived from herbs and people around the world use a large variety of herbal medicines to treat ailments of many kinds. In some countries, Germany for example, these types of medicaments require a prescription. Are they then prescription drugs and the herbalists that produce and prepare them actually pharmaceutical manufacturers—part of the pharmaceutical industry?

Over the years there has been a tremendous amount of merger and acquisitions (M&A) activity within the pharmaceutical and related industries. Not only does this open the door to consider thousands of financial analysts, accountants, lawyers, patent attorneys, and others as part of the pharmaceutical industry, but it complicates the definition of the industry at a much more general level. It has become much more difficult to know who owns what, or what a company's major lines of business are, its subsidiaries, etc. Furthermore, with a global industry like the global pharmaceutical industry, inter-firm transfers across national boundaries can complicate the study of industry dynamics because of the manner in which data on such transfers is accounted for and maintained.

Pharmaceuticals come from many sources, including petroleum, coal-tar, plant, animal, and mineral resources, etc. Approximately 50% of the world's steroid supply comes from soybeans. As another example, corn is used to manufacture "Cephalosporin C," the basic starting material for the entire class of Cephalosporin Antibiotics, See Figure 2-1. Ingredients or "precursor materials" are being manufactured on a worldwide basis in thousands of tons. Thus, as a basic feedstock, there is a relationship between the agribusinesses that produce these crops and the pharmaceutical products manufactured from them; but where does the agriculture industry stop and the pharmaceutical industry begin? Several years ago, a concept known as the "life sciences concept" swept through the pharmaceutical industry. This will be discussed at length in a later chapter, but for now suffice it to say that many pharmaceutical companies were buying and selling all forms of "life sciences" companies, including agricultural firms and agricultural processes. Consider the process depicted in Figure 2-1.

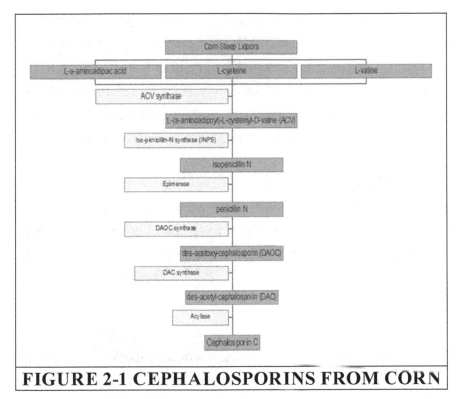

FIGURE 2-1 CEPHALOSPORINS FROM CORN

Whether or not the individual companies involved are owned or controlled by a so-called pharmaceutical company, should this process in some way, in whole or in part, be included in our definition of the pharmaceutical industry?

SOURCES OF PHARMACEUTICALS

The focus of this book is largely, though not exclusively, on ultra-pure, high-potency, synthetic and semi-synthetic pharmaceuticals that require a written prescription by a licensed physician (typically, in the United States and other countries) in order to be dispensed by a licensed pharmacist. These prescription pharmaceuticals are referred to as *ethical* drugs, and their purity is rigidly defined by a national formulary or pharmacopoeia. Drugs that do not require a prescription are called *over-the-counter* (OTC), or sometimes *proprietary* drugs because they are usually marketed under a brand name or proprietary trademark. In the broadest possible terms, therefore, we should recognize two general types of pharmaceutical products, those that require a prescription, and those that do not require a prescription.

Regardless of whether or not a prescription is required, there are six basic sources of modern pharmaceutical products. These are listed in Figure 2-2. Some of these have been known since ancient times; others are of much more recent origin.

PLANT EXTRACTS

Medicinal plant extracts frequently contain alkaloids or carbon-based chemicals that also contain nitrogen and are usually biologically active in small quantities such as caffeine and quinine. Plants are also a source of steroids or steroid-like chemicals (e.g., having an affinity for the estrogen receptor in mammalian cells) and have a complex classification scheme, sometimes referred to as polyphenols: such as isoflavones, phytosterols, saponins, and tanins. A large percentage of the starting material for the world's steroid supply comes from soybeans **and** the Mexican yam. For example, Diosgenin is isolated in tonnage quantities and used to synthesize commercial progesterone, which is converted into *cortisone* on a large scale, through a process that begins with microbial oxidation by a soil organism *Rhizopus arrhizus*. The plant digitalis contains cardiac steroids that have been used as poisons and heart drugs since at least 1500 B.C.

- 1. Plants and plant extracts
- 2. Animal extracts
- 3. Minerals
- 4. Chemical Synthesis
- 5. Fermentation
- 6. Biotechnology

FIGURE 2-2 SOURCES OF PHARMACEUTICALS

ANIMAL EXTRACTS

Animal extracts are a major source of hormones and other steroids. For example, the drug *Premarin,* which until recently was the top-selling prescription drug in the world, is obtained from the urine of pregnant mares. Prior to the discovery of recombinant DNA technology, which is now the major source, the primary source of *insulin* for human consumption used to be the pancreases of slaughtered animals. Similarly, hormones of the adrenal cortex, such as *aldosterone,* were originally obtained from slaughtered animals. As another example, the skins of some toads contain medically useful cardiac steroids that were used as poisons for the tips of arrows. The bones of slaughtered animals are also a major source of calcium and other minerals.

MINERALS

Mineral requirements for human beings are divided into two groups, which are listed in Table 2. The first is *macrominerals,* which are required each day in amounts measured in grams, and the second is *microminerals* (or trace minerals), which are required each day in amounts measured in milligrams or micrograms. Of the macrominerals, both sodium and chloride are required to maintain an acid-base balance, osmotic pressure, and blood pH levels. Sodium is also important in muscle contractility, nerve transmission, and as a pumping mechanism across the cell membrane. Chloride is important to kidney function. Potassium is important in muscle activity, nerve transmission, intracellular acid-base balance, and water retention. Calcium is important in both bone and tooth formation, blood coagulation, neuromuscular irritability, muscle contractility, and myocardial conduction. Phosphorous is important in bone and tooth formation, acid-base balance, and is an important component of nucleic acids and essential to energy production. Magnesium is important in bone and tooth formation, nerve conduction, muscle contraction, and enzyme activation.

Among the microminerals, iron is an essential component of hemoglobin and also important in myoglobin formation, cytochrome enzymes, and iron-sulfur proteins. Fluorine is important in bone and tooth formation. Zinc is a component of various enzymes, important in skin integrity, wound healing, and growth. Copper is an important enzyme component, important in the formation and development of blood cells in the bone marrow, and bone formation. Chromium is important in the promotion of glucose tolerance. Selenium is a component of glutathione peroxidase and thyroid hormone iodinase. Manganese is a component of many manganese-specific enzymes such as the glycosyltransferases, phosphoenolpyruvate carboxykinase, and manganese superoxide dismutase. Molybdenum is an important component of the coenzyme for sulfite oxidase, xanthine dehydrogenase, and one aldehyde oxidase.

TABLE 2 ESSENTIAL MINERALS			
Macrominerals		Microminerals	
Required in gram quantities per day		Required in milligram or microgram quantities per day	
1.	Sodium (Na)	7.	Iron (Fe)
2	Chloride (Cl)	8.	Iodine (I)
3.	Potassium (K)	9.	Fluorine (F)
4.	Calcium (Ca)	10.	Zinc (Zn)
5.	Phosphorous (P)	11.	Copper (Cu)
6.	Magnesium (Mg)	12	Chromium (Cr)
		13	Selenium (Se)
		14.	Manganese (Mn)
		15.	Molybdenum (Mo)

CHEMICAL SYNTHESIS

Chemical synthesis has been a major source of pharmaceuticals since the late nineteenth century. It is used to produce a wide variety of modern medicines from analgesics, antacids, and antidepressants to antihistamines, diuretics, and tranquilizers. In terms of tonnage, more drugs are derived from chemical synthesis than any other source, so we will focus considerable attention on a large number of commercial chemical syntheses and their importance to the structure and dynamics of the global pharmaceutical industry.

FERMENTATION

Fermentation has been used for thousands of years to produce such products as alcohol (beer, wine, etc.), bread, cheese, and vinegar. It is a major source today of a large number of drugs, especially antibiotics. Some of the important classes of antibiotics made by fermentation include the penicillins, cephalosporins, tetracyclines, and macrolides. Numerous other drugs are made by chemically altering fermentation products through chemical synthesis.

Various classes of microorganisms are used in commercial fermentations, including molds and yeasts (which are both fungi and thus have a well-defined central nucleus), and bacteria (which lack a true nucleus but have an independent metabolism and also contain plasmids). Bacteria are a higher form of existence than viruses, and viruses are a higher form of existence than plasmids, but in the general scheme of things, fungi are a higher form of existence than bacteria. Indeed, in some classification systems fungi are considered plants, whereas bacteria are neither plant nor animal.

BIOTECHNOLOGY

In addition to the fact that fungi, bacteria, viruses, and plasmids are together responsible for an exceptionally large number of diseases, these and other distinctions are important to the field of biotechnology because they represent alternative forms of encapsulated genetic material. For this reason especially, formal definitions taken from *Dorland's Medical Dictionary* (28th edition) are as follows in Table 3.

TABLE 3 VARIOUS FORMS OF ENCAPSULATED GENETIC MATERIAL	
Bacteria	In general, any unicellular organism that lacks a true nucleus (prokaryotes) and that commonly multiplies by cell fission and whose cell is typically contained within a cell wall. They may be aerobic or anaerobic, motile or nonmotile, and may be free-living, saprophytic, parasitic, or even pathogenic. In former systems of classification "bacteria" was a division of the kingdom Procaryotae that included all prokaryotes except the blue-green algae, which are capable of photosynthesis. There have been several classification systems for the kingdom Procaryotae based largely on whether or not the organism is capable of deriving energy from light through photosynthesis. More recently the Procaryotae kingdom has been arranged in four divisions based on biochemical and genetic analysis and the presence or absence and type of their cell walls. These four divisions are the Gracilicutes, Fermicutes, Tenericutes, and Mendosicutes. The Tenericutes do not have a cell wall and the Mendosicutes have a faulty cell wall. The Gracilicu are gram-negative and the Fermicutes are gram-positive.

TABLE 3 VARIOUS FORMS OF ENCAPSULATED GENETIC MATERIAL	
Fungi	A kingdom (or in some systems of classification a subdivision of the Plant kingdom) consisting of eukaryotics (organisms whose cells have a true nucleus, i.e., one bounded by a nuclear membrane, within which lie the chromosomes combined with proteins, and that exhibit mitosis). Eukaryotic cells also contain membrane-bound compartments or organelles in which cellular functions are performed, heterotrophic (not selfsustaining; said of a type of nutrition in which organisms derive energy from the oxidation of organic compounds either by consumption or absorption of other organisms) organisms that live as saprobes (feeding off dead matter) or parasites, including mushrooms, yeasts, smuts, molds, etc. Fungi lack chlorophyll, have a cell wall composed of polysaccharides, polypeptides (sometimes), and chitin. They reproduce either sexually or asexually, and have a life cycle that ranges from simple to complex.
Plasmid	An extrachromosomal self-replicating structure found in bacterial cells that carries genes for a variety of functions not essential for cell growth such as antibiotic resistance; the production of enzymes, toxins, and antigens; and the metabolism of sugars and other organic compounds.

TABLE 3 VARIOUS FORMS OF ENCAPSULATED GENETIC MATERIAL	
Virus	One of a group of minute infectious agents that, with certain exceptions (e.g., poxviruses), are not resolved in the light microscope, and are characterized by a lack of independent metabolism and the ability to replicate only within host cells. Viruses are able to reproduce with genetic continuity and the possibility of mutation. They exist in a variety of shapes, some of which give rise to a crystalline structure. Viruses are customarily separated into three subgroups on the basis of host specificity, namely bacterial viruses, animal viruses, and plant viruses.

TYPES OF PRODUCTS

The two most basic types of pharmaceuticals are prescription and nonprescription. A prescription is a written or oral description for the preparation and administration of a remedy. In most jurisdictions, only a licensed physician can issue a prescription. Furthermore, only a licensed pharmacist, or other authorized health care professional can fill a prescription. Prescription pharmaceuticals are usually designated by the **Rx** symbol, indicating that a prescription is required.

While it is useful to think of pharmaceutical products in terms of prescription versus nonprescription, it is also simplistic. Many people tend to think of all nonprescription pharmaceutical products as over-the-counter (OTC) medications, a term that is generally synonymous with medicines that do not require a prescription. However, there are many reasons for delineating pharmaceuticals into more than just the prescription and OTC (nonprescription) categories.

In the first place, countries differ on whether or not a prescription is required for a particular pharmaceutical product. Second, some pharmaceuticals are sold in one dosage that requires a prescription, and another dosage that does not require a prescription, both within the same country! For example, in the United States ibuprofen is sold OTC in 200 mg doses and by prescription-only in 400 mg doses. Third, there are two different types of prescription pharmaceuticals, "legend" and "generic," which are marketed very differently and have significant implications for market structural analysis. Of particular significance to the marketing of pharmaceuticals: they can be either branded or unbranded and the implications here for market structural analysis are equally as significant, if not moreso.

Fourth, there are several different types of pharmaceutical products, also with very different marketing strategies within the overly broad conceptualization of OTC medications referred to above. For example, medicinal herbs and other botanicals tend to be marketed to different consumer segments than aspirin and aspirin-related products.

Fifth, certain countries require prescriptions for herbal medications, while others do not. Furthermore, in some countries many people prefer herbal medicines and other medicinal botanicals to synthetic or semi-synthetic pharmaceuticals, whether or not the synthetics require a prescription; China is a good example, and so is India, as well as parts of Latin America and Africa.

Sixth, vitamins and minerals are regulated differently in different countries and they tend to be marketed differently within countries, differently than other so-called OTC medications such as analgesics, laxatives, and cold preparations.

As you can probably by now detect, classifying pharmaceutical products in the most useful manner possible with respect to the structure of the industry can be a difficult task. Additionally, long histories of legal battles, promulgated and overturned regulations, new legislative activities intended to clarify existing or proposed definitions, prohibited or exempt specific products, and subsequent court actions by various affected interests have resulted in a complex maze of terminology that is only marginally useful in a general context. Moreover there are much more subtle, but significant differences equal to or exceeding those concerning markets and marketing practices described above; in general, these subtleties are seen in terminology across legal jurisdictions and regulatory agencies from one country to another.

Many of these details will be discussed in a later chapter where they are more relevant to the subject at hand. For the moment, however, simply to facilitate a general introduction to the industry, we will categorize the broad realm of pharmaceutical products into ten major sectors. It must be realized that there will be many cases, situations, and contexts in which this particular scheme will not apply equally well. It is intended to represent the broadest possible level of abstraction. Any attempt to add detail or specificity at this point would run the risk of obfuscating the more general principles intended to be conveyed. Some authors refer to such broad schema as "divisions." We will refer to them as "sectors," as in "sectors of the pharmaceutical industry." In many usages the two words ("divisions" and "sectors") are synonymous. Furthermore, the use of the word "pharmaceutical" itself is problematic.

CLASSIFYING INDUSTRIES

As discussed, categorizing and classifying industries and the various activities that occur within an economy is a difficult task. Industries are relatively large groupings of similar or related business activities. As already mentioned, business activities historically have consisted of either manufacturing, trade, or both. But such characterizations are no longer as useful as they have been in the past. In the modern world, industries tend to be very complex and are characterized by high levels of specialization and skill when categorized across a wide range of business-classification areas, and also individual job descriptions. Economically developed nations, such as the United States, the United Kingdom, Germany and Japan support literally hundreds of different industries and industry groups.

One of the most developed and useful schemes for dividing and subdividing an economy into industry groups and subgroups has been the SIC system, which evolved in the United States during the period of World War II when industries where mobilized on a national scale for the war effort. It is based on the idea that related industries use similar raw materials and production techniques.

Although the SIC system is now being phased out in favor of the North American Industry Classification System (NAICS), mandated by the North American Free Trade Agreement (NAFTA) among the United States, Canada, and Mexico; and although the United States adopted the Harmonized Coding System in 1989 for imports and exports; the SIC system has been employed by the U.S. Department of Commerce in the Economic Census of the United States since 1947, and is therefore the basis for an enormous amount of statistical information collected, analyzed, reported, and used throughout the world since that time. However, because of the speed of technological innovation and the pace with which entirely new industries were being created, the SIC category "not elsewhere classified" had become the fastest-growing industrial sector in the United States by the mid-1990s and the SIC system, as it then was, had become obsolete. Rather than modify the SIC system again, as had been done previously, the decision was made to abandon it all together in favor of NAICS, but full implementation will be a long and tedious process.

TABLE 2-4 TWO USEFUL CLASSIFICATION SYSTEMS

SIC versus NAICS

Historically, an "<u>Industry</u>" has been represented by a 4-digit code.

➤ SIC CATEGORY	SIC CODE	➤ NAICS CATEGORY	NAICS CODE
➤ Manufacturing	20-39	➤ Manufacturing	31-33
➤ Chemicals and Allied Products	28	➤ Chemical Manufacturing	325
➤ Drugs	283	➤ Pharmaceutical and Medicine Manufacturing	3254
			32541
		➤ Pharmaceutical and Medicine Manufacturing	
➤ Medicinal Chemicals And Botanical Products	2833	➤ Medicinal and Botanical Manufacturing	325411
➤ Pharmaceutical Preparations	2834	➤ Pharmaceutical Prepration Manufacturing	325412
➤ In Vitro and In Vivo Diagnostics Substances	2835	➤ In-Vitro Diagnostic Substance Manufacturing	325413
➤ Biological Products, Except Diagnostic Substances	2836	➤ Biological Product (except Diagnostic) Manufacturing	325414

The U.S. Economic Census is the responsibility of the United States Department of Commerce, Economics and Statistics Administration, Bureau of the Census. Title 13 of the United States Code (USC) directs the Bureau of the Census to take the Economic Census every five years, covering years ending in 2 and 7. In addition to supervising the Economics and Statistics Administration, the United States Department of Commerce also includes the Patent and Trademark Office (PTO) and the International Trade Administration (ITA), which are of particular interest, as well as many other important administrations, bureaus, institutes, offices, and services. When studying the economic structure of the pharmaceutical industry, the United States Department of Commerce is more important than the U.S. Food and Drug Administration (FDA). Of course the FDA is more important when studying the regulation of the industry.

MAJOR INDUSTRY GROUPS WITHIN THE MANUFACTURING DIVISION

The manufacturing division of the economy includes a number of major industry groups, or sectors, consisting of establishments engaged in the mechanical or chemical transformation of materials or substances into new products. These establishments are usually described as plants, factories, or mills and characteristically use power-driven machines and materials-handling equipment. Establishments engaged in assembling component parts of manufactured products are also considered manufacturing if the new product is neither a structure nor other fixed improvement. Also included is the blending of materials, such as lubricating oils, plastics, resins, and liquors.

The materials processed by manufacturing establishments include products of agriculture, forestry, fishing, mining, and quarrying as well as products of other manufacturing establishments. The new product of a manufacturing establishment may be finished in the sense that it is ready for utilization or consumption, or it may be semi-finished to become a raw material for an establishment engaged in further manufacturing. As an example, let's look at copper. In addition to being a micronutrient necessary for life and required by humans in milligram quantities, there are a whole host of manufacturing and other uses for copper throughout the economy and the pharmaceutical industry. The product of a copper smelter becomes the raw material used in electrolytic refineries. Refined copper is the raw material used by copper wire mills. Copper wire is the raw material used by electrical equipment, medical device, and catalyst manufacturers, among many others.

Table 2-5 presents the Major Groups (2-digit SIC codes), or Sectors, within the Manufacturing Division of the U.S. Economy. Please make special note of the fact that SIC code 28 is "chemicals and allied products," which contains "drugs," suggesting, at least by this system of classification, that the pharmaceutical "industry" is part of the chemical "industry."

The raw materials used by these manufacturing establishments may be purchased directly from producers, obtained through customary trade channels, or secured without recourse to the market by transferring the product from one establishment to another that is under the same ownership (not necessarily an "inter-firm transfer" if ownership, or effective control, is considered at levels other than the individual firm; see the definition of "ownership" below, later). Production by manufacturing establishments is usually carried on for the wholesale market, for inter-plant transfer, or to order for industrial users, rather than for direct sale to the domestic consumer.

SIC CODE	**TABLE 2-5 MAJOR INDUSTRY GROUPS, OR SECTORS, WITHIN THE MANUFACTURING DIVISION** (SIC Codes 20-39)
20	Food and Kindred Products
21	Tobacco Products
22	Textile Mill Products
23	Apparel and other Textile Products
24	Lumber and Wood Products
25	Furniture and Fixtures
26	Paper and Allied Products
27	Printing and Publishing
28	**Chemicals and Allied Products**
29	Petroleum and Coal Products
30	Rubber and Miscellaneous Plastics Products
31	Leather and Leather Products
32	Stone, Clay, and Glass Products
33	Primary Metal Industries
34	Fabricated Metal Products
35	Industrial Machinery and Equipment
36	Electronic and other Electric Equipment
37	Transportation Equipment
38	Instruments and Related Products
39	Miscellaneous Manufacturing Products

The Chemicals and Allied Products Group

This major group includes establishments producing basic chemicals, and establishments manufacturing products by predominantly chemical processes. Establishments classified in this major group manufacture three general classes of products: (1) basic chemicals, such as acids, alkalis, salts, and organic chemicals; (2) chemical products to be used in further manufacture, such as synthetic fibers, plastics materials, dry colors, and pigments; and (3) finished chemical products to be used for ultimate consumption, such as drugs, cosmetics, and soaps; or to be used as materials or supplies in other industries, such as paints, fertilizers, and explosives.

The mining of natural alkalies and other naturally occuring potassium, sodium, and boron compounds, of *natural* rock salt, and of other *natural* chemicals and fertilizers are classified as mining (industry group 147). Thus, consider certain naturally occurring fertilizers such as the feces of bats. Bat dung has historically been used as a source of biguanides, used in anti-diabetic medications. Classified as a product of a mining operation, this historically important raw material for the pharmaceutical industry would not be considered part of the "industry" or industry group (sector) until processed by a chemical process firm to isolate the biguanide for resale. The same can be said for macronutrients such as calcium and magnesium, micronutrients such as copper, and the trace elements. However, as will soon become apparent in this book, we will examine mining, primary metals, petroleum and coal products, as well as agriculture, because important sources of raw materials for the pharmaceutical industry are not all contained in the chemicals and allied products group, or similar categories in similar classification systems.

SIC CODE	TABLE 2-6 THE CHEMICALS AND ALLIED PRODUCTS INDUSTRY GROUP (SIC 28)
281	Industrial Inorganic Chemicals
282	Plastics Materials and Synthetic Resins; Synthetic Rubber; Synthetic and Other Manmade Fibers; Except Glass
283	**Drugs**
284	Soaps, Detergents, and Cleaning Preparations; Perfumes, Cosmetics, and Other Toilet Preparations
285	Paints, Varnishes, Lacquers, and Enamels
286	Industrial Organic Chemicals
287	Agricultural Chemicals
289	Miscellaneous Chemicals

Establishments primarily engaged in manufacturing nonferrous metals and high-percentage ferroalloys are classified in major group 33; those manufacturing silicon carbide are classified in major group 32; those manufacturing baking powder, other leavening compounds, and starches are classified in major group 20. Of equal importance, if not moreso, is the fact that establishments primarily engaged in packaging, repackaging, and/or bottling of purchased chemical products, but not engaged in manufacturing chemicals and allied products, per se, are classified in the wholesale or retail trade divisions. This fact is particularly important when considering whether or not to include pharmaceutical packagers and repackagers in our conceptualization of the pharmaceutical industry.

Drugs SIC 283

This group includes establishments primarily engaged in manufacturing, fabricating, or processing medicinal chemicals and pharmaceutical products. Also included in this group are establishments primarily engaged in the grading, grinding, and milling of botanicals, diagnostic substances, and biological products.

SIC CODES	TABLE 2-7 THE INDUSTRIES WITHIN THE DRUG GROUP
2833	Medicinal Chemicals and Botanical Products
2834	Pharmaceutical Preparations
2835	In Vitro and In Vivo Diagnostic Substances
2836	Biological Products, Except Diagnostic Substances

Medicinal Chemicals and Botanical Products SIC 2833

Here we find establishments primarily engaged in (1) manufacturing bulk organic and/or inorganic medicinal chemicals and their derivatives and (2) processing (grading, grinding, and milling) bulk botanical drugs and herbs. Included in this industry are establishments primarily engaged in manufacturing agar-agar and similar products of natural origin, endocrine products, manufacturing or isolating basic vitamins, and isolating active medicinal principals such as alkaloids from botanical drugs and herbs.

Pharmaceutical Preparations SIC 2834

These are establishments engaged in manufacturing, fabricating, or processing drugs in pharmaceutical preparations for human or veterinary use. The greater part of the products of these establishments are finished in the form intended for final consumption, such as ampoules, tablets, capsules, vials, ointments, medicinal powders, solutions, and suspensions. Products of this industry consist of two important lines, namely: (1) pharmaceutical preparations promoted primarily to the dental, medical, or veterinary professions, and (2) pharmaceutical preparations promoted primarily to the public.

In Vitro and In Vivo Diagnostic Substances SIC 2835

These are establishments engaged in manufacturing in vitro and in vivo diagnostic substances, whether or not packaged for retail sale. These materials are chemical, biological, and radioactive substances used in diagnosing or monitoring the state of human or veterinary health by identifying and measuring normal or abnormal constituents of body fluids or tissues.

Biological Products Except Diagnostic Substances SIC 2836

These are establishments engaged in the production of bacterial and virus vaccines, toxoids, and analogous products (such as allergenic extracts), serums, plasmas, and other blood derivatives for human or veterinary use, other than in vitro and in vivo diagnostic substances.

Thus, in the SIC system of classification, the class known formally as the "drugs" group is really what we sometimes mean when we refer to the pharmaceutical industry, at least from a manufacturing perspective, and then only with specific reference to these four particular "industries." The drugs category is a group of these related four "industries."

THERAPEUTIC MARKETS AND PRODUCT MARKETS

For reasons that will become apparent later in the section on terminology used within the pharmaceutical industry, it is important to differentiate early on between what are referred to as therapeutic markets and product markets, as they relate to the structure and dynamics of the pharmaceutical industry. These are introduced next and more fully developed later in the book.

Note Figure 3 below. It depicts the overall economy as consisting first and foremost of economic divisions, then industrial sectors, etc., until we arrive at the innermost two circles of the figure, which depict first therapeutic markets, and then product markets. In other words, therapeutic markets consist of (usually) more than one product market. The pharmaceutical industry is depicted as consisting of many therapeutic markets.

Although, as we will see when we discuss terminology, the various schema in use for therapeutic markets can differ considerably, Figure 3 uses the example of something called "cardiovascular preparations" as a specific therapeutic market. The example used for a specific product market (ACE Inhibitors) is a type, or sub-category of cardiovascular preparations. Even though it is not shown in Figure 3, individual product markets, e.g., ACE Inhibitors, can be broken down further into the individual brands of ACE Inhibitors on the market. The level of the individual brand is of crucial importance to understanding industry structure and dynamics.

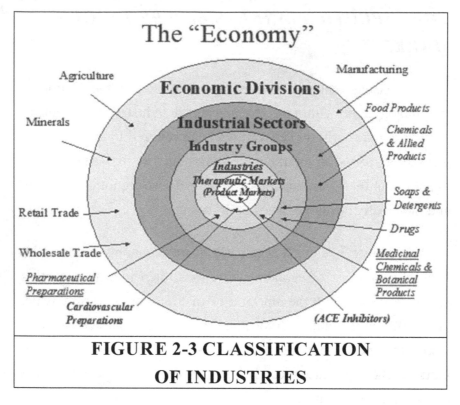

The "Economy"

Economic Divisions

Industrial Sectors

Industry Groups

Industries

Therapeutic Markets
(Product Markets)

Agriculture

Minerals

Retail Trade

Wholesale Trade

Pharmaceutical
Preparations

Cardiovascular
Preparations

Manufacturing

Food Products

Chemicals
& Allied
Products

Soaps &
Detergents

Drugs

Medicinal
Chemicals &
Botanical
Products

(ACE Inhibitors)

FIGURE 2-3 CLASSIFICATION
OF INDUSTRIES

Industry Structure and Dynamics

In this section the subjects of industry structure and dynamics will be introduced. These are very complex subjects and their study can be confusing. Although it may seem overly simplistic without further background material being laid down first, the subjects of structure and dynamics are introduced in terms of the two great economic paradigms of the world, generally speaking neoclassical economics, i.e., capitalism, and Marxist/Socialist economics, i.e., communism. It is hoped that by introducing structure and dynamics in this way at the beginning, the reader will be able to more succinctly absorb the first five parts of the book in preparation for a more detailed development of these subjects in Part VI.

The Meaning of Industry Structure

What is meant by the structure and dynamics of an industry? At least to some extent, when one is asked this question, the answer given should depend upon who is asking the question. Overall, it is the "internal organization" of an industry that is important in the meaning of the term "structure" and the influence of this internal organization on market prices; however, the basis for organization within an industry, or the reasons why it is "structured" in such a manner, are frequently ignored. In a general sense, the conventional concept of industry structure relates to the pattern of ownership (who owns what), intensity of competition (how many competitors there are), and economic power (ability to dictate price) of industry participants (firms or companies).

The conventional concept of industry structure relates to:

- the pattern of ownership (who owns what),
- intensity of competition (how many competitors there are)
- and the economic power (ability to dictate price) of industry participants (firms or companies).

FIGURE 2-4 THE CONCEPT OF INDUSTRY STRUCTURE

Traditionally, industry structures have been characterized by terms such as pure competition, monopolistic competition, oligopoly, duopoly, or monopoly. In general, such terms reflect the number of competitors comprising a particular industry, with pure competition at one extreme reflecting a large number of competitors, and monopoly at the other extreme reflecting but a single firm. However, there is much more to the idea of industry structure than simply the number of competing firms. It really concerns the power that individual companies have to dictate the prices markets will pay for their products. In an industry characterized by pure competition, individual firms are little more than "price takers." Each firm contributes only a small percentage of overall industry production of virtually identical goods and is, therefore, powerless in its own right to set, establish, or influence industry prices. In an industry comprised by only a single firm, however, that one firm may set whatever price it so desires, without fear of a lower price being offered by competing firms, because its offering is essentially unique; i.e., there is no competition. A duopoly describes an industry comprised of just two companies, while an oligopoly describes an industry comprised of a few firms. In each case, competitors have less power than would a monopoly, but more than would pure competition. Consumer markets tend to be described by monopolistic competition, a term that at first appears somewhat confusing. It describes a situation that is more like pure competition than anything else, but with the additional characteristic that companies are able to slightly differentiate their goods from those of competing firms and attempt, often in vain, to monopolize this difference or at least be the first to bring it to market. Such "first-mover" advantages can be very lucrative. In fact, there is often what is referred to as an "order-of-entry" effect whereby the first firm garners a generally sustainable advantage (at least for a period of time) over the second, third, and fourth firms respectively. With all other things being considered equal (ceterus paribus), each of these, in turn, has a significant advantage over subsequent entrants.

Economists often talk about various barriers to entry (the ease or difficulty of new firms entering a particular industry or market). These are barriers that perpetuate the power of existing firms by providing them with de facto control over both supplies and prices. This is how economists view the structure of an industry— as how strong, or powerful company control is in effecting the level of pricing within an industry. In general, the more competitors there are within an industry, the lower is their individual ability to control price.

To others besides economists, industry structure involves the *perceptions* of companies *by* their customers, consumers, other businesses, institutions, and government agencies. Have you ever heard the term "perception *is* reality"? Well, the meaning applies here too, in that different groups of people perceive industries in very different ways. People tend to see an industry as structured or organized around issues that are of primary concern to them. They view industries in these terms and describe the behaviors of firms as influenced primarily by these factors, for example, around therapeutic areas, knowledge, or intellectual property, not to mention the major divisions of labor that are sometimes used to characterize the internal organization of an industry. As we shall see, the division of labor is perhaps the single most important concept in the entire field of economics.

The structure of the pharmaceutical industry can be seen as a function of the scientific specializations found within companies, an idea that is related to the division of labor concept, though we tend not to view microbiologists, cardiologists or chemical engineers, etc., in the same context as we do manual labor. It may be accumulated "corporate knowledge" that defines organizations and the behaviors of firms within an industry. From a managerial perspective, the pharmaceutical industry may be seen as structured around the major tasks that must be completed toward the discovery, development, manufacturing, and marketing of new and improved drugs. Someone, somewhere within the industry, must perform these tasks. In this way, the industry is perceived as being organized around job descriptions, or task-related performance objectives (i.e., the division of labor). Finally, some very clever people view the pharmaceutical industry as structured around the intellectual property rights represented by defensible patents and patent law, rather than as any form of abstract "corporate knowledge," per se. Each of these and other perceptions are important because each defines some relationships as being more important than others in motivating and directing the dynamics of pharmaceutical companies.

In this book, we will consider the social and historical context in which the industry has developed. We will be examining industry structure or organization from the perspective of national and international economies ("macro-analysis) and in terms of the individual organizations of participating firms ("micro-analysis") and their relationships (both social and economic) to one another. We will concentrate on their strategic competitive advantages and relative market shares, their sustainable rates of growth, costs, profitability, and pricing power. To understand the actions undertaken by firms, or the internal "dynamics" of the industry, all of these factors should be well understood and considered from the perspective of rational business decision-making, particularly strategic or long-term business planning and policy-making on a global scale.

THE WORLD'S TWO GREAT ECONOMIC PARADIGMS

For over 150 years, the world has been characterized by two opposing economic paradigms and their minions:

(1) the classical and neoclassical idea of the <u>separability</u> of economic actors from the realms of political and social influence; and

(2) the alternative that social, economic, and political ideas and institutions are <u>inseparable</u> from what a mode of production, industry or economy and its actors are understood to be at any given time.

As already emphasized, these two opposing views will be discussed in detail later. For the moment it is important to realize that as a result, at least two conceptualizations of industry structure in its broadest possible context are possible:

(1) in terms of an infinite number of autonomous and rational economic actors, driven by individual interests constantly measuring costs and benefits, whose sole interaction is through a set of interdependent markets moving toward general equilibrium, and whose entire relationship is fully contained in *price*; and

(2) in terms of qualitatively different social relationships and unequal influence among economic actors that cannot be characterized by a single variable (such as price) or a single interactive context (such as a set of markets, whether or not they are moving toward general equilibrium).

INDUSTRY STRUCTURE & DYNAMICS

When considering the dynamics of the pharmaceutical industry from the perspectives of classical and neoclassical economics, as with many other industries, the key ideas <u>are</u> individual brands and their prices.

In the pharmaceuticals-related chemicals industries there typically is no branding. Prices are more a function of whether or not a particular chemical falls into one of three general categories. These three categories are presented along with pharmaceutical products (a fourth category) in Figure 2-5.

The Chemical Process <u>and</u> Pharmaceutical (Drug) Industry Groups

- <u>Bulk or Commodity Chemicals</u>:
  - Sold on a price-per-weight basis.
- <u>Specialty Chemicals</u>:
  - Sold based upon performance-in-use characteristics.
- <u>Fine Chemicals</u>
  - Sold as precise chemical structures of very high purity.
- <u>Pharmaceutical Products</u>:
  - 11 Categories.

FIGURE 2-5 CATEGORIES OF CHEMICALS-RELATED PRODUCTS

Hank Laskey

A Finer Gradation of Industry Subsectors

- 1) **Legend pharmaceuticals:** patented, brand name, prescription drugs:
  - ➤ *Lipitor, Prevacid, Risperdal, etc.*
- 2) **Generic pharmaceuticals:** non-patented, prescription drugs, with "bioequivalence" to the legend pharmaceuticals:
  - ➤ *Atenolol, Alprazolam, Metoprolol, etc.*
- 3) **Biologic & Biological Poducts:**
  - ➤ *Vaccines, serums, toxoids, etc.*
- 4) **Over-the-Counter Medications and Remedies:**
  - ➤ *Bayer Aspirin, Lanacaine, Zantac 75, etc.*
- 5) **Homeopathic Medicines** (minute quantitites):
  - ➤ *Belladonna, Gelsemium, Nia Vonica, etc.*
- 6) **Vitamins & Minerals.**
- 7) **Diagnostic Substances**
- 8) **Medicinal Botanicals 7 Herbal Medicines:**
  - ➤ *Black Cohosh, Echinacea, Ginseng, etc.*
- 9) **Botanical Extracts & Phytochemcials**
  - ➤ *p-Courmaric Acid, Chlorogenic Acid, Sulforaphane, etc.*
- 10) **Dietary Supplements:**
  - ➤ *Chondroitin Sulfate, Creatine, Shark Cartilage, etc.*
- 11) **Nutraceuticals (to include "Medical Foods").**

FIGURE 2-6 ELEVEN CATEGORIES OF PHARMACEUTICAL PRODUCTS

PATENTS

Patents on pharmaceutical products and processes constitute a particularly important and indeed controversial aspect of the pharmaceutical industry's relationship with government because they grant a period of 20 years' exclusivity to the holder or assignee (usually a pharmaceutical company) for the making, using, or selling of a specific patented product or process. Patents free a company from competitive pressures and market forces. They can have an enormous impact on corporate profits. Pharmaceutical companies invest large sums of money in new medicines because of the economic benefit they expect and are able to derive from the resulting patent protection. Indeed, it is argued that without the possibility of receiving a patent, work in drug discovery and development would grind to a screeching halt. Major changes can take place in the structure and dynamics of the industry, or sectors within the industry as a result of patent expirations.

OWNERSHIP AND PRIVATE PROPERTY

Ownership is defined by the *Oxford Dictionary of the English Language (American Edition 1996)* in terms of an "individual" as the "acknowledged" "possessor," "holder," "proprietor," and/or "user" of "private" "property." We have already discussed the importance of language in the contexts of culture, philosophy, and the understanding of ideas. The language, or "use of words in an agreed way," that is employed by the Oxford Dictionary, as above, uses several interesting words (all shown above in quotes), and listed in Table 2-8.

TABLE 2-8 WORDS USED IN OXFORD DEFINITION OF "OWNERSHIP"
1. Individual
2. Acknowledged
3. Possessor
4. Holder
5. Proprietor
6. User
7. Private
8. Property

Eight words, each with its own meaning, all used together to communicate the meaning of another single word, how strange? Furthermore, notice the use of the word "own" in the immediately past or previous sentence, i.e., its "own" meaning. Does this imply that each of the above eight words has ownership of an individual, acknowledged meaning, that each word is the possessor, holder, or proprietor of a meaning, its acknowledged "user" in the sense of private property? Of course not, many different words can have the same meaning. They are called synonyms. The key here lies in understanding the meaning of the word "individual." Ownership is defined in terms of an individual who is the acknowledged possessor, holder, proprietor, and/or user of private property.

Now let's see what the law has to say about the meaning of the word "ownership." *Black's Law Dictionary, Seventh Edition (1999)* is a widely recognized source of legal definitions, at least within the United States. *Black's Law Dictionary* defines the word "ownership" as follows:

Ownership. The collection of rights allowing one to use and enjoy property, including the right to convey it to others. Ownership implies the right to possess a thing, regardless of any actual or constructive control. Ownership rights are general, permanent, and inheritable.

"Possession is the *de facto* exercise of a claim; ownership is the *de jure* recognition of one. A thing is owned by me when my claim to it is maintained by the will of the state as expressed in the law; it is possessed by me, when my claim to it is maintained by my own self-assertive will.

"Ownership is the guarantee of the law; possession is the guarantee of the facts. It is well to have both forms if possible; and indeed they normally co-exist." John Salmond, Jurisprudence 311 (Glanville L. Williams ed., 10th ed. 1947).

"Ownership does not always mean absolute dominion. The more an owner, for his advantage, opens up his property for use by the public in general, the more do his rights become circumscribed by the statutory and constitutional powers of those who use it." Marsh v. Alabama, 326 U.S. 501, 506, 66 S.Ct. 276, 278 (1946) (Black, J.). Furthermore, there are many forms of ownership, as shown in Table 2-9:

TABLE 2-9 FORMS OF OWNERSHIP
1. Bare ownership
2. Beneficial ownership
3. Bonitarian ownership
4. Contingent ownership
5. Corporeal ownership
6. Incorporeal ownership
7. Joint ownership
8. Ownership in common
9. Qualified ownership
10. Trust ownership
11. Vested ownership

THE UNITED STATES PATENT CLASSIFICATION SYSTEM

The patent laws of the United States are contained in Title 35 of the United States Code. Sections 101-103 of Title 35 deal with patentable inventions and the issues of novelty, and obviousness. Patentable inventions are defined as any new and useful process, machine, manufacture, or composition of matter, or any new and useful improvement thereof.

The first-ever U.S. patent (shown in Figure 2-7 below) was issued on July 31, 1790, to Samuel Hopkins from George Washington: "For the Making of Potash and Pearl Ash by a New Apparatus."

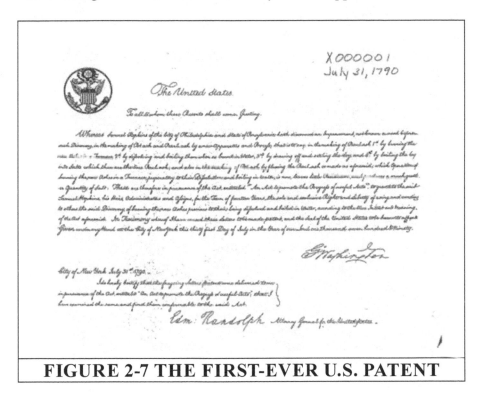

FIGURE 2-7 THE FIRST-EVER U.S. PATENT

The Index to the U.S. patent classification system is maintained within the United States Patent and Trademark Office by the Office of Classification Support. It is an alphabetical list of subject headings referring to specific classes and subclasses of the patent classification system.

There are *utility class titles* and *design class titles* depending on the essential function or effect of the device or the use or application to which the device or composition of matter is put.

INSTRUCTION: After finding an identifying number, refer to the *Manual of Classification* to obtain the precise classification (class). When in doubt about an identifying number, consult the classification *definition* for the class under study.

The *classification definitions* supplement the Manual of Classification in that they contain detailed definitions and illustrations of the kind of subject matter that can be found in each class and subclass, the lines of distinction among classes and subclasses, and they also refer to other classes and subclasses having related subject matter.

Subject headings in the *Index* are not an alphabetical inversion of the *Manual of Classification*. They are a subjective determination of relevant terms, phrases, synonyms, acronyms, and occasionally even trademarks that have been selected over the years as the best identifying description of products, processes, and apparatus of patent disclosures.

The *Index* contains product-related entries, whereas the *Manual of Classification* is descriptive, or nonspecific.

The *Index* is arranged alphabetically with subheadings that can have four levels of indentation.

The following abbreviations are used:

D = Design Class
DIG = Digest – an unofficial collation of related patents.
PLT - Plant Class

Utility Classes

Below are some examples of utility classes, arranged in alphabetical order, which can lead to an initial understanding of the classification of pharmaceutical patents in the United States:

TABLE 2-10 U.S. PATENT UTILITY CLASSES (EXAMPLES)	
Class 8	Bleaching & Dyeing; Fabric Treatment and Chemical Modification of Textiles and Fibers.
Class 15	Brushing, Scrubbing and General Cleaning.
Class 502	Catalyst, Solid Sorbent or Support Therefor: Product or Process of Making.
Class 422	Chemical Apparatus and Process Disinfecting, Deodorizing, Preserving or Sterilizing.
Class 260	Chemistry of Carbon Compounds.
Class 585	Chemistry of Hydocarbon Compounds.
Class 423	Chemistry of Inorganic Compounds.
Class 436	Chemistry: Analytical and Immunological Testing.
Class 204	Chemistry: Electrical and Wave Energy.
Class 429	Chemistry: Electrical Current Producing Apparatus, Product and Process,
Class 71	Chemistry: Fertilizers.
Class 518	Chemistry: Fischer-Tropsch Processes; or Purification or Recovery thereof.
Class 435	Chemistry: Molecular Biology and Microbiology.
Class 530	Chemistry: Natural Resins or Derivatives; Peptides or Proteins; Lignins or Reaction Products thereof.
Class 23	Chemistry: Physical Processes.
Class 209	Classifying, Separating, and Assorting Solids.
Class 134	Cleaning and Liquid Contact with Solids.

TABLE 2-10 U.S. PATENT UTILITY CLASSES (EXAMPLES)	
Class 510	Cleansing Compositions for Solid Surfaces, Auxilliary Composition Thereof, or Processes of Preparing the Compositions.
Class 424	Drug, Bio-affecting and Body Compositions.
Class 514	Same as 424.
Class 44	Fuel and Related Compositions.
Class 55	Gas Separation.
Class 96	Gas Separation Apparatus.
Class 95	Gas Separation Processes.
Class 65	Glass Manufacturing.
Class 588	Hazardous or Toxic Waste Destruction or Containment.
Class 165	Heat Exchange.
Class 336	Induc tor Devices.
Class 725	Interactive Video Distribution Systems.
Class 349	Liquid Crystal Cells, Elements and Systems.
Class 210	Liquid Purification or Separation.
Class 196	Mineral Oils: Apparatus.
Class 208	Mineral Oils: Processes and Products.
Class 89	Ordnance.
Class 532	Organic Compounds – Part of the Class 532-570 Series.
Class 987	Organic Compounds Containing a Bi, Sb, As, or P atom or containing a metal atom of the 6th to 8th group of the periodic system.
Class 930	Peptide or Protein Sequence.
Class 512	Perfume Compositions.
Class 47	Plant Husbandry.
Class 504	Plant Protecting and Regulating Compositions.
Class 111	Planting.

TABLE 2-10 U.S. PATENT UTILITY CLASSES (EXAMPLES)	
Class PLT	Plants.
Class 419	Powder Metallurgy Processes.
Class 623	Prosthesis (i.e., Artificial Body Members), Parts Thereof, or aids and Accessories therefor.
Class 250	Radiant Energy.
Class 430	Radiation Imagery Chemistry: Process, Composition, or Product thereof.
Class 901	Robots.
Class 127	Sugar, Starch, and Carbohydrates.
Class 505	Superconductor Technology: Apparatus, Material, Process.
Classes 128, 600, 604, 606, 601, 607, 602	Surgery.
Class 520	Synthetic Resins or Natural Rubbers – Part of the Class 520-528 Series.
Class 386	Television Signal Processing for Dynamic Recording or Reproducing.
Class 26	Textiles: Cloth Finishing. (19, 68, 38, 66, 28, 57, 139).
Class 1	This class contains patents with no data.
Class 131	Tobacco.
Class 378	X-Ray or Gamma Ray Systems or Devices.

Design Classes

Below are some examples of design classes arranged in alphabetical order and shown in Table 2-11.

TABLE 2-11 U.S. PATENT DESIGN CLASSES (EXAMPLES)	
Class D28	Cosmetic Products and Toilet Articles.
Class D1	Edible Products.
Class D13	Equipment for Production, Distribution, or Transformation of Energy.
Class D10	Measuring, Testing, or Signaling Instruments.
Class D24	Medical and Laboratory Equipment.

Index to Classification

Below are some examples taken from the *Index* (December, 2000), in alphabetical order in Table 2-12.

TABLE 2-12 U.S. INDEX TO CLASSIFICATION (EXAMPLES)

Abietic Acid – 562 / Subclass – 404+

    Esters – 560/7

    Naturally Occurring Mixtures – 530/200+

Abietyl Alcohol – 568/714

Acetals – 568/590+

    Cyclic 5 Membered Ring – 549/430+

    Cyclic 6 Membered Ring – 549/369+

Acetosalicylic Acid – 560/143

Acetylation (See Acetate)

    Amines – 564/137+

    Ketene Production – 568/301

    Phenols – 560/130+

    Textiles – 8/121

Acetylene (See Triple Bond Hydrocarbon)

    Aldehydes from – 568/458

    Burner Lantern – 363/160

    Cylinder – 206/.6+

    Electrostatic Field or Electrical Discharge Production – 204/17

    Esters from – 560/242

    Separating from Gases – 95/145+ (95/238)

    6-Membered Hetero N Compounds from – 546/253

    Synthesis of – 585/534+

    Vinyl Halides from – 570/233

Manual of Classification

Below, in Table 2-13 are some examples taken from the *Manual of Classification*, Revision #7, June 30, 2000.

TABLE 2-13 U.S. MANUAL OF CLASSIFICATION (EXAMPLES)		
Class 424 – Drug, Bio-affecting and Body Treating Compositions:		
Subclass	Indents	Description
1.11		RADIONUCLEOTIDE OR INTENDED RADIONUCLEOTIDE CONTAINING; ADJUVANT OR CARRIER COMPOSITIONS; INTERMEDIATE OR PREPARATORY COMPOSITIONS.
1.13	·	In Aerosol, Fine Spray, Effervescent, Pressurized Fluid, Vapor or Gas, or Compatible Composition thereof.
1.17	·	Attached to or within Viable or Inviable Whole Micro-Organism, Cell, Virus, Fungus, or Specified Sub-Cellular Structure thereof (e.g., Platelet, Red Blood Cell)
1.21	·	Molecular Bilayer Structure (e.g., Vesicle, Liposome).
1.25	·	Dissolving or Eluting from Solid or Gel Matrix (e.g., Capsule, Tablet).
9.1		IN VIVO DIAGNOSIS OR IN VIVO TESTING.
9.2	·	Testing Efficacy or Toxicity of a Compound or Composition (e.g., Drug, Vaccine, etc.

TABLE 2-13 U.S. MANUAL OF CLASSIFICATION (EXAMPLES)		
9.3	·	Magnetic Imaging Agent (e.g., NMR, MRI, MRS, etc.)
9.31	· ·	Clay or Zeolite Containing
9.32	· ·	Particle Containing a Actinide, or Lanthanide Metal (e.g., Hollow or Solid Particle, Granule, etc.)
9.321	· · ·	Liposome
9.322	· · ·	Polymer Containing (e.g., Polypeptide, Synthetic Resin, eyc.)
9.323	· · · ·	Metal is Paramagnetic.
NOTE: Even though 9.323 is indented four (4) times (i.e., it is preceded by four dots), it contains only three (3) digits to the right of the decimal place. The numbers are simply addresses! They are completely unrelated to the number of indents, or preceding dots.		
9.33	· ·	Nitoxide or Nitroxide Containing.
130.1		IMMUNOGLOBULIN, ANTISERUM, ANTIBODY, OR ANTIBODY FRAGMENT, EXCEPT CONJUGATE OR COMPLEX OF THE SAME WITH NONIMMUNOGLOBULIN MATERIAL.
141.1	·	Monoclonal Antibody or Fragment thereof (i.e., Produced by any Cloning Technology).
142.1	·	Human.
143.1	· ·	Binds Receptor.
144.1	· · ·	Receptor Integral to or Derived from a Lymphocytic or Lymphocytic-like Cell (e.g., NK Cell, etc.)

TABLE 2-13 U.S. MANUAL OF CLASSIFICATION (EXAMPLES)		
145.1	··	Binds Hormone to Other Secreted Growth Regulation Factor, Differentiation Factor, or Intercellular Mediator (e.g., Cytokine, etc.); or Binds Serum Protein, Plazma Protein (e.g., tPA, etc.), or Fibrin.

INTERNATIONAL TRADE AGREEMENTS

Industrialists have long conceptualized the world into three major economic regions (industrial "centers" and their respective "peripheries"). These are generally referred to as: (1) the western hemisphere, dominated by the United States and formalized in part by the North American Free Trade Agreement (NAFTA); (2) Europe and Western Asia, dominated by Germany and formalized in part by the European Union (EU); and (3) the Pacific rim and Eastern Asia, dominated by Japan and formalized in part by the Association of Southeast Asian Nations (ASEAN); as well as other international agreements.

THE GLOBAL CHALLENGE

According to the editors of the influential journal, *Foreign Affairs*, an article published in the journal in 1993 by Samuel P. Huntington entitled "The Clash of Civilizations" stirred up more controversy and debate than any other article they had published since the 1940s. Four years later, in 1997, Huntington followed up his article with a book entitled *The Clash of Civilizations and the Remaking of World Order*, in which he intended to clarify much of the material he believed had been misinterpreted in his original article, as well as to elaborate upon a number of his highly controversial ideas and themes.[5] This book has been called "one of the most important books to have emerged since the cold war" by former U.S. Secretary of State, Dr. Henry Kissinger. It is an extremely thought-provoking work.

It is important, in the face of Huntington's powerful and influential work, to recognize that the development of our discussion here will not follow Huntington's ideas exactly; however, the discussion here is

---

[5] These ideas include the concept of civilizations; the question of a universal civilization; the relation between power and culture; the shifting balance of power among civilizations; cultural indigenization in non-Western societies; the political structure of civilizations; conflicts generated by Western universalism; Muslim militancy; the Chinese assertion; balancing and bandwagoning responses to the rise of Chinese power; the causes and dynamics of fault line wars; futures of the West and of world civilizations; the crucial impact of population growth on instability and the balance of power; clashes of civilizations as the greatest threat to world peace; and an international order based on civilizations as the surest safeguard against world war.

not inconsistent with his ideas either. In a sense, Huntington's ideas are built upon the general character of the ideas that are presented in the paragraphs that follow and indeed throughout this chapter on the global challenge. Huntington's ideas are definitely politically oriented. We are concerned with politics only to the extent that it impacts the structure, dynamics, and regulation of the pharmaceutical industry.

ALTERNATIVE CULTURES

To understand the global challenge that faces the pharmaceutical industry it is necessary to understand the concept of culture and how cultures can be dimensionalized. In other words, what are the dimensions by which cultures differ? Huntington's work is based upon the idea that they do differ and develops from that point forward. It is more useful to the global pharmaceutical industry, in a general sense, to examine the dimensions by which they differ. In this sense, it is useful to think about cultures in terms of their value-orientations, or the dimensions upon which succeeding generations within a culture tend to place value and around which they tend to structure their belief systems. This approach is more germane to a variety of applications, including Huntington's global political application where he argues that culture and cultural identities at the broadest level *are* civilization-identities and shape patterns of cohesion, disintegration, and conflict in the world today; i.e., the post-cold war world.

The idea of culture employed here is the same as that employed by Huntington, which he appears to have adopted from Adda B. Bozeman's work, *Civilizations Under Stress*. A culture involves the "values, norms, institutions, and modes of thinking to which successive generations in a given society have attached primary importance." We will focus on values as being of primary importance. We will use the scheme employed by Hawkins, Best, and Coney (1983).

As shown in Figure 3-1, there are three basic categories of cultural values dimensions.

Self-Oriented Values

Other-Oriented Values

Environment -Oriented Values

Source: Hawkins, Best, and Coney (1983)

FIGURE 3-1 THE VALUES DIMENSIONS OF CULTURE

ENVIRONMENT-ORIENTED VALUES

1. Cleanliness.

2. Performance - Status.

3. Tradition - Change.

4. Risk Taking - Security.

5. Problem Solving - Fatalism,

6. Nature

Source: Hawkins, Best, and Coney (1983)

FIGURE 3-2 ENVIRONMENT-ORIENTED VALUES

Cleanliness

Is cleanliness next to "godliness," or is it a relatively minor matter? Many people in Southeast Asia consider black and discolored teeth desirable! Thus, pharmaceutical products to correct the diseases associated with this condition would probably not be valued by this group.

Performance - Status

Are opportunities, rewards, and prestige based on an individual's performance or associated with the person's family, position, or class? Status-oriented societies tend to prefer high-priced brand names. Japan, Hong Kong, Singapore, the Philippines, Malaysia, and Thailand are all status-oriented societies.

Tradition-Change

Is tradition valued simply for the sake of tradition? Is change or "progress" an acceptable reason for altering established patterns? "All innovation is the work of the devil," is a quote which has been attributed to Mohammad. Given that innovation is of crucial importance to the pharmaceutical industry, this valuation has far-reaching implications for the industry.

Risk Taking - Security

Do the "heroes" of a culture meet and overcome obstacles? Is the person who risks established position or wealth admired or considered a fool? What action should one take when one contracts an illness, condition, or disease? Is the "tried and true" medication appropriate (perhaps an over-the-counter product), or is a new, experimental drug to be tried? The society that does not admire risk-takers is unlikely to develop entrepreneurs to achieve economic growth and change.

Problem Solving - Fatalism

Do people react to obstacles and disasters as challenges to be overcome? Or do they take a "c'est la vie" attitude? Is there an optimistic "we can do it" attitude? In the Caribbean "no problema" actually means "there is a problem but you can't do anything about it, so why worry?"

It is very difficult to get people to plan or anticipate unforeseen circumstances in fatalistic cultures.

Also, there tend to be much lower complaints about unsatisfactory products in these cultures: Dominican Republic, especially, and also Mexico.

Nature

Is nature assigned a positive value, or is it viewed as something to be overcome, conquered, or tamed?

Americans have historically considered nature as something to be overcome or improved on.

Animals were either destroyed as enemies or made into heroes or pets.

Horses and dogs are romanticized in the U.S., but few would feel comfortable eating them.

In Thailand, animals are a lower form of creation. Thais are not attracted to advertising using animal themes.

OTHER-ORIENTED VALUES

1. Individual - Collective.
2. Romantic Orientation.
3. Adult - Child.
4. Masculine - Feminine.
5. Competition - Cooperation.
6. Youth - Age.

Source: Hawkins, Best, and Coney (1983)

FIGURE 3-3 OTHER-ORIENTED VALUES

Individual - Collective

Individual rewards versus cooperation and conformity.

Best example is U.S. versus Japan.

Romantic Orientation

A "love conquers all obstacles" concept.

It begins with boy. Boy has a problem. Boy cannot solve his problem. Boy meets girl. Together they solve boy's problem. Then they live happily ever after.

Best example is U.S. versus Thailand (arranged marriages).

Adult -Child

To what extent do primary family activities focus on the needs of children? What role, if any, do children play in family decisions? What role do they play in decisions that primarily affect the child?

Best example is U.S. versus Britain (parents don't take advice from children).

Masculine - Feminine

Are rank and important social roles primarily assigned to men? Can a female's life pattern be accurately predicted at birth? Does the husband, or wife, or both make important family decisions? **Basically, we live in a male-dominated world!**

Best example is "Dutch" versus Muslim (even have male secretaries).

Competition - Cooperation

Do individuals or groups obtain success by forming alliances with other individuals or groups? Does everyone admire a winner?

Australia: "Don't be greedy, mate; you've had yours for this time. Reckon I've got to save some for the next chap. Fair shares for all you know."

Effects: Sales force compensation, motivation, comparative advertising, etc.

Youth - Age

Are prestige, rank, and important social roles assigned to "younger" or "older" members of society? Are behavior, dress, and mannerisms of the "younger" or "older" members of society emulated or imitated by the rest of society?

Confucian concept (Korea) emphasizes age. Germans associate youth with "inexperience." European women aren't in their prime until age 30+.

SELF-ORIENTED VALUES

1. Active - Passive.
2. Material - Nonmaterial.
3. Hard Work - Leisure.
4. Postponed - Immediate Gratification.
5. Sensual Gratification - Abstinence.
6. Humorous - Serious.

Source Hawkins. Best, and Coney(1983)

FIGURE 3-4 SELF-ORIENTED VALUES

Active - Passive

A physically active approach to work and play.

French women: "Fireside chats with friends are my favorite way to spend an evening."

American women: "I like parties where there's lots of music and talk."

Norwegian women spend two to four times as much time participating in sports than American women. Advertising themes reflect this.

Material - Nonmaterial

Is the accumulation of wealth a positive good in its own right?

Instrumental materialism – enables the owner to do something.

Terminal materialism – ownership is an end in itself.

Both U.S. and Japanese ads are materialistic, but the Japanese ads are terminal, whereas U.S. ads are instrumental.

Hard Work - Leisure

Is work valued for itself, independent of external rewards? Or is work merely a means to an end? Will individuals continue to work even when their minimum economic needs are satisfied?

Latin America – work is a necessary evil.

Swiss women – reject ads emphasizing time and effort saved in household tasks. Instant coffee in Germany ("boil, steep, then stir").

Brazil – Tang is not convenient but fun and comes in many colors.

Postponed Gratification - Immediate Gratification

"Save for a rainy day" versus "Live for today."

In Germany and The Netherlands: Credit living is living beyond one's means. (Discount rate cuts are not as significant.)

Sensual Gratification - Abstinence

Is it acceptable to pamper one's self, to satisfy desires for food, drink, or sex beyond the minimum requirement?

India – "use moderation in all expressions of life."

Russians – "lusty hedonists."

France – limited use of toothpaste, deodorant, and bath soap. Excessive concern and handling of the body is immoral. (Catholic and Latin traits too.)

Humor - Serious

Most Europeans and many Latins don't mix the two. Americans co-mingle jokes with seriousness (examples are Jay Leno, David Letterman; Mr. Bean, and Benny Hill).

Perhaps most importantly, differences in what is considered humorous can be <u>extreme</u> between cultures.

ALTERNATIVE LANGUAGES

Language is the most important aspect of culture. The scientific study of language is known as *linguistics or philology.* Linguists have long noted similarities among the words and structures of various different languages. For example, the *"deus"* group of words: Latin (deus), Italian (dio), Spanish (dios), French (dieu), German (gott), English (god), Dutch (god), Swedish (gud), Russian (bog), Polish (bog), Czech (buh).

GERMANIC LANGUAGES

	German	Dutch	Swedish	Danish	English
1	einz	een	en	en	one
2	zwei	twee	tva	to	two
3	drei	drie	tre	tre	three
4	vier	vier	fyra	fire	four
5	funf	vijf	fem	fem	five
6	sechs	zes	sex	seks	six
7	sieben	zeven	sju	syv	seven
8	acht	acht	atta	otte	eight
9	neun	negen	nio	ni	nine
10	zehn	tien	tio	ti	ten

ROMANCE LANGUAGES

	French	Spanish	Italinn	Latin
1	un	uno	uno	unus
2	deux	dos	due	duo
3	trois	tr85	tre	lr8$
4	quotre	cuatro	quanro	quattuor
5	cinq	cinco	cinque	quinque
6	six	seis	sei	sex
7	sept	siete	sane	septem
8	huit	ocho	otto	octo
9	neuf	nueve	nove	novem
10	dix	diez	dieci	deeem

SLAVIC LANGUAGES

	Russian	Polish
1	adin	jeden
2	dva	dwie
3	tri	trzy
4	chetyre	cztery
5	pyat	piec
6	shest	szesc
7	sem	siedem
8	vosem	osiem
9	devyat	dziewiec
10	desyat	dziesiec

Linguists have thus classified the languages of the world into eleven language families:

Linguists have classified the languages of the world into eleven language families:

- » 1. Indo-European
- » 2. Sino-Tibetan
- » 3. Afro-Asian
- » 4. Uralic and Altaic
- » 5. Japanese and Korean
- » 6. Dravidian
- » 7. Malayo Polynesian
- » 8. Mon Khmer
- » 9. Black African
- » 10. American Indian
- » 11. Unusual

Each language family is subdivided into branches. For example, the Indo-European family has eight living branches:

The Indo-European family has eight living branches:

» <u>Germanic</u> - English, German, Dutch, Danish, Icelandic, Norwegian, and Swedish.

» <u>Romance</u> - French, Spanish, Portuguese, Italian, and Romanian.

» <u>Balto-Slavic</u> - Russian, Ukrainian, Polish, Czec, Slovak, Serbo-Croatian, Slovenian, Bulgarian, Lithuanian', and Latvian.

» <u>Indo-Iranian</u> - Hindi, Urdu, Bengali, Farsi, and Pashto.

» <u>Celtic</u> - Irish (Gaelic), Scots Gaelic, Welsh. & Breton.

» <u>Greek</u>

» <u>Albanian</u>.

» <u>Armenian</u>.

Indo-European is the world's most important language family. About half of the world's population speaks languages in this family.

All Indo-European languages have the same original structure, based on *inflections*. They all have clearly defined parts of speech: nouns, pronouns, adjectives, and verbs, which take endings to show gender, number, case, person, tense, mood, or voice.

The earliest Indo-European language of which we have a record is Hittite, followed by Greek and Sanskrit. Later in this book we will talk about the Hittite Iron Monopoly as causal in this domination of Indo-European languages.

Sino-Tibetan is second in numerical importance with about 1.1 billion speakers. It includes Chinese (with its many dialects, such as Cantonese and Mandarin), Thai, Burmese, and Tibetan.

The Sino-Tibetan languages consist of one syllable words. Speakers show the different meanings of otherwise identical words by changing their tone of voice.

Afro-Asian includes Arabic and Hebrew, Berber (North Africa), Amharic (Ethiopia), Galla, and Somali. About 220 million people speak Afro-Asian languages.

Uralic and Altaic languages include Finnish, Hungarian (Magyar), Turkish, Mongol, Manchu, and most of the languages spoken in the Asian part of the old Soviet Union. About 130 million people speak Uralic and Altaic languages.

Japanese and Korean form a family with about 181 million speakers. They are spoken in different styles according to social situations. They have both inflected and uninflected words. All words end in vowels or the letter *n*. Differences in pitch are the distinctive feature of words and phrases. Vowels and consonants are usually soft (*Ling*). There are no exact expressions for yes and no.

The Dravidian family is located in southern India and parts of Sri Lanka, consisting of Tamil, Telugu, and others. The Dravidian languages have about 210 million speakers.

The Malayo-Polynesian family includes the languages of Indonesia, the Philippines (*Tagalog*), Hawaii, New Zealand, Madagascar, and most other islands of the Pacific and Indian Oceans. There are 270 million speakers.

The Mon-Khmer family has about 80 million speakers in Southeast Asia and parts of India. This family is also called "Austro-Asiatic."

Black African languages are spoken in areas south of the Sahara and west of the Sudan, Ethiopia, and Somalia. The three main branches are Nilo-Saharan, Niger-Kordofanian, and Khoisan. These three branches have about 430 million speakers.

American Indian languages number over 1,000. But they are difficult to classify because of the great differences among them. Their total number of speakers does not exceed 20 million. They appear in isolated areas of North, Central, and South America.

Unusual languages and dialects include the Pidgin and Creole tongues spoken in many parts of the world. Examples include Melanesian Pidgin English of the Solomon Islands and New Guinea, and Haitian Creole based on French.

People have long been interested in having one language that could be spoken throughout the world. Over 600 universal languages have been proposed. Esperanto is the most successful universal tongue. About 10 million people have learned Esperanto since its creation in 1887. Currently, people in about 90 countries speak Esperanto. Over 100 magazines and newspapers are published in Esperanto.

ALTERNATIVE RELIGIONS

CHRISTIANITY

Has its basis in the life and teachings of Jesus Christ, who was born a Jew in what is today Israel. Christianity grew out of Judaism, and its sacred teachings spring both from the Jewish Old Testament and the New Testament of the Bible which records the life and teachings of Jesus Christ.

Most Christians believe that Jesus Christ is God incarnate, sent to the world to enable people to gain salvation by repentance for their sins.

As in Judaism, the Ten Commandments form the basis of moral law for Christianity. Various creeds express Christian doctrines.

Christians make up the world's largest religious group, about one-third of the world's population, about 2 billion people.

Christianity has three major branches: (1) Roman Catholicism, with about 970 million followers; (2) Protestantism, with about 400 million; and (3) Eastern Orthodoxy, with over 200 million.

Christianity is the major religion of Europe, the Western Hemisphere, and Australia, but many Christians also live in Asia and Africa. The Western world, largely Christian by faith, has spearheaded the development of modernization, for reasons outside the scope of this book. An important factor, however, in the development of modernization, was the formulation of civil law, the work of jurists in seventeenth-century France as a result of religious strife between

Catholics and Protestants. This was important in creating the "secular society," a mark of developed countries.

It has been claimed that the Protestant faith, by motivating its adherents to the values of hard work and thrift, has instigated movement toward capitalism and economic development (the "Protestant work ethic"). But other non-Protestant, non-Christian nations, i.e., Japan, have also had enormous economic growth through capitalism.

JUDAISM

Judaism, the religious faith of the Jews, is the oldest living religion in the Western world. According to tradition, sometime between the fifteenth and thirteenth centuries B.C., the patriarch Abraham moved with his flocks north and west from Mesopotamia into the area later called Palestine. Eventually, Abraham's descendants moved into Egypt, where they were held in bondage. In the thirteenth-century B.C., the prophet Moses led them out of Egypt and unified them under the worship of Yahweh.

Judaism was the world's first religion to teach monotheism. Both Christianity and Islam drew on the central tenets of Judaism in their development. Today there are over 14 million adherents of Judaism, mainly in North America, Europe, and Israel.

The Hebrew Bible, especially the first five books (Torah), is the source of basic beliefs. The revelations received by the patriarchs Abraham, Isaac, and Jacob, as well as the Ten Commandments received by Moses, are an important cornerstone of Jewish law.

These laws are codified in the Talmud, a fifth- and sixth-century compendium of Jewish religious life and legal decisions, couched in parables, fables, sermons, and homilies.

Judaism today has four main branches: Orthodoxy, Conservatism, Reform, and Reconstructionism. Orthodox Jews are least likely to assimilate into secular life, but are influential in Israeli politics and Jewish communities worldwide.

Jews, like Muslims, shun pork and do not mix meat and milk.

Historically, Jews were persecuted in Christian countries.

In medieval Europe, they were not allowed to hold property. Many jews consequently settled in large cities and became active in commerce. Today, Jewish communities in many countries are prominent in world commerce.

ISLAM

The Muslim religion, Islam, dates back to the early seventh century A.D. and began during the lifetime of the prophet Mohammed.

It is practiced in about 30 countries, mainly in North Africa and the Middle East, and has over 1 billion adherents. Indonesia has the largest Muslim population in the world, about 180 million worshipers. Islam is split into two major groups, the result of a disagreement over who should succeed Mohammed: Sunnis (about 90%) and Shi'ites or Shi'ahs (about 10%).

The major precept of Islam is submission to the will of Allah (Islam means "to submit"). The primary text is the Koran or Qu'ran. The Koran contains the divine revelations of the prophet Mohammed. Much of the power of the Koran derives from the beauty of its prose. Over and above its (religious) content per se, the prophet's use of the Arabic language is said to be stunningly gorgeous. It is an art form in its own right.

The Koran is the source of the legal and social codes that constitute Islamic law. Muslims typically do not eat pork, drink alcohol, or smoke tobacco. In the strictest Islamic societies, such as Libya and Iran, there are no nightclubs, bars, or casinos.

- Muslims have five main duties: 1. To profess the faith, that there is no God but Allah, and Mohammed is the prophet of Allah. 2. To pray five times each day at a specific time, no matter where one is. 3. To abstain from food, drink, and any worldly pleasure from dawn until dusk during the month of Ramadan. 4. To give to the poor. Because Mohammed was himself a poor orphan, the Muslim faith dictates that all followers should give 2.5% of their annual income to the poor. This practice is known as "Zakaat." 5. To make a pilgrimage to Mecca at least once in life. Mecca, located in Saudi Arabia, is the birthplace of Mohammed.

Islam dictates not only religious behavior but also social etiquette. Islamic societies are male dominated. In Shi'ite countries such as Iran, women must cover themselves from head to foot and must wear veils when they go outside. In Saudi Arabia, women are not allowed to drive cars.

HINDUISM

Hinduism had its beginnings about 1500 B.C. when Aryan invaders swept into what is today India and conquered its people.

The Aryans brought with them their beliefs in many gods and goddesses who rule nature, and these beliefs were blended with local practices over time to produce Hinduism. Hinduism today claims about 780 million adherents and 85% of India's population.

At the heart of Hinduism are the sacred Vedas and the Upanishads, which Hindus believe reveal the basic truths of life and the individual's place in the universe. The unifying philosophy is that birth, life, and death are all passing events in a cycle of births and rebirths, and that individual status is determined by how well or ill one lived in previous lives (karma).

The Aryans established the Hindu practice of caste, a system by which all Hindus are born into a specific social and occupational class. There were originally three castes: the Brahmins, or priestly caste; the Kshatriya, or warrior caste; and the Sudra, or peasant and laborer caste.

Below these three castes are the lowest of the low, then as today, the "outcasts" (out of the caste system), the "untouchables". *A similar concept exists in Japan.*

Hinduism does not have a body of authoritative doctrine, but it does provide a guide for correct conduct. The caste system was officially abolished in India in the mid-twentieth century; many castes nevertheless exist now. The caste system is very intricate and affects all relationships.

BUDDHISM

Buddhism was founded in the early sixth century B.C. by Siddartha Gautama, a member of a wealthy, warrior-caste family in India. His search for spiritual enlightenment took him beyond the sacred Hindu texts and into a harsh life of self-mortification, where he denied himself nearly to starvation. After years of self-denial and meditation, he achieved an understanding of life contained in what came to be known as the "Four Noble Truths":

1. Everything in life is suffering and sorrow.
2. The cause of suffering and sorrow is desire and attachment to worldly goods and goals, which bring disappointment, more sorrow, and more desire.
3. The way to end pain is to avoid desire.
4. The means to reach this end is by following the "Fightfold Path" between self-indulgence and self-mortification: right knowledge, right purpose, right speech, right action, right living, right effort, right thinking, and right meditation.

Following the eight-fold path leads to *nirvana* – the total release of selfish cravings and desires, release from the cycle of rebirths (Buddhism began as Hinduism).

Today, Buddhism has over 300 million followers who have split into two major sects: the Theravada (stricter of the two sects), which is prominent in Sri Lanka, Vietnam, Laos, Cambodia, Burma, and Thailand; and the Mahayana, which is prominent in Hong Kong, Korea, Singapore, Taiwan, and Japan (all fast-growing economies).

SHINTOISM

Shinto is the state religion of Japan (known as "high Shinto"). There is also "folk Shinto," and "modern Shinto;" these are practiced among common people, in small towns and rural areas. Shinto is a uniquely Japanese religion. It combines elements of Confucianism, Taoism, and Buddhism.

Japan has probably always had folk (cult) Shinto, which names over forty thousand gods who preside over mountains, villages, kitchens, etc., and give people good fortune. In the era of the seventh and eighth centuries A.D., the Japanese emperor and his court set about "enriching" Japan with the "high culture" their amazed envoys had observed in China.

Japan adopted Buddhism wholesale from China as a religion "excellent for protecting the state." Shinto changed somewhat as a result, but proved amazingly resilient in its core beliefs. During the Meiji Reform (1868; ended the Tokugawa period), State Shinto was taught in the schools. State Shinto became the history of Japan from the age of the gods and the veneration of the emperor, "ruler from ages eternal." It was state-supported and state-regulated. It had its own bureau in the Home Office and its priests and ceremonies and shrines were supported by the state.

Elements of Confucianism within Shinto are clearly evident in its prescribed hierarchy of social relationships. Taoism is evident in the extreme focus manifest in, for example, "the sweat of *muga*." Shinto has no holy books, just legends, fables, stories, and other folklore, which illustrate the principles Japanese live by.

ALTERNATIVE LEGAL SYSTEMS

Man is a social animal. The family is at the heart of his personal relationships. In general, familial relationships, the laws of inheritance (property rights), etc., are governed by what is known as Personal Law, or sometimes Family Law. Personal Law is used in most questions of domestic relations, marriage and divorce, maintenance and alimony, the "legitimization" of minors, the "inhibition" of the aged and incompetent persons, the administration of the property of absent persons, etc. It should thus seem natural that much later as the Commercial Law developed, it would include many of the concepts that formed the basis of Personal Law. Most business relationships are governed by what is generally known as Commercial Law. The specialty area known as Corporate Law is part of the more general body of Commercial Law. A highly developed system of Corporate Law developed in England during the era of the British East India Company (circa 1600–1860). Modern Corporate Law has its roots in this system.

CODE LAW

Present in continental Europe and many other countries that have "Westernized," such as Japan, Turkey, and Latin America. There have been three major periods of influence:

Prior to the Byzantine or Roman Emperor of the East, Justinian (A.D. 527–565), this was the living, changing, evolving law of Rome and the combined Roman Empire (which had been divided administratively by the Emperor Diocletian in A.D. 286). The living law evolved primarily from the "Laws of the Twelve Tables" (450

B.C.), the de-facto Constitution of the Roman Republic. The Byzantine Emperor, Justinian, later (A.D. 533) compiled the "Code and Digest," which contained the essential legacy of imperial legislation and juristic writings of the Romans from the founding of the Republic to the invasion and destruction of the city of Rome and collapse of the Empire of the West by the Visigoths (a Germanic tribe) in A.D. 476.

In the eleventh century A.D., however, Justinian's works were rediscovered and studied extensively in Italian universities, in monastaries by monks, and by other scholars. They then spread widely via missionaries throughout Europe (even across the channel into medieval England) and have significantly influenced the development of judicial thought and terminology ever since.

Next came the period of codification that began with the French *Code Napoleon* in A.D. 1804 at the height of Napoleon's military and political power. "The greatest codification of law that the world has ever known was never the law of any state at any time."

Problems of ownership, obligation, exchange, contract, and debt occupied the largest portion of Roman law. Ownership came either by inheritance or acquisition and materialism was at the very heart of Roman society. Acquisition came by formal gift or sale before a witness, or as the result of a suit at law. Obligations could arise as the result of non-contractual wrongs (torts) or through contract. Verbal promises before a witness were considered binding. Debts were incurred by loan, mortgage, deposit, or trust. In its final form, the Roman law of property is considered the most perfect part of the Roman code.

COMMON LAW

This is the law in Britain, Canada (not Quebec), the United States (not Louisiana), Australia, and New Zealand. Much Common Law (civil, criminal, and commercial) is still in force in India and parts of Africa.

Common Law or "English Law" is largely of Norman-English growth. The Normans, like the Romans, were tough soldiers, great architects, and inspired lawyers. Anglo-Saxon law (prior to A.D. 1066) was more Germanic, but has had little continuing influence. Continental lawyers refer to the Common Law (the law common to all of England) as "the law that nobody knows."

The Norman conquest of England established a system in which the royal court was only the highest stratum of a society administered by smaller landowners and their "petty entourages" (assemblies of citizens). During the first two centuries following the Norman Conquest, professional lawyers and judges gradually replaced patrons and civil servants.

It is important to realize that some important Roman (Code) Law principles have been adopted by the Common Law, e.g., in tort, the apportionment of loss according to the respective fault of the parties, also divorce law, and probate law.

Roman Law flowered under pagans. English Law is the product of Christian culture; but the Norman concept of separation of church and state stemmed the influence of the church. Nevertheless, early English judges were in holy orders.

English Common Law constitutes a classic system of case law or judge-made law. This means that under the Anglo-American system, courts have played, and continue to play, a leading part in creating new law, plus having the authority to give binding pronouncements on the true interpretation of statutes passed by legislatures. Note here that the law is thus made retroactively, hence "the law that nobody knows."

MARXIST/SOCIALIST LAW

The classic Marxist view of the legal system of any state is that it expresses and sub-serves the interests of the dominant class, and is therefore merely a cosmetic pretense, not at all impartial and inherently inequitable.

Marxists believe that when classes finally disappear altogether, under perfect communism, then the law and the state will be redundant and will wither away.

In a purely Marxist system, there is no private property, and there is no private enterprise. The core concept underlying this legal system concerns the exchange of commodities.

The owner of commodities is said to have a will toward alienation through exchange transactions and to profit from it. A legal contract is seen as the means of expression of such a will toward alienation. Through the process of "contractual bargains," relatively small numbers of persons were seen to engross large areas of economic activity. Legal institutions are seen strictly as mechanisms for expropriation under other names.

Thus, all areas of economic activity are transferred to public legal control, leaving to the private sphere only items for personal consumption.

At various times, and in various countries, the death penalty has been imposed for "economic crimes," such as corruption or embezzlement in state enterprises. Beginning with the 22nd Party Congress in 1961, "social morality" began to creep into the law. Stiff penalties were imposed for "parasitism," an idle, socially useless way of life; disobedience to the "inner voice" of social obligation.

Just prior to the dissolution of the USSR in 1989, Yevgenyi Smolentsev, Chairman of the Supreme Court of the USSR, wrote in an essay: "Democratic and humane socialism is only possible in a state ruled by the law which is based on two fundamental principles - the supremacy of the law and the division of power into legislative, executive, and judiciary. Our court reform is aimed at guaranteeing the independence of the judicial authority, and strengthening the foundation of a law-based state".

ISLAMIC LAW

Known as the "*Shari a.*"

Islam began with the teachings of the prophet Muhammad in A.D. 622 in Medina. It is not really an entirely new code of law, but rather an attempt to modify the existing Arabic tribal law in certain particulars. It largely concerns the relationships between men and women (*Personal Law*); and it grants women certain important rights.

Islam imposes a penalty of flogging for an unproved accusation of illicit sexual relations. Furthermore, Muhammad directed dowries to be the possession of the wife, not her father. It continues to allow men to terminate their marriages, but requires men to compensate their ex-wives. Particularly important are the inheritance laws with respect to women's rights. Arabic tribal law was strictly patrilineal and patriarchal. Traditional succession to property at death was traditionally confined to male agnate relatives. The Qur'an gives repeated emphasis to the closer family ties between parents and children, including daughters.

The Qur'an gives rights of inheritance to certain other close female relatives too: wives, mothers, and sisters.

Because of the influx of wealth that resulted from the numerous, rapid, military conquests of Islam, a popular and practical concern developed over its distribution and inheritance. In the famous case of Sa'd, his widow complained directly to Muhammad himself. His brother was claiming all of her dead husband's property. The prophet thus gave one-eighth to the widow and two-thirds to his daughters; the brother the residue.

The remarkable thing is that the brother got anything at all. This is called the "golden rule" of the Islamic Law of inheritance. In this way, the two classes of heirs (the new and the traditional) were merged into a composite system. The rights of the traditional heirs were diminished, but preserved. This preservation of the traditional Arabic tribal rights is an important characteristic of the general legal development of the Medina period.

After the death of Muhammad, Islam was a vast military empire with its central government at Damascus. Local governors were appointed to administer the provinces. These governors delegated judicial powers to officials known as the *Qadis* who produced a particularly interesting diversity of Islamic legal rulings. Ibn Hujayra, the Qadi of Cairo (A.D. 688–702) said that men must compensate their ex-wives with three dinars, and this was obligatory.

A subsequent Qadi of Cairo, Tawba ibn Namir, reversed this ruling and said that payment was up to the man's individual conscience and a husband who refused to pay could not be compelled to do so. Soon after, his successor made the payment a strict legal obligation again.

In contemporary Islam, the so-called Islamic Law is by no means exclusively Islamic. On the grounds of practical necessity, Muslim states and societies have recognized and applied laws whose terms are contrary to the religious doctrine. Laws imported from foreign, and particularly European sources now govern an ever-increasing field of legal relationships; however, the *Shari a* remains the symbol of ideological unity.

CHINESE LAW

"If I should ever leave England to live in China, I should go mad. The mere antiquity of Asiatic things, of their institutions, etc. I am terrified by modes of life placed by feelings deeper than I can analyze. I would sooner live with lunatics, or brute animals." (Thomas De Quincey May, 1818).

The Communists achieved victory in China in **1949** and changed institutions derived from the beliefs of farmers along the Yellow River 4000 years ago.

Of all the legal counselors to the rulers of China, one name stands out supreme, that of K'ung Fu-tzu, "Master K'ung" or "Confucius" (Latinized by seventh-century Jesuits). He lived between 551 and 479 B.C. Chief among his beliefs was that the best provision a man can make for his declining years is to beget sons to support him.

Also, a particularly Chinese idea is that humankind is so organically a part of the universe that human society not only depends on natural forces, but these forces are in turn affected by human conduct. Thus, the sexual instinct naturally leads to procreation and children are naturally subject to parental authority. Homosexuality is an abomination, which will upset the harmony of the seasons and bring drought or floods.

Penal codes were alien to Confucius' way of thinking. For him, the correct way to induce men to social functions was by education and example. During the unification of China under various dynasties, governments attempted to base the law on commands of the ruling emperors, but rebellions would soon sweep the tyrannical regimes from the land. Dynasties would rise and fall, but Confucianism remained.

Imperial China, then, for two thousand years down to the abdication of the last emperor in 1912, was governed according to Confucian principles. However, even though there is nothing bearing even the faintest resemblance to a civil code, the anti-Confucian notions of all those dynasties that attempted to rule by the will of the sovereign still exist in many legalistic specifics.

One fairly consistent legalistic specific of Chinese law is that a man can only have one wife. "Whoever has a second wife shall receive ninety blows, and his second wife shall be sent back home."

The husband and wife are of equal dignity, with the male being the active and dominant element. The male exercises parental powers, but after death they pass to the widow.

The clan has always been the most important source of private law. Another important source of law has been the guilds, regulating the affairs of trades and professions. The rules in guilds are fixed, much like a code. Only recently has the idea of a majority vote appeared in some cities. In general, courts do not welcome litigants. Custom largely governs business contracts.

HINDU LAW

It is applied as a part of the law of the land in India, Pakistan, Burma, Malaysia, Singapore, Aden, Kenya, Uganda, Tanzania, but (curiously) not Ceylon. It is largely *Personal Law*. There are two major schools, differing in minor aspects of marriage, inheritance, and females' rights in family property. It is recognized before British courts. "Hindu," in this context, means an Indian by racial extraction that is not a member of Muslim, Christian, Zoroastrian (Farsi), or Jewish religions.

Like Judaism, Hindu Personal Law will govern a child of a non-Hindu father and a Hindu mother. The law is as old as Indian civilization; traces are found in the Vedic literature of about 1500 B.C. Fundamental rules date from about 500 B.C. to 200 A.D.

Examples of legal postulates include a division of function between the judges and the assessor who recommended a judgment. There are "eighteen titles of law," serving as chapters of the court law. The legal system's key word is *duty* (originally of members of social groups in diverse, small kingdoms*)*, and was developed by the intellectual elite of the Brahmin caste.

When the Portuguese, the French, and the British acquired territory in India, *the British East India Company* became de facto sovereign of Bengal, Bihar, and Orissa in 1765. European-style courts were set up (especially English). Foreign judges until 1864 obtained opinions on Personal Law from native professors appointed to the court for this purpose (Pundits), afterward judicial knowledge of the system was assumed.

Appeals from the British-Indian High Courts were heard by the Privy Council in London (also heard appeals on French law from the Canadian province of Quebec, Roman-Dutch law from South Africa and Ceylon, and Islamic law from elsewhere); from French-Indian territories, cases went to the *Cour de Cessation* in Paris. The law thus evolved, and it is interesting to recognize that many members of the Privy Council tended to be Scots.

As an example of the convoluted nature of the resulting law is the *unchaste widow*. Traditional Hindu law intended her to be divested of her husband's estate. But British courts were averse to divesting a *vested* title, thinking in-laws would perjure themselves to take her property. Thus, if she remarried she became divested, also if she was unchaste at the time of his death; but being unchaste following his death does not deprive her.

AFRICAN LAW

Like Chinese law, the main source of rules for African law has been ancestral custom. African law is not one common body of law, but a family of systems of law, which share no traceable common parent.

Nevertheless, the systems reveal a striking similarity in procedures, principles, institutions, and techniques. Differences point out interesting reactions to unique variations in environment. Firstly, all African legal systems are unwritten; hence there is no written legislation, nor juristic analyses. Secondly, some African societies exclusively recognize matrilineal succession, others patrilineal. This affects differences in parental authority, the structure of the corporate family, and rights of inheritance.

Most African law is very formal with respect to the creation of a marriage, the transfer of property, and the disposal of an estate. It is less formal with respect to other matters and often employs a leader or counselor as chief spokesperson or advocate in discussions, or judge and arbiter in disputes or quarrels. Among the Kikuyu of Kenya, he is *"muthamaki wa chira."* To the Arusha of Tanzania, he is known as *"olaigwenani."*

In general, African law is public knowledge. It is not the "exclusive monopoly of an aristocracy or judicial oligarchy."

During the latter part of the nineteenth and first part of the twentieth centuries, highly organized legal systems were superimposed on

Africa, developed in utterly different environments, motivated by different objectives, backed-up by administrative systems, and military and police forces.

JEWISH LAW

Jewish law is an all-embracing body of religious duties, regulating all aspects of Jewish life. It comprises, on an equal footing, norms of worship and ritual, rules of private and social behavior, **and** laws, which nowadays are enforced by the courts.

Jewish law is part of the law of modern Israel in so far as it forms the *Personal Law* of Jewish citizens. It is also given status in some foreign countries, e.g., the United Kingdom. Some of the concepts of Jewish law have infiltrated pieces of Israeli legislation (influence).

Jurisdiction is vested in rabbinical courts, always composed of three members. Rabbinical courts are also frequently used to settle arbitration cases. In these cases, it is important to note that judgments can only be enforced through execution by the civil courts, and they sometimes refuse to act.

Most of the provisions of Jewish law do not apply to Gentiles living in the Jewish community.

ALTERNATIVE POLITICAL AND ECONOMIC SYSTEMS

THE POLITICAL ENVIRONMENT

The sovereignty of nations is a generally accepted facet of international relations: supreme and independent power or authority within a state. It is assumed that the country's overall goals for its economic, political, and social systems reflects, or is consistent with the base of its political environment. The most important factor facing international marketers is the **stability** of a prevailing government's policies, regardless of which particular party is in power.

POLITICAL RISKS

Governments can exert total control over any activity occurring within their borders. Regardless of the specific nature of a particular regime, it is the **stability** of government policies that is most important to foreign businesses.

Instability, or change, usually occurs as the result of action by political parties. Monitoring the philosophies of all major political parties is, therefore, very important to marketers. Nationalism is the largest possible threat to international marketing.

Between 1960 and 1980, a total of 1,535 firms from 22 different capital-exporting countries had been expropriated in 511 separate actions by 76 different nations. *Confiscation* is the seizing of a company's assets without payment of any kind.

Expropriation is the seizing of a company's assets with some, usually minor, form of reimbursement, although the actual, physical worth of the assets is often in dispute.

Domestication is the gradual (it varies) transfer of a company's assets to local or governmental ownership or control. Domestication can be insidious, occurring through a series of apparently unrelated government decrees.

In the worst-case scenario, the local police, local governmental authorities, national military, national police, or the armed representatives of any number of other organizations, will simply show up at your place of business and either kill you outright, take you into custody, or ask you to leave immediately, often forbidding you to take any personal possessions whatsoever, or contact any other person prior to leaving the country.

Today, it is much more common for governments to require foreign business interests to share the ownership, and/or management of an enterprise with nationals as a condition of entry or continued and/or expanded presence in the country. These terms often include mandates with respect to local content (supply) requirements, and/or the use of domestic labor.

Ironically, many earlier confiscated, expropriated, and nationalized businesses are now being privatized. Privatization has been a major worldwide trend. Privatization is seen by many governments largely as a source of much-needed capital, technology, and management/marketing expertise.

ECONOMIC/POLITICAL RISKS

Governments can also impose economic restrictions for essentially nationalistic reasons, often in the name of "national security."

–Exchange controls

–Local-content Laws

–Import restrictions

–Taxation policies

–Price controls

–Other labor-related issues/risks

ENCOURAGING FOREIGN INVESTMENT

Foreign governments – eliminate conditions for entry, exchange controls, taxation, content and labor requirements, etc.

U.S. Government:

Export-Import Bank – insurance against political risks in selected countries, i.e., inconvertibility, war, confiscation, civil disturbances, cancellation or restriction of import or export licenses.

Foreign Credit Insurance Association – insurance against a buyer's obligation due to political reasons.

The Agency for International Development (USAID) also issues insurance for political risks, but only in support of "essential" projects in approved countries.

Overseas Private Investment Corporation – insurance against political risks in less-developed countries.

Private Insurance Sources – Lloyd's of London.

REDUCING POLITICAL VULNERABILITY

Good corporate citizenship: minimize capital flight, invest in the local economy.

Do not try to "Americanize" your customers or employees.

Use the local language in all sales and business transactions, including advertising and sales promotion.

Invest or contribute to local public projects.

Train executives and their families in the local culture.

Staff local offices with foreign nationals and supervise the operation from the U.S.

Other strategies:

Joint ventures with locals and other third-country MNCs.

Expand the investment base with local investors and local or third-country banks.

Maintain control of marketing and distribution overseas.

License technology, etc., from a distance.

Planned domestication.

ALTERNATIVE MEDICAL SYSTEMS

Since earliest times, natural remedies have been used throughout the world. Medicinal plants account for approximately 20% of all prescriptions in developed countries and 80% of all prescriptions in developing countries.

(The World Health Organization has compiled a list of over 20,000 common medicinal plants used in different parts of the world.)

NATURAL REMEDIES

The association between disease and nutrition is well established in modern medicine. About 400 B.C. the Greek physician Hippocrates (460–377 B.C.) said, "Let food be your medicine and medicine be your food." In addition to diseases associated with general malnutrition, modern science recognizes the difference between those nutrients that can be synthesized by the body and those that must be supplied from an external source. The essential nutrients include vitamins, minerals, amino acids, and some form of carbohydrate as a source of energy.

Much of modern medicine has only recently begun to recognize the therapeutic value of some of these natural remedies as there have

Of considerable importance is the Chinese system, which is based on a theory of dynamic interplay and homeostasis between the viscera of *Yin* (corresponding to the functions of the heart, liver, spleen, kidney, and lung) and the *Yang* (corresponding to the function of the bowels, gall bladder, stomach, large and small intestines, and urinary bladder).

Other systems of equal standing, in terms of both their theory and logical development include: (1) the Unnani-Tibb system, on which considerable documentation is still available in the original Turkish script in Istanbul; (2) the ancient medical theories of the Babylonian-Assyrian period; (3) those from the Egyptian civilization, up to and including the theories of Hippocrates (460–377 B.C.); and (4) the works of Galen (A.D. 130–200), which were practiced up until the period of the American Civil War. There are also the medical theories of the indigenous peoples of the Latin American region, found to be relatively rich in concepts and structure.

Because of the existence of large populations today where a significant proportion uses traditional herbal therapies and where such therapies are socially accepted and believed in, the Ayurvedic system and the Chinese system warrant particular attention. These two systems of medicine share some concepts that developed independently in other cultures having no known communication with each other. One such concept is that disease is caused by a change in the "balanced state" of the body. This idea is not in conflict with the central tenets of modern medical science.

The main objective of Ayurveda is the restoration and maintenance of metabolic equilibrium.

Economic Development of Medicinal Plants

The World Health Organization has compiled a list of over 20,000 common medicinal plants used in different parts of the world. And, as already mentioned, medicinal plants account for approximately 20% of all prescriptions in developed countries and a whopping 80% of all prescriptions in developing countries.

Two major issues that confront the global medicinal plant industry are *national development* and *technical assistance*. These are very complicated issues because of the multidimensional nature and interdependence of the industry. Large-scale agricultural production, the extraction of active ingredients, formulations, dosing, manufacturing, and marketing all require significant levels of technical expertise. Underdeveloped nations frequently lack such expertise and are therefore dependent on the more developed nations for technical assistance. Furthermore, special situations exist in many countries, such as China and India, where fresh, dried, and partially processed medicinal plants are found. There are markets in the developing world for each of these products. In the developed world there is a sophisticated array of herbal preparations, impressively formulated and aggressively marketed. In order for national development to occur in and around this industry, a great deal of technical assistance is needed **from** agribusiness professionals and chemists **to** customer satisfaction and marketing specialists.

In Asia, Africa, Latin America and the Pacific Islands, only about 20% of the population benefit from **modern drugs**. Traditional, natural remedies are the norm in such places. The merchants of medicinal plants and essential oils (aromatic plants), wishing to obtain large profits, do not **protect nature** and maximally exploit existing stocks. In programming the *renewable* exploitation of medicinal and essential oil plants, it is important not to neglect the additional role of some plants, trees and shrubs, in favoring the multiplication of birds, or insects, or animals that are useful in natural pest control and maintaining a productive ecological balance among natural processes, and especially their complex interactions.

In many areas where medicinal plants thrive, conventional transportation is difficult and distances to industrial centers are great. The location of drying equipment, post-harvest conditioning, primary processing, and storage are all important economic and development considerations. There appears to be a large and growing market for such products, even in the industrial world where the terms "natural" and "organic" have taken on sharply important characteristics, and a profitable demand.

From the point of view of an industrializing society, however, providing labor opportunities in remote areas of the world, as well as water, electric power, food, medicines, and fuel are also very important and frequently difficult considerations. So too are the important specialty areas described below a major concern.

Chemotaxonomic selection:

This is the segregation and propagation of selected medicinal plants at the expense of others, based on high active substance content. It requires an in-depth knowledge of genetics and the importance of multiplying plants with a greater yield of the specific active ingredient desired over other active ingredients that might also be present. Some elements of industry frequently prefer, strangely enough, a plant with less foliage yield and less essential oil content, such as French varieties of lavender, preferred because of their lower essential oil, but higher ester content.

Economic mapping

This is the quantitative and qualitative determination of the profit potential of a given geographic area. For medicinal plants, it is the determination of the potential to profitably develop organization, collection, drying and conditioning centers, as well as pharmaceutical industrial units for the extraction of active substances. Economic mapping also locates existing, small-scale processing plants at which collecting and drying operations take place. Economic mapping notes soil conditions, soil moisture and pH, calcium, potassium, nitrogen and trace elements present in the soil.

THE AYURVEDIC SYSTEM OF MEDICINE

Health in Ayurveda is defined as the dual state of a well-balanced metabolism and a state of well-being in the mind, body, and senses. Disease is recognized as being four-fold: adventitious (the result of external injury); physical (caused by nutritional or metabolic imbalances, for example, growths, inflammatory conditions and infections); mental (including states of imbalance caused by anger, pride, greed, hate, uncurbed desires, etc.), and natural (which covers naturally occurring phenomena, such as birth, aging, hunger, thirst, sleep, etc.).

Therapeutic approaches to disease are dependent upon the category of disease. Broadly speaking, the adventitious diseases call for surgical methods. Physical diseases are treated medically; mental diseases are treated psychologically; and natural diseases are treated spiritually.

The Ayurvedic concept of the treatment of disease is a three-pronged approach consisting of therapeutic agents, diets, and spiritual practices. The physiological symptoms and the pathogenesis of disease are explained in terms of the three basic constituents of the human system. These three elements cannot easily be rendered into modern medical terminology. Very crudely, therefore, the first element, *vata*, is responsible for the utilization of energy by cells and organs for the growth process, and also controls the movements of the other two elements and, therefore, all functions and activities of the body. The second element, *pitta*, is body energy and so is the agent of metabolic changes and the governing force behind the entire body chemistry. The final element, *kapha*, has to do with the cell structure of the body and, therefore, its physical well-being and effectiveness.

Whereas, in Ayurveda, health and disease are based on the normality and abnormality of the functioning of vata, pitta, and kapha, amelioration of disease, or return to the state of normality, is dependent on the reconversion of any abnormality in these three *doshas*. Besides the three doshas (vata, pitta, and kapha), which are analogous to the system of "humors" in the Greek system of ancient medicine (which was still widely practiced at the time of the American Revolutionary War), the human body consists of seven *dhatus* and several *malas*. The seven dhatus are (1) body fluids, (2) blood, (3) muscle, (4) adipose tissue, (5) bone, (6) nerve tissue, and (7) generative tissue (sperm and ova). The malas consist of body wastes including (1) stools, (2) urine, (3) sweat, (4) hair, (5) nails, (6) mucous, and (7) miscellaneous.

The Ayurvedic definition of health is a state of equilibrium or dynamic balance between the three doshas, the seven dhatus, and the seven malas, and any imbalance results in disease for which appropriate therapy consists of measures to restore the balance. It is a holistic rather than a symptomatic approach.

The regulation of diet is an inseparable part of Ayurvedic treatment and foods are classified as either "heaty" or "cold." The two types are indicated depending on whether a particular disease is associated with an imbalance caused by a "cold-factor" or a "heaty-factor," respectively. This concept of diet and classifications of food as therapy is present in other systems of traditional medicine as well, notably the Chinese system. It is an interesting and noteworthy concept that should be taken into consideration when evaluating therapies that originate in these systems of medicine.

CHINESE TRADITIONAL MEDICINE

Ancient Chinese concepts bear a close formal resemblance to those generated independently by other civilizations. In classical Chinese concepts, the body is seen as composed of a number of interrelated functional entities or *orbs*, and there is a dynamic interplay of these in the body. There are two categories of orbs: *yin* and *yang*. The yin orbs correspond to the functions of the body organs such as the heart, liver, spleen, kidney, and lung, and are associated with the storing of life constituents. The yang orbs correspond to the functions of the bowels, gall bladder, stomach, large and small intestines, and urinary bladder, and are associated with the digestion and transport of body nutrients. It is important to recognize that it is the orbs themselves that are the functional entities, while the corresponding organs are merely the substrates or carriers. Each orb is not defined by any anatomical role but rather by its specific function such as processing, storing, and distributing energy.

According to the basic concepts of Chinese medicine, the well-being of the human body depends on maintaining homeostasis, a balance or equilibrium. The fundamental concept is that there is coordination between the various parts of the body that can adapt it to variations in the environment, and disease is the consequence of a confrontation between the harmful effects of a pathogen and the intrinsic resistance of the body. Disease results when such a confrontation succeeds in breaking down the states of balance and equilibrium.

The pathogenic factors in Chinese medicine are classified into categories such as the atmospheric factors: wind, cold, damp, dryness, fire, etc.; the emotional factors: joy, anger, melancholy, anxiety, grief, fear, etc.; and other factors: strain, stress, trauma, irregular meals, improper diet, etc. Diet is an important aspect of traditional Chinese medicine.

Traditional Chinese medicines for these syndromes are arranged into the eighteen categories as shown in Table 3-1

TABLE 3-1 CATEGORIES OF DRUGS IN CHINESE TRADITIONAL MEDICINES

1. Drugs for dispelling pathogens from the exterior of the body, i.e., diaphoretics.
2. Antitussives, anti-asthmatics, and drugs for resolving phlegm.
3. Drugs for clearing internal heat, i.e., antipyretics.
4. Drugs for dispelling internal wind dampness, i.e., anti-rheumatics.
5. Warm drugs for dispelling internal cold.
6. Aromatic drugs for resolving dampness.
7. Diuretics and hydrogogues.
8. Drugs for regulating the flow of vital energy.
9. Drugs for regulating blood condition and circulation.
10. Aromatic drugs for stimulating resuscitation.
11. Drugs stabilizing the spirit, essentially sedatives and tranquilizers.
12. Drugs for subduing hyperactivity of the hepatic orb and endogenous wing.
13. Drugs reinforcing vital functions, i.e., tonics and aphrodisiacs.
14. Drugs arresting discharges, including astringents and hemostatics.
15. Digestives and evacuants.
16. Purgatives and laxatives.
17. Anthelminthics.
18. Drugs for external use.

INDUSTRY BACKGROUND

The modern pharmaceutical industry, based on synthetic and semi-synthetic organic chemistry, began in Germany in the later part of the nineteenth century. The industry has had, therefore, a relatively short (in a general context) but dynamic history. Natural products from both plant and animal sources have been used as medicines for thousands of years.

Pierre Pelletier and **Joseph Caventou** established the first modern pharmaceutical company to produce *pure quinine* from imported cinchona bark in 1826.

FIGURE 4-1 THE FIRST MODERN PHARMACEUTICAL COMPANY

The pharmaceutical industry, which developed in the late 1880s, consolidated diverse interests and emerged during a very specific phase of history. The industry did not develop in isolation, but as an integral part of a multitude of events that have shaped the course of world and regional histories in general. The pharmaceutical industry began less than 30 years after the birth of industrial-scale, synthetic organic chemistry, which had begun in 1856 with the discovery of the first of the aniline dyes by a young Englishman by the name of William Henry Perkin.

THE BIRTH OF INDUSTRIAL-SCALE, SYNTHETIC ORGANIC CHEMISTRY

William Perkin made his famous discovery in 1856 while trying to synthesize quinine (see figure 4-2), a drug that could be obtained only from the bark of the cinchona tree and which grew, at the time, only in Bolivia and Peru despite costly attempts by Britain and Holland to grow it elsewhere. Quinine had been used by Europeans as part of raw cinchona bark since 1629 when it was discovered among the Indians of the new world, and had first been isolated in 1820 by the French, i.e., Pelletier and Caventou.

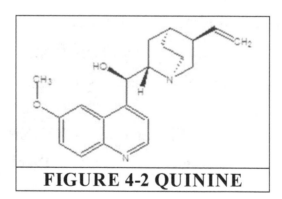

FIGURE 4-2 QUININE

Quinine was in exceptionally high demand and therefore expensive as the only known treatment for malaria, which was rampant throughout the world in India, Russia, Australia, New York, Philadelphia, Florida, New Orleans, and the Carolinas. British imperialists found malaria to be their greatest hindrance to colonization. No one had yet made the link between the disease and mosquitoes.

It was generally known, by Perkin and others, that quinine was an alkaloid,[6] like caffeine in coffee beans and both morphine and codeine in opium (see Figure 4-3).

Caffeine $C_8H_{10}O_4N_2$	Morphine $C_{17}H_{19}NO_3$	Codeine $C_{18}H_{21}NO_3$

FIGURE 4-3 SOME IMPORTANT ALKALOIDS

It was also known that the molecular formula for quinine was similar to compounds that could be extracted from coal tar, such as naphthalidine, a two-ring aromatic molecule with nitrogen attached as part of an amine group (see Figure 4-4). Perkin's teacher, Dr. August Wilhelm von Hofmann, had realized earlier that the amine group continues to manifest the basic character of its ammonia parent whenever it is attached to a number of other, though simpler molecules. So it was natural for him to imagine that aromatic ring systems derived

---

[6]   Alkaloids all contain nitrogen and therefore tend to behave as nitrogenous bases in chemical reactions. Alkaloids occur naturally in many forms of plant life and can have strong physiological effects when administered in small quantities. There was considerable demand for better methods of analyzing alkaloids and a great many scientists of the period were involved in research either directly or indirectly related to questions of whether or not such substances could be synthesized from materials that are not derived from living things, e.g., coal tar extracts.

from coal tar and having an amine group attached, such as aniline and naphthalidine (see Figure 4-4), would react with a variety of acids and oxidizing agents to form entirely new chemicals with their aromatic ring(s) still intact. Hofmann had been doing these kinds of experiments for over 15 years when Perkin made his discovery.

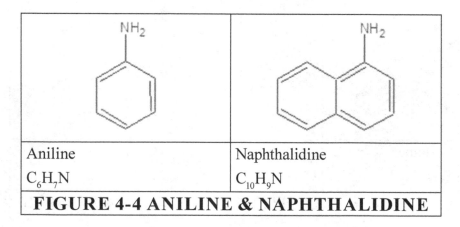

Aniline C_6H_7N	Naphthalidine $C_{10}H_9N$

FIGURE 4-4 ANILINE & NAPHTHALIDINE

In the end, Perkin was working in his home laboratory with compounds he had synthesized from coal tar when he saw that by oxidizing one of these compounds (aniline) with potassium dichromate, he had in fact synthesized a new, multi-ring compound with a magnificent purple color (see Figure 4-5). He soon found it to be an excellent colorfast dye and rushed into commercial production.

Perkin's new synthetic dye, called "mauve" by the French, was the first of the so-called *aniline dyes*.[7] It marks the beginning of large-scale, synthetic organic chemistry and led to the development of a whole host of other colors, including fuchsine or "magenta red" in 1858, and "bleu de Lyon" in 1860 (both synthesized in France).

[7]   Aniline was first discovered in 1826 by Prussian chemist Otto Unverdorben as one of several products he obtained from the distillation of the natural vegetable dye indigo. In 1834, Friedlieb Runge obtained it from the distillation of coal tar.

Hank Laskey

Although Perkin's discovery took place in England, it spread rapidly to the European continent where, soon after, German chemists and the emerging German industrial machine took over. Later, using fuchsine as a base, August von Hofman developed violet, "Perkin green," and "Manchester brown." Eventually, the industrial synthesis of alizarin (the natural red dye obtained from the madder plant, cultivated in commercial quantities in southern France), and indigo (the natural blue dye obtained from the indigo plant, grown in India) by chemical giants BASF and Hoechst in Germany, resulted in the complete disappearance of the natural dyestuffs from the marketplace and the total annihilation of large-scale madder production in southern France, as well as serious problems for the British-controlled indigo trade with India.

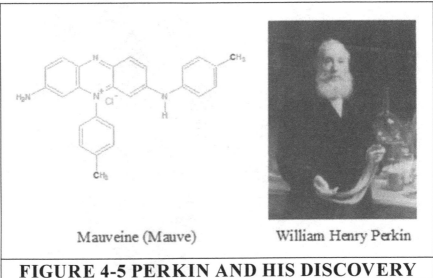

Mauveine (Mauve)   William Henry Perkin

FIGURE 4-5 PERKIN AND HIS DISCOVERY

Most importantly, it was Perkin's discovery that made aniline the intermediate for pharmaceutical manufacturing that it is today. Aniline has been the starting point for a large number of pharmaceutical products developed since Perkin's discovery, including analgesics, anti-anxiety agents, anti-inflammatory agents, antibacterial agents, antipyretics, hypnotics, and tranquilizers.

THE ANILINE REVOLUTION

Aniline was found to be so useful in organic synthesis that many new companies were formed to set up aniline production, i.e., large-scale, synthetic organic chemistry. Table 4-1 presents a list of some of the many companies that were established just to make it, or who started making it and/or using its many derivatives in the years following Perkin's discovery.

TABLE 4-1 ANILINE COMPANIES

Company	Country	Year
K.G.R. Oehler (Griesheim Elektron)	Germany	1856
Perkin & Sons	Britain	1857
Renard Freres (Societe la Fuchsine)	France	1858
Read Holliday	Britain	1858
Girard et Georges de Laire	France	1860
Alexandre Clavel (Gesellschaft fur Chemische Industrie Basel – CIBA)	Switzerland	1860
J.J. Muller (Geigy)	Switzerland	1860
J. Poirrier (S.A. des Matieres Colorantes et Produits Chimiques de Saint Denis)	France	1861
Badische Anilin und Soda Fabrik (BASF)	Germany	1861
Meister Lucius & Bruning (Farbwerke Hoechst)	Germany	1862
Durand & Huguenin	Switzerland	1862
Friedrich Bayer (Farben Fabrik vormals Friedrich Bayer)	Germany	1863
Kalle & Co.	Germany	1864
Leopold Cassella & Cie.	Germany	1867
Aktien Gesellschaft fur Anilin Fabrikation (AGFA)	Germany	1867
Schoellkoph Aniline & Chemical Co.	USA	1879
Benzol Products	USA	1910
DuPont	USA	1916
Calco	USA	1916
Dow	USA	1916
National Aniline and Chemical Company	USA	1917

THE FIRST SYNTHETIC PHARMACEUTICALS

Shortly after the Franco-Prussian War, around 1872, in the newly unified German empire, Robert Koch discovered that different aniline dyes could be used to selectively color different strains of bacteria. This suggested that aniline dyes or their derivatives could be used to treat disease. Koch was also the first to identify which bacteria caused specific diseases, including the rod-bacillus of anthrax, and in 1882, the bacillus of tuberculosis. In 1884, he developed purified tuberculin serum as a possible cure for tuberculosis and sold the rights to German dyestuffs manufacturer, Hoechst, for the outrageous sum of one million marks. It was later found to be useful only in the diagnosis of tuberculosis, rather than a cure; nevertheless, his method is still used today, and Hoechst went on to become a pharmaceutical powerhouse.

BAYER ASPIRIN

Bayer Aspirin (acetylsalicylic acid) was the first truly successful synthetic pharmaceutical (shown in Figure 4-6).[8]

---

[8]   Acetylsalicylic acid was <u>first</u> synthesized in 1853 in Strasbourg (at that time, a French city) by professor Dr. Frederic Charles Gerhardt in a reaction between salicylic acid and acetic anhydride. Gerhardt's work remained obscure until 1860 when German professor, Dr. Adolf Hermann Kolbe, at the University of Marburg (east of Bayer's facility in Leverkusen), synthesized salicylic acid from phenol. Kolbe's student, Friedrich von Heyden, first produced it commercially as a food preservative almost two decades later, after the Franco-Prussian War, and it is still used as a food preservative today. Also, acetylsalicylic acid today is still synthesized according to the method developed by Kolbe, i.e., by reacting phenol with carbon dioxide in the presence of heat, pressure, and sodium hydroxide to yield salicylic

FIGURE 4-6 ACETYLSALICYLIC ACID ("BAYER ASPIRIN")

Bayer Aspirin was introduced in Germany in 1897. It was patented in Germany in 1899. The formulation of *Bayer Aspirin* has remained essentially unchanged since that time. Nevertheless, *Bayer Aspirin* was not the <u>first</u> (or second, third, or fourth for that matter) synthetic pharmaceutical. The <u>first</u> synthetic pharmaceutical was *antipyrine* (Hoechst, 1884) The second was *acetanilide* (branded "Antifibrin" by Kalle & Co., 1886). The third was *Phenacetin* (Hoechst, 1888). And the fourth was *Pyramidon* (Hoechst, 1893). *Bayer Aspirin* was actually the fifth synthetic pharmaceutical.

ANTIPYRINE

The first synthetic pharmaceutical, *antipyrine*, was a drug discovered by Dr. Ludwig Knorr while he was a graduate student

---

acid, and then by reacting the salicylic acid with acetic anhydride. It is not only an antipyretic, but has anti-inflammatory and analgesic properties as well, which made it useful in the treatment of rheumatic fever (now known to be caused by a streptococcus infection), which was a common ailment. Today, aspirin is the only drug manufactured on the scale of an industrial commodity. Over 20 million pounds are produced in the United States each year.

in 1883.[9] He gave the rights to Hoechst, who scaled up and began marketing in 1884.

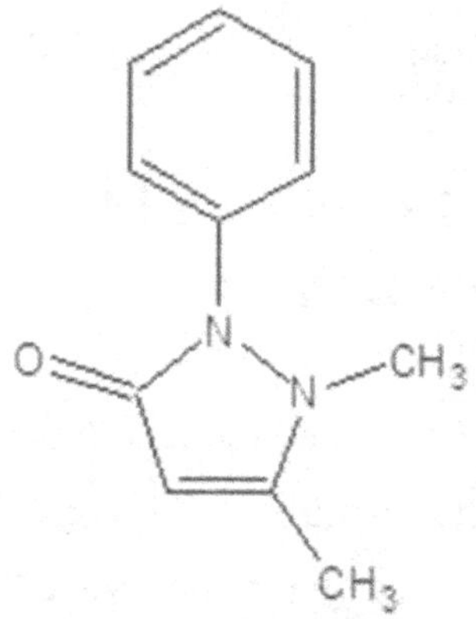

FIGURE 4-7 ANTIPYRINE

Following a suggestion from Knorr, Hoechst began doing large-scale research on the derivatives of pyrazole (see Figure 4-8) as possible pharmaceutical products. As an addition to their dyestuffs business, this involved a significant commitment to pharmaceutical research and development on the part of Hoechst.

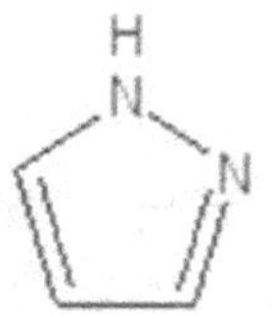

FIGURE 4-8 PYRAZOLE

---

[9]   Knorr had been a student of Dr. Emil Fischer, a natural products chemist who was awarded the Nobel Prize in Chemistry in 1902 for his work on purines and sugars. Between 1899 and 1906, Fischer decomposed proteins into amino acids and then used these to synthesize polypeptides.

ACETANILIDE ("ANTIFIBRIN")

The second synthetic pharmaceutical, *acetanilide*, forms by reacting aniline with acetic acid. The pharmaceutical properties of *acetanilide* were discovered in the (formerly French) city of Strasbourg (which belonged to the German empire in 1886 as a result of the Franco-Prussian War) when two medical interns (Drs. Kahn and Hepp) requested a supply of naphthalene through a local pharmacist to treat a case of intestinal parasites and mistakenly received *acetanilide* instead, which they administered to their patient. They found that it did not cure the patient of parasites, but it did dramatically reduce the patient's fever. Hence, the remarkable antipyretic properties of acetanilide were discovered—by accident!

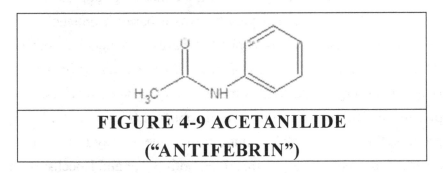

FIGURE 4-9 ACETANILIDE ("ANTIFEBRIN")

This information reached the German Kalle & Co. through Hepp's brother who worked there as a chemist. Kalle & Co. was a specialty dyestuffs manufacturer that began in 1864 across the Rhine from Strasbourg, in Biebrich, Germany. It was Kalle & Co. that had supplied the pharmacist with *acetanilide* in the first place.

Because the process for making *acetanilide* was well-known, and therefore could not be patented, Kalle & Co. came up with the rather innovative idea of simply marketing it under another name. Thus, they began to market *acetanilide* as an antipyretic under the trade name, *Antifebrin*, charging more for it than generic *acetanilide*, which infuriated pharmacists. However, nothing could be done because it was illegal to change the written prescription of a physician who prescribed *Antifebrin* instead of *acetanilide* and, of course, Kalle & Co. marketed *Antifebrin* to physicians and not *acetanilide*. Kalle & Co. became (and is today) a subsidiary of Hoechst, and thus is today a part of the German/French conglomerate, Aventis.

PHENACETIN

The same year in which *Antipyrine* was introduced to the market, 1884, Bayer formally hired Dr. Carl Duisberg to direct its own research and development efforts. Bayer was generating approximately 30 thousand kilograms per year of waste para-nitrophenol from its dyestuffs business. Knowing that para-nitrophenol is similar to *acetanilide* and that sales of *acetanilide* and *Antifibrin* were rising, Duisberg instructed his researchers to come up with a new pharmaceutical product from para-nitrophenol (Figure 4-10). In the process, Bayer was to make a huge commitment away from its core dyestuffs business. Thus, by this time, both Bayer and Hoechst were making large investments in pharmaceuticals. In 1890, Bayer had over six times more chemists (90) as in 1881. However, all was not smooth. In their book, *The Aspirin Wars*, Charles Mann and Mark Plummer describe the situation at Bayer as follows:

> *"Duisberg kept stuffing workers into Bayer's crude, overcrowded research quarters. Lab tables were scattered everywhere in the facilities, with foul-smelling experiments being conducted in corridors, bathrooms, and an abandoned woodworking shop.*

Lucky researchers had access to sinks; unlucky ones worked outdoors, in the river fog. They wore clogs because the muddy ground was full of harmless-looking puddles capable of disintegrating leather shoes. They had no chemical storeroom, no technical library, and little equipment – nothing but a platoon of boys who cleaned retorts and vials." (Mann and Plummer, p. 24)

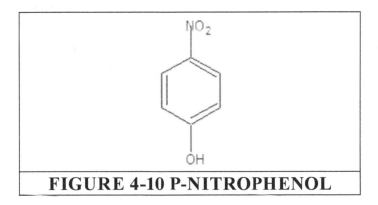

FIGURE 4-10 P-NITROPHENOL

The result of Duisberg's dogged ambition at Bayer was *Phenacetin (Figure 4-11)*, the third synthetic pharmaceutical to hit the market. Like *Antifibrin, Phenacetin* was a trade name, and Bayer developed a sales force to market the new product internationally.

A major influenza epidemic swept across the Northern Hemisphere in 1889, the year after *Phenacetin* was introduced, and Bayer was able to reap huge profits from *Phenacetin* sales throughout Europe, Russia, and the United States. With significantly fewer side-effects than *Antifibrin, Phenacetin* cost consumers much more than *Antifibrin.*

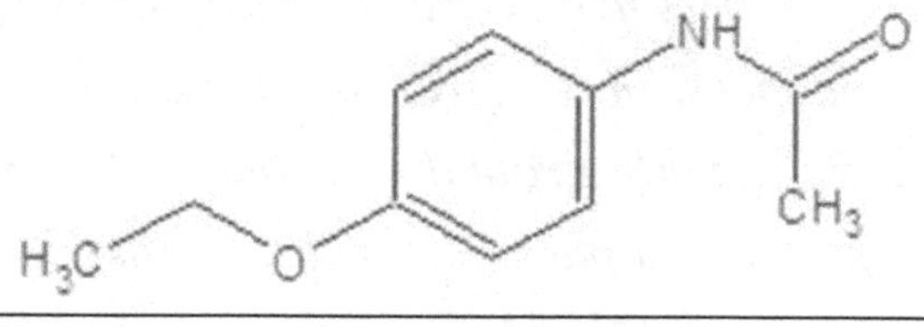

FIGURE 4-11 PHENACETIN

PYRAMIDON

In 1887, Giessen University professor, Dr. A. Laudenheimer became the head of research at Hoechst. This marks the beginning of a strong pharmaceuticals tradition at Hoechst, with what was to become a strong commitment of resources. In 1893, Hoechst introduced the fourth synthetic pharmaceutical to the market, Pyramidon.

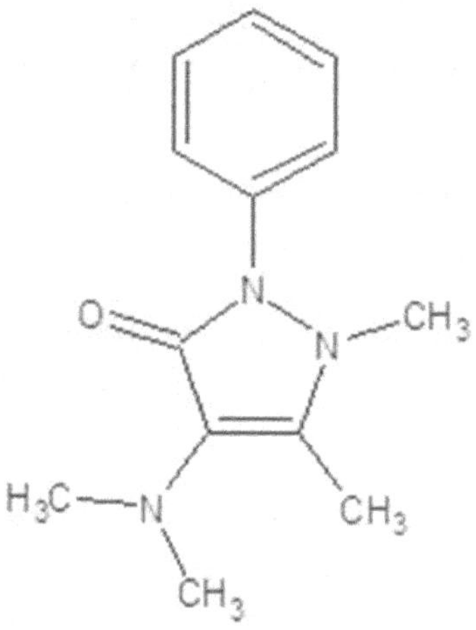

FIGURE 4-12 PYRAMIDON

Under the leadership of Laubenheimer at Hoechst and Duisberg at Bayer, the two became the dominant pharmaceutical companies in the world, and together created the modern pharmaceutical industry.

Bayer and Hoechst created the modern pharmaceutical industry beginning in the 1880s.

FIGURE 4-13 BIRTH OF THE INDUSTRY

EARLY PHARMACEUTICALS

The dominance of Hoechst and Bayer through the period of World War I can be seen in Table 4-2, which lists successful drugs from the period of 1884 through 1964.

TABLE 4-2 EARLY SUCCESSFUL DRUGS

Date	Drug	Category	Company
1884	Antipyrin	antipyretic	Hoechst
1886	Antifebrin	antipyretic	Kalle
1888	Phenacetin	analgesic/antipyretic	Bayer
1893	Pyramidon	analgesic/antipyretic	Hoechst
1898	Aspirin	analgesic/antipyretic	Bayer
1902	Diphtheria antitoxin	antitoxin	Hoechst
1904	Veronal	hypnotic/sedative	Bayer/Merck
1905	Novocaine	anesthetic	Hoechst
1909	Salvarsan	anti-syphilitic	Hoechst
1922	Insulin	hormone/diabetes	Hoechst
1928	Progynon	hormone/estrogen	Schering
1935	Prontosil	antibacterial	Bayer
1938	Sulfapyridine	antibacterial	May and Baker
1938	Sulfathiazol	antibacterial	May and Baker
1939	Dolantine	analgesic	Hoechst

1941	Chloroquine	antimalarial	Winthrop
1942	Sulfamethazine	antibacterial	ICI
1942	Penicillin (C)	antibacterial	Merck, Pfizer, etc.
1946	Paludrine	antimalarial	ICI
1948	Streptomycin	antibacterial	Merck
1954	Hibitane	antibacterial	ICI
1956	Norethindrone	contraceptive	Syntex
1957	Fluothane	anesthetic	ICI
1959	Tolbutamide	antidiabetic	Hoechst
1961	Ampicillin	antibacterial	Beecham
1962	Tolazamide	antidiabetic	Upjohn
1964	Inderal	antihypertensive	ICI

It is important to realize that the Allied powers made German patents public property as a result of both World Wars I and II. Take, for example, Winthrop's launching of Chloroquine in 1941. This drug had been protected by German patent 683692 issued in 1939. Furthermore, there was an unprecedented and massive combined effort on the part of both American and British companies to develop Penicillin during World War II. The incredible upheaval that occurs across society when nations go to war is, therefore, acutely indicative of widespread scientific, social, and economic transformations. However, such transformations are not uniquely associated with war.

THE TIMING OF SCIENTIFIC, SOCIAL & ECONOMIC TRANSFORMATIONS

Selecting a moment in time from which to begin the telling of the history of any subject should depend in large measure on the prior knowledge and beliefs of one's intended audience.

For example, it would probably be inappropriate to begin the history of the global pharmaceutical industry in the year 1850–1851 if one's audience did not fully grasp the major events leading up to this particular time-frame, or the conditions that then existed. Furthermore, if an audience tended to believe that the economic supremacy of France had finally been decided in favor of Great Britain with Wellington's defeat of Bonaparte at Waterloo, then there might be little merit in discussing (rehashing) their relative advantages in international shipments of medicinal raw materials during the Napoleonic wars, and perhaps more advisable to simply begin with the premise that by 1850–1851 Britannia ruled not only the seas but most of the world's sources of raw materials and her overseas markets for finished products. Additionally, if one believes that the greatest universities and medical schools prior to 1850–1851 were in France, and that chemistry was essentially a French science that was in some sense "stolen" by the Germans, then there would probably be little receptivity to arguments concerning the relative merits of the German university system prior to the great "theft," or to the role of the German patent and banking systems, the availability of credit, etc.

It is quite common for students seeking to compare the industrial development of the major European economies, such as Britain, France, and Germany, to begin their analyses approximately midway through the nineteenth century, for a number of reasons, but especially because the Napoleonic Wars (which had so completely changed virtually every aspect of European life) ended approximately 30–35 years earlier by this time, and the Franco-Prussian War was still another 20–25 years in the future. Furthermore, the American Civil War had not yet begun which, even though an ocean away, would still have a differential impact on the economies of Europe, and a baseline should therefore be established beforehand.

To be sure, the mid-nineteenth century was not a particularly static period in the overall history of Europe. There was a great deal of social unrest during this time and governments were being forced to draft new constitutions (though not necessarily to issue them), and to consider the granting of new freedoms, indeed to grant new freedoms at an unprecedented pace.

There were serious riots in Paris, which spread to Vienna, Berlin, and other cities in 1848, but by 1850 these had all quieted down with important consequences for the relative rates of industrialization and growth in each country. Finally, with the recovery of the French economy from the costs associated with the Napoleonic Wars, there was again what seemed to be a balance of power in Europe. Therefore, the mid-nineteenth century is frequently chosen, for these and other reasons, as the starting point for comparative analyses of the developments that led to the modern era.

Nevertheless, for the express purpose of examining the growth and development of the global pharmaceutical industry, it is necessary (for reasons that will soon become apparent), to consider the conditions of each nation's chemical industries; mining, forestry, and agriculture industries; textile and dyestuffs industries; systems of administrative, scientific, and technical education; financial, banking, and credit systems; prevailing conditions of disease and health care; patent and legal systems; and a whole host of other political, social, and economic factors that have created the structure of the global pharmaceutical industry as we now know it. It is preferable to begin our discussion of the development of the national pharmaceutical industries of

Europe at different points in time for each country. This is because different sets of factors were important, and more influential in each case. Further, it will be beneficial to bring each set of factors into full perspective with a broader view of history, in general, in order to more fully realize why each nation's pharmaceutical industry followed its own relatively unique trajectory.

There will be a number of commonalities for sure, that will become readily apparent; but the differences are equally important, if not more so because, as we all too often are forced to learn the hard way, overgeneralization almost always leads to bigger problems than we are faced with initially. Nevertheless, in the final analysis, it is important in the context of social transformations that affect industry structure to realize that the **discoveries** discussed here occurred around the time of the Franco-Prussian war (1870 1871), with their concomitant implications for the development of the pharmaceutical industry in the aftermath.

INDUSTRY, TECHNOLOGY & WORLD AFFAIRS

There is a <u>strong</u> connection between the synthetic dyestuffs that are used to color textiles (cloth, apparel, household furnishings, etc.) and the development of the modern pharmaceutical industry. This relationship should never be underestimated. When it has been underestimated, it was proven disastrous. Many of the chemical intermediates that are used in the dyestuffs industry, or that are generated as by-products of the dyestuffs industry are the exact same intermediates required in the manufacture of modern synthetic pharmaceuticals. Both the modern synthetic dyestuffs industry and the modern synthetic pharmaceutical industry, which Germany dominated, were developed from coal tar technology, i.e., extracts generated as a by-product in the making of coke (essentially pure carbon) for steel production.

Although petroleum is the dominant worldwide feedstock for the chemical process industries today, including pharmaceuticals, there was no petroleum-based chemical process or petrochemicals industry anywhere in the world until after the invention of the internal combustion engine and mass production of gasoline-powered automobiles (roughly 1901–1902). Prior to this time, some petroleum distillates had been used for heat and light, while the "useless" gasoline fraction was discarded, thrown away as "waste," frequently in open ditches or on barren soil, much as coal tar had been discarded as an unwanted by-product of the coking process earlier. Coke is relatively pure carbon that is produced in the destructive distillation of coal, and is used extensively in the smelting of iron and other metal ores. Therefore, there is also a strong link between the development of metallurgy and the development of synthetic organic chemistry.

Hydrocarbons are the backbone of organic chemistry, the modern pharmaceutical industry and biotechnology. The petroleum-based chemical process industries were slow to develop, however, up until the time of World War II, when emphasis was placed on new methods of petroleum refining in the United States in order to produce jet fuels capable of increasing the speed of fighter planes.

Thus, German coal tar technology, which came to be based on acetylene chemistry, ruled the day until long after World War I, when the Allies had appropriated all German Patents. It wasn't until 1920 that Standard Oil of New Jersey first produced propylene, and then isopropyl alcohol from petroleum. Most important was that a man by the name of George Curme, working for Union Carbide Corporation, developed a method for obtaining acetylene, ethylene, and propylene (the so-called olefins, or unsaturated aliphatic hydrocarbons) through electric-arc cracking of petroleum distillates, although he ultimately settled in favor of thermal cracking. From this point forward, the petrochemical industry (beginning in the United States) experienced strong growth, based almost entirely on the chemistry of ethylene, mainly because it was so much easier to handle and transport than the more explosive acetylene chemistry developed in Germany.

The reasons that things evolved as they did had as much to do with the political, legal, financial, and educational institutions that evolved (or were created) in each country as they did with any perceived difference in mind-set, work ethic, culture, religion, class structure, or social organization within any society. Yet, the role of these cannot be ignored. The idea of large organizations created solely for the purpose of economic gain or personal profit was slow to develop in the minds of men. The concept of an economic world that was separate from the world of social, political, and religious life was essentially beyond the capabilities of the human mind until relatively late in our life on this planet.

The profit motive, as we know it today, is only as old as modern man. Such an idea requires an abstract conceptualization of things like a set of markets where everyone pursues his own self-interest, yet replicable patterns develop, on a large scale, which are as predictable as the sun rising each morning and setting at night. An abstract conceptualization of value is also required (sometimes called marginal value), as is abstract labor, capital, and land sufficient to povide all together an excess of value (a marginal value) that is reliably convertible into observable and tangible profits for those who do not directly participate in the production process.

Perhaps, it will be helpful to imagine two men, each painting his own house. Six days are required for them to finish the job. But, if the two men were to join forces and together paint the first house and then the second house together as a team, they might finish in five days. Here, we have the concept of a savings in abstract labor (a marginal increase in productivity and abstract value); abstract because the savings does not really involve labor at all. The two men simply work better as a team than they do alone. Now, the question becomes, can we capture that abstract labor as something of value to be converted into real profits? The answer is clearly yes, and is a rather simple concept to grasp with only two men painting two houses. But, what about 30,000 men and women with many different levels of skill discovering, developing, manufacturing, and marketing pharmaceutical products all over the world? Just exactly where is the abstract value in that scenario? And how do we convert it into real money?

Large organizations have a nasty tendency to become *bureaucratic* and inflexible. Whatever marginal value they might have generated is usually lost in the dull round of calm that surrounds a regular paycheck and unchecked shirking.

The years following World War II (1939–1945) saw enormous change in the political, economic, and financial systems of the new world community that survived and resolved never to let it happen again. The agreements reached in 1944 at Bretton Woods, New Hampshire, and later that same year at Dumbarton Oaks in Washington, D.C. created the United Nations, the World Bank, and the International Monetary Fund. NATO was formed in 1949 (the

North Atlantic Treaty Organization) to provide for the common defense of Western Europe against a possible attack by the Soviet Union. NATO's counterpart in the East, the Warsaw Pact, was formed in 1955 by the U.S.S.R., Albania, Bulgaria, Czechoslovakia, East Germany, Hungary, Poland, and Romania. Although China did not sign the Warsaw Pact, it pledged its support to the member countries.

The Treaty founding the European Coal and Steel Community in 1952, followed by the Treaty forming the European Atomic Energy Community in 1957, and culminating with The Treaty of Rome, also signed in 1957, all together formed the enabling legislation of the European Economic Community, and eventually, today, of the 15 member (at present) nation European Union. The eight rounds of the General Agreement on Tariffs and Trade (GATT), which began shortly after World War II and lasted for over thirty years, culminated with the Uruguay Round in the 1980s which resulted in the creation of a new world institution as the guarantor of free trade, the World Trade Organization (WTO).

Many of these events seemed to occur so quickly, under such dynamic leadership and public support, that many companies were slow to realize their implications. Some companies had not fully converted to petroleum-based feeds when the first oil crisis of 1973–1974 threatened to severely change the new world economic order. Then, when the second oil crisis hit in 1979, following the revolution in Iran, a decade or more of social and economic upheaval ensued throughout Europe and a deep-seated uneasiness persists today.

This was the era of Margaret Thatcher in Great Britain and Ronald Reagan in the United States. It was the period when Britain sent 800 war ships to recapture the Falklands from Argentina and the United States began the largest military build-up in the history of humankind. When Ronald Reagan met with Mikhail Gorbachev, the General Secretary of the Communist Party of the Soviet Union, at Reykjavik, Iceland, and suggested the two men go for a walk alone, the stage was set for the Soviet Union to dissolve itself without fear of military intervention by the United States. Now, Russia is a Junior Member of NATO. To say that the world has changed would be an understatement. But does the realization go with it that such change has occurred throughout the history of humankind and the ability to learn from history is the best preparation for making profits in a fast-paced future?

We will look at the evolution of pharmaceutical science, discovery research, pharmaceutical manufacturing, strategies and marketing practices, as well as the responses of companies to public concerns and government regulations leading to the current economic structure of the industry within this historical context. In the end, we will not only understand the structure and dynamics of this very important industry, but we will have also gained the perspective and tools necessary to work beneficially and assume higher levels of responsibility within the industry.

ECONOMICS THEORY

Economics is a field of scientific inquiry, a "science" that deals with the allocation of scarce resources, i.e., the production and distribution of wealth. The so-called disciplines of business are subfields of the science of economics, and include: accounting, finance, management, marketing, production operations, and so forth. To go one step further, and by way of example only, marketing is the process of planning and executing the conception, pricing, promotion, and distribution of ideas, goods, and services to create exchanges that satisfy individual and organizational goals. There are a number of subdisciplines of marketing that are generally recognized, including: advertising, publicity, public relations, and personal selling, which, together, are often referred to as "promotion." Marketing also includes the so-called distribution subdisciplines of logistics, transportation, warehousing, wholesaling, retailing, etc. Furthermore, product conceptualization, design, and pricing decisions are also included under the rubric of marketing. Thus, it can be seen that the science of economics, as well as the disciplines and subdisciplines of business are exceedingly broad in scope and include a large number of activities related to the production and distribution of wealth, consumption, and even the by-products, recycling, and waste disposal associated with such highly specialized activities.

Although there had long been undercurrents and criticisms of various business activities from outside the realm of formalized economics, it was not until the latter half of the twentieth century that widespread recognition was given to an area of thought and study described here generally as "business and society." Within this context, the larger realm of business activities, indeed the entire sphere of economics, was cast against a backdrop of higher-order social needs. Profit maximization was no longer viewed in the isolation of mutually beneficial exchange transactions, but from the perspective of a zero-sum game, wherein one party can only gain at the expense of another, or the parties to an exchange transaction gain only at the expense of the larger society. What is more, studies of chaotic motion began to reveal underlying patterns in physical phenomena when considered at a sufficient level of generality. Emergent theories of complexity were then applied to studies of economic behavior. The dreadful zero-sum game is now viewed as an indication of impending structural change, and while market share may have superseded profit maximization as a measure of economic viability in the closing decades of the twentieth century, it too can be viewed as only temporary when the underlying structure of an economy begins to evidence the early stages of chaotic motion.

THE DOMINANT ECONOMIC PARADIGM

Some potentially relevant and interesting ideas are contained in certain somewhat unconventional theories of economic history, political and social dynamics. These contrast sharply with what is referred to as the *dominant economic paradigm*. For over 150 years, this paradigm has been dismissed in capitalist societies as untenable, that is: widespread, purely rational behavior by autonomous economic actors. This inflexible doctrine of impersonal exchanges between calculating and rational players has tended to denigrate, confuse, and

ECONOMICS THEORY

obfuscate other forces (social forces) **held to be important** in diverse economic relations by well-experienced theorists.

Though the specifics of interpretation differ from one school of thought to another, it might be worth considering the idea that social forces, other than those that are purely economic, might have an impact on industrial growth and development. We then can conceptualize these "other" forces as having at least the potential for a cause and effect relationship with the dynamics and structure of an industry. One must be very careful in making such a consideration, however, because the suggestion that anything other than purely rational economic behavior, especially when derived from within or extracted from the "social" domain, has been all too often associated with Marxist/Leninist/Communist ideology. The point made earlier about the need to discern an author's basic philosophical orientation, especially when expressed in subtle terminology or an expansive treatise becomes paramount.

In addition to rational and autonomous economic actors, the dominant economic paradigm <u>also</u> suggests that any multitude of rational actors, each engaged in independent behavior, will ultimately give rise to a maximally efficient, harmonious, worldwide community of compatible interests absent of conflict and/ or lingering strife.

Some critics of the dominant paradigm have referred to this convergence idea as "the naïve view of the end of history" (Boyer, translation 2002, p. 7). What they mean by this so-called end of history is a condition or state of nature known to economists as *general market equilibrium*. A series of dynamic market crises, abnormalities, or "disequilibria" (a series of infamous economic "short runs") can and do (often) take place along the road to this

Hank Laskey

141

happy end-state of affairs. Economic actors therein relate to one another principally through the medium of price, forming an all-encompassing bond or the entirety of any and all relationships between rational subjects experiencing the uniform constraint of scarce resources. In other words, price becomes the sole element and all-meaningful building block of a matrix, complex, network, or structure of relationships among all economic actors.

According to the dominant economic paradigm, industry structures evolve through a series of short-run initiatives to increase efficiencies, reduce costs, and implement product and pricing strategies in dynamic market environments. The immutable essence of human beings everywhere ensures that such short-run initiatives will occur as <u>essential</u> components of the lock-step march toward general market equilibrium.

CONSTRUCTIVISM

By "Constructivism," we mean a juxtaposition of a number of more or less unconventional social, political, and economic ideas contained in the theory of "structural analysis," as opposed to the singular idea that price is a necessary <u>and</u> <u>sufficient</u> basis for deciphering the structure of an industry, or indeed of an entire economy. Several of the ideas underlying this theory have the rather odd tendency of unexpectedly appearing at important junctures in international or cross-cultural expositions of seemingly unrelated industry dynamics. They become crucial in understanding cross-cultural relations.

A good definition of constructivism was presented by Gary Herrigel, in 1996, on the sources of German industrial power. Here, he argues what I maintain is the largely unconventional view of a small but growing number of scholars in the United States that several incredibly robust subsystems of industrial governance existed in nineteenth-century Germany during the period when the large German chemical and pharmaceutical companies of today first came into existence, and that these subsystems and the networks of small businesses they supported played a dominant role in Germany's spectacular economic growth and development from the period of the Franco-Prussian War (1870–1871) and continuing right up to today. His argument and the evidence he presents are surprisingly similar to those presented by David Friedman in his 1988 text on Japanese industrial development. Furthermore, as described by Herrigel, this key ingredient of the industrial structure of Germany, small business, was also specifically cited by Kurt Lanz in his book, 1978, as being "so characteristic" of the German chemical industry of the 1930s (when <u>he</u> first joined the global behemoth I.G. Farben in 1937).

The works by Herrigel and Friedman stand in sharp contrast to the so-called <u>American</u> model, which is known primarily to foreign scholars as *Fordism,* and, paradoxically, previously argued by most influential writers on German industrialization to have been the very model adopted by Germany for industrial growth at that time. It will be discussed in detail later, but for the moment, a brief description of Fordism would include the idea of the fundamental desirability of big business based on a division of labor and economies of scale. A second and very important concept associated with Fordism is the "buy-in" of organized labor to an inherently capitalist system. Organized labor's buy-in is based on an agreement between management and labor that the wage rate will be sufficient for employees to purchase and enjoy the benefits of an increased industrial output—that will enhance or improve the overall standard of living of their individual lives, and result throughout the economy. It is essentially a guarantee of the "American dream" based on their mutual promise to renegotiate the wage rate in good faith whenever it is suggested by government economic indicators.

Herrigel defines the Constructivist approach as viewing *both* the social realm of an economy "and the organizations and institutions that populate and govern it as the outcome of historically specific struggles among social actors over the constitution of the social division of labor." While most influential Western economists have tended to think of the realm of direct production as separate and distinct from the realm of politics and other social institutions, the Constructivist approach defined by Herrigel views "historically specific social, economic, and political ideas and institutions" as *inseparable* from what an industry is "understood to be at any given time and what the identities of the actors within these social spaces are." Constructivism sees an integrated, unified, or at least overlapping, social, economic, and political space that favors big business, but not to the exclusion of small business; in fact, quite the opposite.

It is important to realize that the more "conventionally" held view of the *separateness* of these three spheres has survived a long and tortuous history of intense debate and petty bickering. It has survived so well, in fact, as to be found quite frequently at the bottom of heated arguments over concepts of corporate governance and economic polity between industrialized and unindustrialized, or ideologically opposed world communities.

In this vein, it is illustrative to consider the results of a multi-year research program conducted by a team of nine cross-national scholars and researchers (Martinelli, 1991). Their study concerned economic polity, social institutions, and the industrial governance of global chemical companies. They had hypothesized an expansive and pervasive but practically invisible influence of big business-style capitalism on world politics through a "dense network of well-organized self-governing interest associations with multiple institutional arrangements for negotiation and intermediation between public and private interests." They obtained what they considered extensive evidence to suggest that in spite of the structural advantage that big companies might have in market economies, they are unable to significantly promote their interests without resorting to such convoluted behavior. They argued that this inability is a function of three major factors: 1) the political mobilization of organized labor, 2) the devastating consequences of cut-throat competition from foreign competitors in domestic markets, and 3) systematic increases in state interventionism and the regulation of economic processes by democratic political institutions.

It is particularly interesting, therefore, that in the final analysis, these researchers seem to discount the primacy, or at least the overall importance of this form of big business influence. Their alternative seems to be that increasing internationalization and economic concentration within national economies have allowed global firms to establish and exploit, through closely held coordination, a diversified work-process existing across different countries. By organizing and managing such co-dependent production operations across national boundaries, large global firms have gained substantial leverage in bargaining with national governments and their politically active trade unions.

A substantial body of research that seems to be motivated in similar fashion to the study just described would appear to be rather neatly subsumed under the more general Régulation Theory that is described next. Regardless of the perceived generality, however, or the particular attractiveness of any one theory or any one body of evidence, **our discussion** of world pharmaceutical markets, global, international, and domestic pharmaceutical companies, regulatory agencies and other important government or private and social institutions related to health care, managed care, employee benefits, welfare, social security, national insurance programs, prescription drug coverage, socialized medicine, etc.; and particularly the influence of these on the strategies of pharmaceutical companies, indeed the entire structure and dynamics of the global pharmaceutical industry, **will benefit** if we maintain a keen focus on the underlying precepts of the Constructivist approach. In other words, the most general issue is the one argued by Herrigel (1996), i.e., the potential for individual small to medium-size firms to play an *essential*, largely independent and thoroughly sustainable, profitable role over the long term within an integrated, or at least overlapping economic, political, social, and historical context that might appear to largely favor big business.

RÉGULATION THEORY

The essence of Régulation Theory is that capitalism tends to periodically reinvent itself, and is therefore not exactly the one-way, highly deterministic mode of production described by Karl Marx in *Das Kapital*, one that would eventually lead to its own demise. Régulation theory sees capitalism as capable of many different trajectories and thus dissipates what has always been the most basic argument of capitalism's critics.

It is important to realize that what is meant by a society's general laws has nothing to do with its legal code, or system of jurisprudence. These are "social" laws, in the sense developed by Marx and others, to include economics. They represent the relationships that structure society and govern the production and distribution of goods and services within social groups and organizations. Régulation theory is thus a theory of economics based on the transformation of social relations to create new forms of capitalism. Examples of its general laws are the Law of Competitive Forms and the Law of Monetary Forms.

One additional and equally unconventional (in the U.S.) collection of ideas, that should benefit our discussion and ultimate understanding of the structure and dynamics of the global pharmaceutical industry, is the one most fervently argued by the so-called Parisian school of French Régulationists, founded by Michel Aglietta in his analysis of the evolution of the U.S. economy from the period of the American Civil War (1862–1865).

Régulation Theory is a complex systems approach to economics, although it is based upon only five key relationships, and has very little in common with the meaning of the English word "regulation." It is unfortunate that the same word is used in both English and French to represent such very different meanings because it tends to give English-speaking peoples the wrong idea about Régulation Theory right from the start.

The implication for more satisfying explanations of industry structural changes, and indeed, more reliable predictions of future changes, lies in the manner in which capitalism tends to reinvent itself. Capitalism is reinvented according to specific relationships among a society's general laws. These five key relationships will always be present in any reinvented form of capitalism. Changes in their morphology or composite structure, in the sense of a system, complex, or network of integrated relationships are defined to be changes in the "form" of Régulation. In other words, capitalism can reinvent itself by essentially reproducing its previous morphology, with changes occurring only within the relationships themselves. These changes in relationships will be according to a matter of degree only, rather than as any qualitative change in the nature of the relationships themselves, or in the relative levels of their influence, i.e., without changing, reprioritizing or reintegrating the overall system, its structure, or *form* of Régulation. Alternatively, capitalism can reinvent itself by changing its underlying *form* of Regulation or morphology. Only when one or more of the five key relationships is deleted from the system does capitalism cease to exist. Thus, while Marx saw capitalism itself as the determining factor in only one possible, inevitable social trajectory, Régulation Theory sees the relationships among a society's general laws as determining a range of possible trajectories.

CLASSICAL ECONOMICS

The old classical economics saw government as, at best, a hindrance. Consider Adam Smith for example:

ADAM SMITH

Smith focused on wealth as a function of productivity (production). Smith stressed the primacy of market forces and the importance of productive activity by autonomous entrepreneurs. He saw government as, at best, an obstructive force. A key in Smith's ideas is that productivity is increased when complex jobs are divided into specialized tasks (division of labor).

DIALECTICAL MATERIALISM

The so-called *dialectic* is based on evidence presented by Karl Marx of historic class struggles over the division of labor.

KARL MARX

Marx saw capitalism as capable of only one, single, unavoidable trajectory. That trajectory of a division of labor and a focus on productivity can have only one outcome. Constant productivity gains in the form of technological progress by competing, capitalist firms will always ultimately come into conflict with social and political structures.

THE RISE OF SOCIALISM

Capitalism seems capable of reinventing itself; therefore, there is the possibility of multiple trajectories.

JOSEPH A. SCHUMPETER AND CREATIVE DESTRUCTION

Large-scale enterprise and industrial concentration can be vehicles for classical economic growth as the result of innovative or "creative" entrepreneurs breaking away from large-scale organizations and a short-term optimizing strategy of *adaptive behavior*. These entrepreneurs engage in activities that result in organizational change and technological innovation to create new advantages. "Adaptive behavior" accepts the given constraints of an existing order as binding, lacks motive force, and makes only a limited contribution to growth, whereas *creative behavior* is capable of sustaining enterprise over the long-term because it does not accept such constraints as binding. Thus, new, more efficient organizations and technologies will replace less efficient ones in irregular and evolutionary waves of change.

INSTITUTIONALISM & MANAGED ECONOMIES

ALEXANDER GERSCHENKRON

Political intervention need not always play an obstructive role in economic processes. Nations can improve their position in the international division of labor through political and institutional adaptation. Market forces alone cannot produce the elements needed for economic progress. The nation-state is the appropriate unit of analysis for understanding the process of economic development. Institutions and institution building are essential to economic progress.

BUSINESS AND SOCIETY

SEARCHING FOR ORDER AND
MEANING IN SOCIAL HISTORY

While it may seem obvious to some groups of people today that the world of practical affairs is inextricably linked to political, social, and religious life, the majority of people would probably agree that the world of our own everyday lives is mostly a function of what we can afford to buy and when we can afford to buy it.

COMPARATIVE NATIONAL CULTURES

The development of the worldwide pharmaceutical industry has proceeded at different times and at different rates in different countries and regions of the world. This development has been dependent upon a number of factors that are much broader in scope than what is usually discussed in the context of economic theory. The entire complex of social, economic, political, and cultural characteristics of nations is related to their propensity for industrial development in general and high technology industrial development in particular; to include a viable pharmaceutical industry. In many ways, France constitutes an excellent example of this idea. Professor Lucien Bélay of the world-famous Sorbonne University in France attempts to describe the peculiar mindset of the French people in this way: "People and nations are abstract, general concepts." He goes on to say that the very nature of the words "people" and "nations" reflects a historical sequence of enormous efforts by successive generations of largely anonymous citizens. He argues that it is this collective, anonymous effort, never forgotten, which carries, supports, and encourages the men and women who have made the history of France. His primary point is that without the "obscure strength" of the French people, no one would have been able to invent, build, or create what has come down to us. Bélay argues that the obscure strength of the French people was freely given to their monarchs and the bond between king and people, especially his justice, was so strong for so long because the people shared with their King a common past and a common destiny. For many years, as Louis XIV himself declared openly (perhaps the greatest of all the monarchs of France): "I am the State," meaning that the King was one with the nation, must be one with the nation, and would be nothing without the soul of France enclosed in his own body.

When the revolution finally came and the people beheaded his great grandson, King Louis the XVI on January 21, 1793, the people, now sovereign themselves, held such a powerful image of France as a strong, centralized nation-state that it was inevitable, according to Professor Bély, that they would feel compelled ultimately to confirm its position in a form little changed from the old. No one knew this better than the little Corsican who would be Emperor of Europe by joining hands with his men and giving sway to that very obscure and anonymous "soul" what she so richly deserved. In the entire course of history, there have been perhaps five men who were so revered by their soldiers: Alexander the Great of Macedonia, Hannibal of Carthage, Caius Julius Caesar of Rome, Charles the Great (Charlemagne) of Aachen in Lotharingia, Genghis Kahn of Mongolia, Robert E. Lee of Virginia, and General George S. Patton, Jr., of the U.S. Third Army.

Patton's men swept so rapidly across France, Belgium, southwestern Germany, Czechoslovakia, and Austria, that their supply lines simply could not keep up with them and they had to be supplied from the air. (When the war finally ended, Patton's men were in firm control of most of what would become the American occupation zone). For the average Frenchman, down through the ages, it has never been about the money, the land, or the power. It has always been about an idea; well *three* ideas really: Liberte, Egalite, and Fraternite. (Liberty, Equality, and Brotherhood.) It was and still is the soul, the spirit, the memory, the history, and the essence, and the dreams of France.

STRATEGY AND ORGANIZATIONAL STRUCTURE

One very basic idea that is important to recognize early on is that industry dynamics are seen as a function of industry structure. We will therefore seek to define the structure of the pharmaceutical industry in order to understand the behaviors of the companies within the industry. Industry dynamics are also seen as a function of the external environment faced by an industry. The most important external factor faced by the pharmaceutical industry is government regulation. Thus, structure and government regulation are seen as the two most important factors influencing the behaviors and activities (dynamics) of modern pharmaceutical companies.

In order to understand the organization of an industry and, therefore, industry dynamics, it is important to understand the internal structures of individual corporate organizations and their strategic alliances with other companies and other industries. Corporate organizations are formed and then organizations change in order to implement strategies that are intended to pursue corporate mission statements, or long-term goals within changing environments. A mission statement defines a company's fundamental reason for being and is related to the vision of senior managers and/or company founders. Strategies intended to implement mission statements in changing environments are thus dynamic rather than static. Over time, strategies are developed in response to changes in the environment that can affect a company's ability to pursue its mission, and, as strategies change, the new ones frequently require concurrent changes in organizational structure.

To summarize, you first have a company with a vision and a mission statement that has been developed in terms of a particular environment and the likelihood of changes occurring within that environment. Then, you have a strategy and a corporate organization to achieve that mission in that environment. Next, you have changes in the environment that can lead to changes in strategy and organization. Beyond these essential and fundamental principles, the internal culture and behaviors of employees are developed and motivated through policies, standard operating procedures (SOPs), and incentive programs. These further elements of an internal organization determine its adaptability to change, flexibility, innovativeness, and speed in bringing new products to market.

INDUSTRY ASSOCIATIONS

The United States, Japan, and the European Union (EU) together represent a large percentage of the worldwide market for pharmaceuticals. In each of these three markets, there are industry associations that represent the industry's interests to the various regulatory authorities and the general public. In the United States, most pharmaceutical companies are members of the Pharmaceutical Research and Manufacturers Association. In Japan, they are members of the Japan Pharmaceutical Manufacturers Association. In Europe, they are members of the European Federation of Pharmaceutical Industries Association. Each of these three associations is in turn a member of the International Federation of Pharmaceutical Manufacturers Association, which is essentially a worldwide association of associations. Each of these associations has played a major role in efforts to standardize international drug regulations.

THE WORLD HEALTH ORGANIZATION

The World Health Organization (WHO) was formed in New York in 1946 to attain the highest possible level of health for all people. The WHO has headquarters in Geneva, Switzerland and 191 countries are members. The definition of "health" stipulated by the WHO does not mean simply an absence of disease or infirmity, but a state of complete physical, mental, and social well-being. In pursuit of this very worthy ideal, the WHO acts as a coordinating authority on all matters pertaining to international health. It assists governments on request to improve the quality of their health systems through a wide variety of technical advice and other services. Of special importance to the global pharmaceutical industry, the WHO has also sought to stimulate the development of international standards for biological, pharmaceutical and similar products.

Under the auspices of the WHO, world regulatory officials have, for many years, discussed the possibility of standardizing their regulations. In 1989, the WHO held a conference in Paris for drug regulators. Following this conference, regulators approached the International

Federation of Pharmaceutical Manufacturers Association to explore the possibility of a joint industry-regulatory initiative to harmonize drug regulations around the world. A number of major international conferences have since taken place at different locations around the world to work toward harmonizing international drug regulations.

INTERNATIONAL CONFERENCES ON HARMONIZATION

In Brussels in 1990, the European Federation of Pharmaceutical Industries Association hosted a meeting of industry representatives and regulators, which began a formal process to harmonize drug regulations in the United States, Japan, and the European Union. A Steering Committee was formed consisting of the regulators and industry associations representing the United States, Japan, and Europe. Five International Conferences on Harmonization (ICH) followed: 1991 in Brussels, 1993 in Orlando, 1995 in Yokohama, 1997 in Brussels, and 2000 in San Diego.

With a major impact for the industry, the San Diego ICH promulgated a Common Technical Document (CTD) for submitting marketing applications to regulators in the United States, Japan, and the EU. The CTD was designed to meet the requirements of all three regulatory authorities, and was approved and forwarded to them for implementation according to their own respective procedures. It is important to recognize that implementation of the CTD is only one step toward full harmonization of worldwide pharmaceutical regulations, but it is remarkably significant in terms of international cooperation and good will between regulators and industry. A following ICH was held in Osaka, Japan in 2003.

ORGANIZATIONAL THEORY

We begin our discussion of organizations, firms, companies, etc., and their dynamics by defining an organization as a codification of both economic <u>and</u> social relationships. Here we throw a dart into the heart of the difference between neoclassical economics, on the one hand, and Marxist/Socialist economics on the other. Yet, anyone who has ever tried to create an organization from scratch and then make it operate efficiently will certainly see the fundamental truth in such a definition. The actors within any organization bring a lot of "excess baggage" with them. Furthermore, to say that such actors may or may not be acting <u>rationally</u> in their own self-interest and that they may or may not be behaving according to <u>rules</u> imposed from within and/or outside of the organization throws a second dart into the middle of microeconomic and macroeconomic theory. Yet anyone who has ever managed an organization must surely see the merit in considering both possibilities.

Organizations begin with individual actors having a common interest in obtaining a common goal and, in most cases, a common set of objectives (to include the element of time). Agreements are made, obligations are incurred, <u>and</u> rules are developed that constrain the behavior of the actors. Such rules may be established, at least in part, as a function of the incoming social status of the actors, stemming from the social hierarchy of the society at large; i.e., macroeconomics; and they may impose a new social hierarchy, an "organizational hierarchy" upon the actors; i.e., microeconomics. If we assume that the organizational hierarchy is a function of the external social hierarchy, then we enter the world of Marxist/Socialist economics. If we assume that the organizational hierarchy is independent of the society at large and solely a function of autonomous, rational decision-making and behaviors (job or contract-performance vs. a lack thereof) of individual actors, then we enter the world of neoclassical economics. In either event, we are interested in a hierarchy of social relationships within organizations.

Consider, for example, the extent to which the members of an organization, say the employees of a large pharmaceutical company, engage in explicitly and exclusively cooperating behaviors. Is there an almost instinctive urge to cooperate with other members of the firm, or is there only an obedience to the rules coupled with a more fundamental tendency toward self-interest? If we adopt a position that is a little of both, then we enter the realm of "convention theory," a variant of neoclassical economics wherein the rationality of the actors is bounded by their concern to cooperate. Such issues beg the question of "what's in it for me?" and have dramatic implications for compensation schemes, stock options vs. stock vesting, etc., and the recent changes made along these lines within some of the world's largest pharmaceutical companies.[10]

The fabric of society, in general, consists of a dense network of many different kinds of organizations; the memberships of which derive from common interests. Perhaps the most basic of these is

---

[10] In 2005, for example, Pfizer made a major change to its compensation package for salaried employees when it dropped its existing annual stock option benefit in favor of the annual granting of shares in the corporation (following a vestment period). Such changes had long been advocated by ex-chairman of the Federal Reserve Board, Paul Volker.

the family, clan, or tribe. In reality, a close circle of friends might have a greater common interest than those of blood relations; but the history of humankind has consistently demonstrated the tenacity of relationships and organizations involving kinship.

It has been popular among academics, theorists, and other members of the intelligentsia in various parts of the world, especially since the 1960s, to explain major changes in the world's economies as the result of complex activities by intricate networks of capitalist institutions, associations, and interest groups, operating largely outside any conventional notion of a market or set of markets. This is an insidious idea. It differs from other groups of economic actors, such as trade associations, labor unions, and cartels, in the sense that the relationships among the members are extremely subtle, abstract, and very subjective. Some have referred to this idea as "an international management culture" among top executives (Martinelli et al., 1991), yet have also recognized the inadequacy of this idea in describing what also contains an element of intrigue.

These hypothesized and intricate networks or quasi-organizations also possess a seemingly transient characteristic, rapidly emerging and visible, with a keen sense of focus and a succinct, incisive influence, only to evaporate, as if into the mist, once the object of their interest has been sufficiently codified into the fabric of society. There is no formal structure, as with an institution or political party, thus the element of intrigue. The idea of a select circle or exclusive group in society, denoted by the word "coterie," is useful by way of comparison because its primary meaning lies in the "shared interest" of its members, but falls short in its implication of social class or qualitative differentiation, and also the relative permanence with which class-based distinctions are usually associated.

The popular idea is that amorphous, obscure, and transient networks of exploitive profiteers cause major changes in the world's economies. However, such **structural shifts** in both national and global industries, as well as the functional order and integration of the global economic system as a whole, has been difficult for scientists to validate empirically. Such an idea is typically conceptualized within the context of political or socioeconomics, and the theoretical constructs and analytical methods of economics, political science, psychology, sociology, even cultural anthropology, have all been employed in the attempt to validate this popular idea. The undaunted have altered the focus of their research (the unit of their analysis) from individuals, to firms, to industries, to institutions, to nation-states, to geo-political alliances, to social classes and cultures, to economic regions and centers of influence, to the world as an international regime or integrated holistic system governed in some sense by these amorphous networks; i.e., a system of networks being the current paradigm.

It would be a gross misrepresentation to suggest that all of this work, decades upon decades of research and analysis, has resulted in a general failure to prove the existence, indeed the recurrence of such sinister networks of local, regional, and global elitists who constrain the autonomy and rationale of ordinary citizens everywhere. It would also be a gross distortion to suggest that a vast body of evidence now exists that irrefutably demonstrates not only the existence of such networks, but their principle mechanisms of action as well as the names and addresses of their primary operatives and membership roster. What does seem clear, however, is that sufficient "quasi-evidence" exists to argue the point either way.

THE LOGICS OF INFLUENCE & MEMBERSHIP

In theory, both the family and the corporation are seen as organizations with articulated structures involving both degrees of complexity <u>and</u> relative autonomy, i.e., the two fundamental dimensions of organizational development. Furthermore, the "value" of any organization is thought to be a function of the group's ability to present a <u>unified front</u> (i.e., the "logic of influence") as well as the group's ability to advance <u>each member's own self-interest</u> (i.e., the "logic of membership").[11]

THE EFFECTS OF CHANGES IN THE GLOBAL POLITICAL-SOCIAL ENVIRONMENT

THE ROUSSEL FAMILY'S GLOBAL PHARMACEUTICAL BUSINESS

As an example of the type of structural change that can occur within the pharmaceutical industry following the death of a major shareholder, we have the case of Roussel in France. We begin with Dr. Gaston Roussel, a graduate pharmacist who, beginning in 1922, founded a number of commercial laboratories in France with

---

[11]   With respect to the "circle of friends" idea, and the emergence of an "international management culture" among top managers, these may be seen either as 1. "quasi-organizations" with ill-defined operating structures, or 2. as supranational "associations of influence" whose presence is suggested by the relative significance of latent variables in <u>systems of structural equations</u>. The conceptual framework used here to explain degrees of organizational development stems from mainstream organizational theory as applied in the study of global firms in the **chemical industry** by Martinelli, et al. (1991).

foreign subsidiaries in Latin America and elsewhere (e.g., Institut de Sérothérapie Hématopoïétique), specializing in blood agents and serums, such as Hemostyl for the treatment of anemia. He also founded Laboratoires Français de Chimiothérapie, Usines Chimiques des Laboratoires Français (UCLAF) and Société Française de la Pénicilline (SOFRAPEN), specializing in antibiotics. When he died in 1947, just two years after World War II, his son, also a graduate pharmacist, Jean-Claude Roussel, aged 25, seemed to be the heir-apparent.

However, because ownership was distributed throughout the widely branched, French Catholic Roussel family, Jean-Claude only became head of the company 14 years later when he had finally managed through complex negotiations within the family to form Roussel-UCLAF in 1961. Then, Roussel-UCLAF acquired Procida in 1962, the second largest agrochemicals company in France.

Important to France in 1962, the North African country of Algeria finally won its independence from France. Algerian independence, as the independence of many former European colonies, was to have enormous economic consequences for the French because that region of the Sahara had been a major supplier of inexpensive petroleum and natural gas to French chemical companies as a colony, and France had grown heavily dependent on Algeria for its raw materials.

It would appear that from the death of the company's founder, Gaston Roussel in 1947, until the succession of Jean-Claude Roussel in 1961, the various branches of the Roussel family were held together by an organizational structure capable of adapting to their own individual and fragmented **self-interests**. One might assume thereafter that the new organizational structure formed by Jean-Claude Roussel in 1961 was better able to **represent and advance** the combined interests of the family (unified front); however, the rapid selling of shares that followed his untimely death in 1972 suggests something more problematic.

The most important pharmaceuticals subsidiary of Roussel-UCLAF was a new group formed by Jean-Claude, known as Laboratories Roussel. Laboratories Roussel was active in many countries of the world and experienced increasing sales for many years, leading to the formation and acquisition of other companies.

At least by 1968, Roussel-UCLAF had become the **second** largest pharmaceutical manufacturer in France **after Rhône-Poulenc.**[12]

Jean-Claude, and the circle of his friends who were managing the company then entered into negotiations with their counterparts in the German chemical giants, Bayer and Hoechst, to explore the possibility of selling a minority interest (about 10%) in Roussel-UCLAF to a foreign company.

GLOBAL POLITICAL-SOCIAL ANTECEDENTS (1968)

In order to more fully understand what happened at Roussel we digress for a broad consideration of the year **1968**. The year **1968** was pivotal for many reasons. It marked the height of the Vietnam War (South Vietnam had been a part of French Indochina for almost 100 years, since the French first occupied Saigon on February 18,

---

[12]   The President of Rhône-Poulenc in 1968 was Wilfrid Baumgartner, who had interesting connections/relationships, after having been the French finance minister from 1960-1962 and was also an honorary member of the Bank of France.

1859, and signed the Treaty of Saigon on June 5, 1862). In 1968 the United States had about 500,000 troops in South Vietnam when the massive invasion by Viet Cong and North Vietnamese known as the Tet Offensive began on January 30, **1968**.

China - 1968

In China, Chairman Mao Tse-tung had been forced to call out the army in 1967 to restore order after he had endorsed the "Cultural Revolution" (which wreaked havoc on both the government and the economy). Violence had broken out among competing radical groups in major cities, and radicals had also seized control of many provincial and city governments. Some semblance of a central authority had been restored in China, but the country's difficulties were by no means over in **1968**. In 1969, fighting broke out - between China and the Soviet Union - over a border dispute.

Soviet Union and Warsaw Pact - 1968

At this time, Leonid Brezhnev was the leader of the Communist Party in the Soviet Union, having replaced Nikita Krushchev in 1964 following a collapse in Soviet farm policy that forced the Soviets to buy large quantities of grain from the West in 1963. Brezhnev remained leader of the Soviet Union until his death in 1982. Under Brezhnev, between 1965 and 1980, Soviet industrial production nearly tripled, but agricultural production remained a problem and purchases of grain from the West continued. In 1968, Albania withdrew from the Warsaw Pact, and students in Warsaw (Poland) rioted against Soviet policies regarding cultural freedom. Further strikes and riots in 1970 led to the formation of a new communist government in Poland.

India - 1968

Mrs. Indira Ghandi became the first woman Prime Minister of India in 1966, during a period of widespread social unrest resulting from severe food shortages, unemployment, and generalized economic hardship. Mrs. Ghandi was the daughter of Jawaharal Neru (long-term Prime Minister from 1952–1964, and a close associate of the world-renowned Mohandas K. Ghandi, who had led India to independence from Great Britain in 1947, when the independent nation of Pakistan was also partitioned and created from India. M.K. Ghandi was assassinated in 1948, (apparently for his tolerance of Muslims). In 1954, under Prime Minister Jawaharal Neru, France had ceded several of her colonies to India: Karikal, Mahé, Pondichéry, and Yanaon. In 1961, Indian troops had seized the Portuguese colonies of Damão, Diu, and Goa.

Mrs. Ghandi's party suffered large losses in the national election of 1967, but she remained in control of the government. Many members of her party broke away in 1969 to form an opposition party against her leadership. Mrs. Ghandi's party, nevertheless, won a majority of seats in the Parliamentary elections of 1971, which was the same year civil war broke out in Pakistan and, with Indian assistance, the new independent nation of Bangladesh was created from the eastern portion of Pakistan. Indira Ghandi was subsequently found guilty of illegal practices during the 1971 election, but her conviction was later overturned by the Indian Supreme Court.

United States - 1968

Facing widespread anti-war sentiment at home in 1968, U.S. President, Lyndon Johnson (Democrat) announced on March 31 that he would not seek, nor would he accept the nomination of his party for re-election as President of the United States. Thus, having lost to John Kennedy (Democrat) in the closest presidential election in U.S. history up until that time, Johnson in essence had stepped aside and Richard Nixon (Republican) at last became President of the United States on January 20, 1969. Nixon not only ended the Vietnam War through repeated saturation bombings of Hanoi, but also became the first U.S. President to officially recognize China. He also later had the distinction of being the first U.S. President forced to resign from the White House in the wake of the Watergate break-in scandal of the Democrats' National Committee Headquarters.

Civil rights leader, Martin Luther King, Jr., was assassinated on April 4, **1968**, leading to severe riots in more than 100 U.S. cities. The United States Congress, sensing that the country was in crisis, responded by passing the Civil Rights Act of **1968**, culminating the legacy of **both** the Kennedy (assassinated in 1963) **and** Johnson administrations.

On April 11, **1968**, the Soviet nuclear ballistic missile submarine "K-129" mysteriously disappeared approximately 750 miles northwest of the Hawaiian Islands in the Pacific. A little over a month later, on May 21, 1968, the American nuclear attack submarine "Scorpion" also mysteriously disappeared, approximately 400 miles southeast of the Azores in the Atlantic.

Finally, between the beginning of the Tet Offensive in January of **1968** and the announcement in March by Johnson that he would not seek re-election, the President notified Congress in February of his intention to create a new government agency charged with significant worldwide operations. He announced that he would be merging the Treasury Department's Bureau of Narcotics with the Food and Drug Administration's Bureau of Drug Abuse Control into a **new** and more powerful agency to be housed within the Department of Justice and known as the Federal Bureau of Narcotics and Dangerous Drugs. He referred to trafficking in illicit drugs as a "national menace" being conducted by "well organized, disciplined and resourceful criminals who reap huge profits." He also recommended "strong new laws to control dangerous drugs," as well as a dramatic increase "in the number of Federal agents enforcing the narcotic and drug laws." Congress responded with the **Comprehensive Drug Abuse and Control Act of 1970**. Title II is referred to separately as the Controlled Substances Act, including five separate schedules (lists) of controlled substances, according to their ability to do harm. Congress also passed the tough **Racketeer Influenced and Corrupt Practices Act** in 1970, otherwise known as RICO, at least in part as a result of the perceived drug problem.

After taking office in 1969, President Richard Nixon declared a **"war on drugs"** in June of 1971, saying that "the problem has reached the dimension of a national emergency." This was the same month that newspapers published a secret government study on the Vietnam War called *The Pentagon Papers*, which deepened the public's already significant distrust of the government.

Between 1960 and 1970, the number of heroin users in the United States had increased from approximately 50,000 to over 500,000. In the aftermath of French occupation, the U.S. Army estimated that 10–15% of all U.S. enlisted personnel in Vietnam were addicted to heroin, and that in some areas, it was as high as 20%, with entire combat units being made ineffectual by drug addiction. Approximately 85% of all American personnel had been offered heroin with 35% having used it. Furthermore, this was not only an "American" problem. Thailand had as many as 400,000 heroin addicts, far higher than the U.S. on a per capita basis. Both Germany and Spain had a higher per capita number than the United States, and per capita usage had increased ten-fold in Great Britain over the same ten years. The highest per capita consumption of heroin in the world was in Hong Kong, consuming virtually the same amount of the drug as all the addicts in the U.S. combined.[13]

---

[13] The history of heroin, opium, and the opium trade will be discussed later, but for the moment: it is worth noting that the French had run an opium monopoly in French Indochina, with more than 100,000 opium addicts there in 1939. It was also the French who enticed the Hmong tribes of Laos into growing opium during the Second World War; and Laotian opium was flown to Saigon in French Military aircraft for processing and distribution into national and international markets. There were more heroin processing labs in the French Mediterranean port of Marseilles than in any other city in the world. However, it would be wrong to leave the impression that only the French had grown rich in the opium and/or heroin trade. The British East India Company had held a monopoly on all opium produced in India for hundreds of years, and the Dutch had been exporting opium from India since at least 1659, trading it in Indonesia for pepper. Furthermore, during the period of the Ottoman Empire, which was defeated and then disintegrated after World War I, British merchants would barter huge quantities of cotton goods for Turkish opium, which had a higher morphine content and was, therefore, better for pharmaceutical use than Indian opium, which was better for smoking. During the period between 1827 and 1869, over 80% of the opium imported to Britain was of Turkish origin. Most Indian opium was sold by the British, or bartered by them (for silk and/or tea) in China, through middlemen in Hong Kong;

Europe - 1968

On May 13, **1968**, following Lyndon Johnson's calling a halt to the bombing of North Vietnam; U.S. and North Vietnamese representatives began peace talks in Paris, France. There had been widespread demonstrations throughout France, beginning at the University of Nanterre in March **1968**. Then, on the nights of May 10, 11, and 12, **1968**, a series of riots, strikes, and widespread social unrest erupted across France, bringing the country to a virtual standstill within a week.

Of much importance, but occurring without much fanfare, given the crisis that existed in France at this time: on July 1, **1968**, the European Common Market (precursor of the European Union) was established within the European Economic Community.

On August 21, **1968**, the Soviet Union invaded Czechoslovakia, ending Czechoslovakia's considerable democratic reform movement. As mentioned, Brezhnev was the leader of the Soviet Communist Party at this time.

---

or else it was transported there by foreign privateers who had purchased it at the British-run opium auction in Calcutta. The first non-Arabic opium ever to reach China came from the Portuguese, having been grown in the Portuguese colony of Goa, on the west coast of India. The Arabs had traded a small amount of opium with Chinese aristocrats or elitists since first reaching China in the sixth century. The Chinese "mass-market" for opium, however, had never been exploited until first the Portuguese, then the Dutch, and then the British arrived. American involvement in the opium trade began when a Philadelphia ship, commanded by Captain Dobrell, arrived in Macao, the original Portuguese outpost on the southeast coast of China, with a cargo of Turkish opium in 1811. Six years later, Americans shipped $500,000.00 worth of opium to Macao.

On August 24, 1968, France exploded its first H-bomb in Mururoa in the Pacific, having first obtained the atom bomb in 1960. Very importantly, 1968 also marked the final year of approximately 15 years after the Americans dropped atomic bombs on Hiroshima and Nagasaki. It also marked the final year of the Presidency of Charles DeGaulle in France, and the final year of the Christian Democratic Union's rule in West Germany. The **CDU** had been in power continuously since the formation of West Germany in the aftermath of World War II.

DeGaulle and West German Chancellor, Konrad Adenauer (1876–1967), had signed a Franco-German Treaty of Cooperation in 1963, which was regarded widely within each country as a symbol of reconciliation between the two countries that had been traditional **enemies** for hundreds of years.

Unlike previous rulers of Germany under Prussian domination, Konrad Adenauer was a staunch Catholic. Remarkably, he began his 14 years as Chancellor when he was 73 years old, and while he was Chancellor West Germany became part of the European Coal and Steel Community (1952), NATO (1954), the European Atomic Energy Community (1957), and then signed the Treaty of Rome (1957), which was the enabling legislation for the European Economic Community. With respect to the events of **1968**, Adenauer had just died in 1967, although he had retired from being Chancellor in 1963 and was replaced by his Vice-Chancellor Ludwig Erhard.

Willy Brandt, leader of the Social Democratic Party, became Chancellor of West Germany in 1969, and Georges Pompidou succeeded Charles DeGaulle as the President of France. Richard

Nixon (Republican) succeeded Lyndon Johnson (Democrat) as President of the United States on January 20, 1969.

Middle East - 1968

In the Middle East, in May 1967, the United Nations had removed its peacekeeping force from the Gaza Strip and Sinai Peninsula. Egypt then sent troops into the Sinai, and on June 5, 1967, Israeli warplanes and land forces attacked Egypt, Jordan, and Syria in "The Six Day War," capturing not only the Sinai and the Gaza Strip, but also Syria's Golan Heights. This was the period when the Palestine Liberation Organization (PLO) came to prominence in the Middle East. Intense fighting then followed between Israel and Egypt over the strategically important Suez Canal, during the period between April 1969 and August 1970.

In 1969, while North Africa's Libyan King Idris was traveling abroad, his feudal monarchy was overthrown by the Libyan military, and Colonel Muammar Qadhafi became the President of Libya (which borders Algeria on the west and Egypt on the east.)

The battle over the Suez was won by Israel. However what followed was the "Yom Kippur War" between October 6 and October 24, 1973. Although Israel was again victorious, she suffered massive losses in men and material, leading to the resignation of Prime Minister Golda Meir during the war and the election of Yitzhak Rabin as her successor.

A New Class of College Students

Much has been written about the widespread upheavals and social unrest that occurred across college campuses around the world in the late 1960s, including the United States, France, and China. Certainly, the Vietnam War was an issue. When France was defeated by Germany early in World War II, Japan invaded Indochina, but allowed the French to retain control of the government. Following Japan's defeat late in World War II, the French attempted to regain control of the region, and war broke out in 1946. Following the French defeat at Dien Bien Phu in 1954, Vietnam was divided in two countries at the 17th parallel. In 1955, the people of South Vietnam established a republic under the Roman Catholic nationalist, Ngo Dinh Diem. Diem and his brother, Ngo Dinh Nhu, were assassinated together in 1963, during the Vietnam War, apparently on the orders of, or with the consent of U.S. President John Kennedy. Nguyen Van Thieu, a South Vietnamese military officer, was a leader in the overthrow of the Diem brothers. While Thieu had been born a Buddhist, he became a Roman Catholic in 1958. Thieu became President of South Vietnam in 1967 and resigned just one week before the war ended in 1975 when the Communists rapidly took control of South Vietnam.

Even though the Vietnam War was unpopular in the United States, France, and China, **and** was clearly a factor behind much of the student unrest occurring in each country during the late 1960s, some authors have attributed another, more profound cause to the upheaval. Lucien Bély (2001), for example, points to the enormous increase in the number of university students (250% increase in France in just seven years, with similar increases in the U.S. and China), consisting largely of the first persons in their respective families ever to receive such an education. He states that although some students came from families steeped in the university tradition, others were being exposed for the first time to a world of which they knew absolutely nothing. Instead, therefore, of considering the works of Marx, Trotsky, Mao, and other political theorists, within an established context of the global order of society, these young people took such ideas to imply a world consisting primarily of servitude and inequality. They were not persons even vaguely familiar with the contests of Voltaire and Rousseau. They were impetuous, having nothing at risk, precipitous, latently hostile, and antagonistic toward the hand that feeds them. Anarchist tendencies were, therefore, quick to develop in the cognitive void of first apprehending the industrial society.

The Effect of a Changing Political Climate on Family Values

An essential factor in Jean-Claude Roussel's decision to seek a foreign partner was that the political climate in France had become quite dangerous in 1968. The situation stemmed, in part, from the Algerian war for independence, resultant increases in the costs of raw materials, disenfranchised owners of Algerian property, and widespread discontent within the French army. There were also large numbers of French-speaking immigrants from North Africa roaming the streets of Paris looking for work.

As already discussed, there had been a virulent period of student unrest at universities throughout France, beginning with Nanterre in March of **1968**, and supported by many faculty members. Paris in May appeared to be in chaos. Industry and transportation had been paralyzed for many weeks. The country was on the verge of civil war.

Charles DeGaulle, the French President, took no immediate action. His motives have been debated ever since.

General DeGaulle, the leader of "Free France" during World War II, had retired from political life in 1953, but was recalled in 1958, as the people of France feared a violent takeover by the army in Algeria. When the Algerian War broke out, in 1954, over one million Europeans owned property in Algeria and formed the dominant social strata. By contrast, over eight million Muslims lived there and were poorer and less well-educated.

The French obtained a military victory in 1957, but then a large uprising occurred in the capital city of Algiers, in 1958, which seemed to have the support of the French army. As he returned to public service, DeGaulle announced himself "ready to take over the reins of the Republic" (Bély, 2001, p. 119). He would form a new government and submit a new constitution to the people of France for their approval by referendum. Thus began the Fifth French Republic since the revolution toppled the monarchy in 1789.[14]

DeGaulle was elected President of the Fifth Republic in December 1958. Under DeGaulle, France in 1964 was the first power to recognize Communist China; and in 1966, under DeGaulle, France withdrew its troops from the North Atlantic Treaty Organization (NATO), giving impetus to the Soviet invasion of Czechoslovakia in **1968**.

---

[14] The First Republic existed from 1792–1799. The Second Republic from 1848–1852. The Third Republic from 1871–1940. The Fourth Republic from 1947–1959. There have been five Presidents of France during the Fifth Republic: 1) Charles DeGaulle (1959–1969), 2) Georges Pompidou (1969–1974), 3) Valéry Giscard d'Estang (1974–1981), 4) François Mitterand (1981–1995), and 5) Jacques Chirac (1995–present).

DeGaulle, at this time, seemed to be distancing himself from the United States, while strengthening his ties to West Germany and a host of other Third World countries. While in Cambodia in 1966, DeGaulle severely criticized America's intervention in Vietnam. He also vetoed the United Kingdom's entry into the Common Market.

DeGaulle had difficulty getting re-elected in 1965 and a second round of voting was necessary, under the constitution, for him to obtain a simple majority. François Mitterand had already begun to galvanize a revival in the left wing of French politics when he described Gaullist practices as *"a permanent coup d'état"* (Bély, 2001, p. 121).

So, in the end, Jean-Claude Roussel opted to form an alliance with Hoechst rather than Bayer, and an agreement between the two companies was signed on September 30, **1968**. DeGaulle had finally acted to squelch the university uprising and social unrest, but only with the help of Georges Pompidou (who succeeded him as President in the 1969 elections), and the support of the army. Nevertheless, a powerful demonstration of Gaullist supporters marched down the Champs Elysées, waiving the French national flag of tricolors, on January 30, 1969, symbolizing an end to what everyone perceived as a crisis of historic proportions. DeGaulle died the following year as one of the most important figures in the history of France.

François Mitterand succeeded in taking over the leadership of the Socialist Party at the Epinay Conference, in 1971, the year before Jean-Claude Roussel's death; and he allied it closely to the Communist Party in 1972 with a common program of government. Mitterand was not to become President for another 10 years however, but, even so, this alignment in 1972 set the machinery in motion that would ultimately give the Socialists control of the French government.

So, it is indeed interesting that on Sunday, April 9, 1972, Jean-Claude Roussel, not yet 50 years old and a very accomplished aviator, crashed to his death on the side of a mountain while piloting his own private helicopter. He had earlier remarked that although Pompidou had regained full control over the political events of the country, the days were surely numbered for large, family-run industrial companies (Lanz 1980, p. 49). Soon after his death, the Roussel family offered Hoechst a majority of its shares and complete control of the far-flung, Roussel chemical and pharmaceutical enterprise.

The following year, 1973, marked the beginning of the first great oil crisis, followed by the second great oil crisis in 1979. Between 1973 and 1979, a barrel of crude oil jumped in price from about $2.40 to more than $30.00, causing a worldwide economic upheaval, especially in the gasoline and **chemical process industries**.

François Mitterand was finally elected President of France in 1981, together with a landslide Socialist victory in the legislative elections as well. (This was the same year that Ronald Reagan became President of the United States, having been elected in November 1980.) On October 26, 1981, the new French Socialist government voted to nationalize the assets of the wealthy Rothschild family, along with over three-dozen other banks and financial groups, together with five industrial conglomerates. Thus, the end predicted by Jean-Claude Roussel only nine or so years earlier had finally arrived in France.

DIFFERENT TIMES, DIFFERENT PLACES, SAME CONSEQUENCES

In Great Britain, there had been only one Labour (Socialist) Prime Minister between 1935 and 1964 (almost 30 years), and that was Clement Attlee, who succeeded Winston Churchill on July 26, 1945. In fact, some historians have argued that it was the three successive Labour Governments from 1905 through 1922 that may have defeated the Germans in World War I, but made such a mess out of the peace accords, as well as the British economy, that World War II was virtually inevitable. How strange it does thus seem, that at the very moment when Britain stood to gain the most from Churchill's undaunted leadership, they would boot him out on his arse and send in a blooming liberal to negotiate, or at least finalize the next half-century of their lives.

The election of Clement Attlee occurred during the Potsdam Conference (July 17–July 25, 1945) just southeast of Berlin, among the three great Allied powers. Potsdam would set the world stage for the next 50 years and beyond. President Franklin Roosevelt (Democrat), who was the only president in U.S. history to be elected four times, had died on April 12, 1945. So, the conference was attended by: 1) the new U.S. President Harry Truman (Democrat), who had been in office for only about 90 days, 2) Soviet Marshal Joseph Stalin, and 3) British Prime Minister Winston Churchill, who was immediately replaced by Clement Attlee.

The three earlier leaders (Roosevelt, Churchill, and Stalin) had met twice before, at Teheran (November 1943) and Yalta (February 1945), while the war was still in some doubt and had demanded a great cooperative and integrative effort among them. However, at

Potsdam, hostilities had, for the most part, ended in Europe; though the atomic bombs had not yet been dropped on Hiroshima (August 6, 1945) and Nagasaki (August 9, 1945). Attlee had joined Churchill, as his guest, during the first few days at Potsdam; then replaced him all together, when some of the toughest negotiating in the history of the human race was about to occur.

The only leader who had been present at all three meetings was Stalin. Furthermore, the Western Allies had pulled their armies back to positions agreed upon at the two earlier conferences, but the Soviet armies were still advancing. Neither had the Soviets yet declared war on Japan; and they did not do so until August 8, 1945, *after* the two atomic bombs had been dropped on Japan by the United States.

As the Soviet advance continued, millions of refugees poured into the American and British sectors. It was as pivotal a year as **1968** would turn out to be **23 years** later in terms of the changes that occurred in the ideological leadership of so many nations simultaneously. However, even though 1968 was the height of the Vietnam War, as well as the height of the Cold War, and tensions within the Middle East, France, China, and elsewhere were very high, there surely will be those who find this comparison a bit of a stretch. But so too, would some people find any comparison of, say, the Vietnam War with the Persian Gulf War to be a similar stretch. Pointing to such differences in perspective, even among those whose countries are victorious, is indeed an appropriate ending to the subject covered in this section of the text, which began you recall with the title "The Global Challenge."

TERMINOLOGY

Before we delve too deeply into the numerous differences and inconsistencies in convention that make the mastery of pharmaceutical terminology a rather dense undertaking, let's agree upon what we will mean by the words pharmaceutical, drug, and medicine. To begin with, the *Oxford Dictionary and Thesaurus, American Edition* defines these three words and gives synonyms, related words and phrases as follows:

> **drug** /drug/ *n. & v.* ● *n.* **1** a medicinal substance. **2** a narcotic, hallucinogen, or stimulant, esp. one causing addiction. ● *v.* (drugged, drugging) **1** *tr.* add a drug to (food or drink). **2** *tr.* **a** administer a drug to. **b** stupefy with a drug. **3** *intr.* take drugs as an addict. V **drug addict** a person who is addicted to a narcotic drug. **drug on the market** a commodity that is plentiful but no longer in demand. [ME drogges, drouges f. OF drogue, of unkn orig.] + *n.* **1** medicine, medicament, pharmaceutical, remedy, cure, treatment, **2** opiate, narcotic, stimulant, hallucinogen, psychedelic, *sl.* dope, downer, upper. ● *v.* **2 a** dose, medicate, treat. **b** anesthetize, dope, narcotize, knock out, sedate, stupefy, numb, benumb, dull; poison. V **drug addict** see ADDICT *n.* 1.

> **medicine** /médisin/ *n.* **1** the science or practice of the diagnosis, treatment, and prevention of disease, esp. as distinct from surgical methods. **2** any drug or preparation used for the

treatment or prevention of disease, esp. one taken by mouth. **3** a spell, charm, or fetish which is thought to cure afflictions. **V a dose** (or **taste**) **of one's own medicine** treatment such as one is accustomed to giving others. **medicine ball** a stuffed leather ball thrown and caught for exercise. **medicine chest** a box containing medicines, etc. **medicine man** a person believed to have magical powers of healing, esp. among Native Americans. **medicine show** a traveling show offering entertainment to entice a crowd to whom patent medicines, etc. would be sold. **take one's medicine** submit to something disagreeable. [ME f. OF *medecine* f. L. *medicina* f. medicus: see MEDIC¹] + **1** esp. *archaic* physic. **2** medication, medicament, remedy, drug, pharmaceutical, prescription, esp. *archaic* physic; nostrum, panacea, cure-all, V **medicine man** healer, witch doctor, shaman. **take one's medicine** face the music; see also *bite the bullet*.

pharmaceutical /fáarmcsōōtikcl/ *adj. & n.* ● *adj.* **1** of or engaged in pharmacy. **2** of the use or sale of medicinal drugs. ● *n.* a medicinal drug. VV **pharmaceutically** *adv.* **pharmaceutics** *n.* [LL *pharmaceuticus* f. Gk *pharmakeutikos* f. *pharmakeutēs* druggist f. *pharmakon* drug] + *n.* see MEDICINE. VV **pharmaceutics** pharmacy.

In common usage, these three words are often used interchangeably without much thought. However, as can be seen from the above definitions, related words, and synonyms, they have different general meanings or sense-associations. They do not represent a single general idea but three different generalized ideas. The word drug is more associated with narcotics, hallucinogens, and stimulants, which can result in addiction, than is the word medicine. The word medicine is more associated with a disease and its diagnosis, treatment or prevention. The word pharmaceutical, in a sense, combines the meanings of the words drug and medicine, i.e., a medicinal drug. It therefore has a much broader general meaning than either the word drug or medicine. The word pharmaceutical does not necessarily imply addictive substances, but it includes these. Also, the word pharmaceutical does not necessarily imply the diagnosis, treatment, or prevention of disease, but includes them. Thus, when we are talking about pharmaceuticals, it is important to be careful and seek to understand exactly what kinds of substances we are referring to.

PHARMACEUTICALS DEFINED

Given the large number of products that can be included, it seems appropriate to employ a definition for the word pharmaceutical that is more encompassing, yet consistent with what the dictionary definition given above suggests. Henceforth, and for other reasons that will soon become apparent, we will employ the following definition for the word pharmaceutical throughout this text: *a "pharmaceutical" is a non-food, medicinal preparation that, based on good evidence, shows a likelihood of making a positive contribution (benefit) to physical or mental health and well-being, either in general, or with respect to a specific part or organ of the body, including synergistic, reduced risk, and health maintenance effects.*

So, we understand that, around the world, there are significant differences and inconsistencies in the terminology that is used within the pharmaceutical industry. This is particularly true in the way various pharmaceutical products are categorized and classified by the various sources of pharmaceutical information, not to mention the various differences between countries and languages and their various regulatory agencies with differing jurisdictions throughout the world. Furthermore, there are differences within companies themselves, particularly within the larger companies, stemming from numerous mergers and acquisitions that have occurred throughout the industry, and the slow process of integrating, or harmonizing internal record keeping.

Even when the decision is made by senior management to implement uniform systems and procedures throughout newly formed or acquired companies, the process is fraught with difficulties and can require years, and an enormous amount of time and effort by employees throughout the world just to reach some level of understanding on exactly what they are attempting to define, categorize, and classify uniformly in the first place. Moreover, conceptualizing the nature of the problem and identifying existing differences throughout an organization is only the first phase. Reaching agreement on how such differences should be harmonized, without destroying valuable information in the process is another phase entirely. It is unwise to attempt to realize savings in operating budgets by eliminating apparent redundancies, or by forcing changes in standard operating procedures too quickly. In most cases, the procedures currently in place have evolved over many years of trial and error, and it has likewise taken years for highly valued employees to learn to work together effectively using existing procedures.

As an example, consider the manner in which major sources of information on pharmaceuticals classify therapeutic categories. The widely adopted textbook *Goodman & Gilman's: The Pharmacological Basis of Therapeutics,* currently in its 10th edition (2001), documents six decades (60 years) of progress in pharmacology. This popular text presents a critical appraisal of useful categories of therapeutic agents, and detailed descriptions of individual drugs or prototypes that serve as standards of reference in evaluating new drugs within a therapeutic category. It therefore seems like a good place to begin our examination of various schemes for categorizing drugs. Goodman & Gilman's textbook is organized by drug types and their therapeutic uses according to the major headings shown in Table 9-1.

TABLE 9-1 GOODMAN & GILMAN'S MAJOR CATEGORIES OF DRUGS The Pharmacological Basis of Therapeutics
Gene Therapy
Drugs Acting at the Sympathetic & Neuroeffector Junctional Sites Muscarinic Receptor Agonists & Antagonists Anticholinesterase Agents Agents Acting at the Neuromuscular Junction & Autonomic Ganglia Catecholamines, Sympathomimetic Drugs, & Adrenergic Receptor Antagonists 5-Hydroxytryptamine (Serotonin): Receptor Agonists & Antagonists
Drugs Acting on the Central Nervous System General Anesthetics Local Anesthetics Therapeutic Gases: Oxygen, Carbon Dioxide, Nitric Oxide, & Helium Hypnotics & Sedatives Ethanol Drugs for Depression & Anxiety Disorders Drugs for Psychosis & Mania Drugs for the Epilepsies Drugs for CNS Degenerative Disorders Opioid Analgesics

TABLE 9-1 GOODMAN & GILMAN'S MAJOR CATEGORIES OF DRUGS
The Pharmacological Basis of Therapeutics

Autacoids; Drug Therapy of Inflammation
Histamine, Bradykinin, & Their Antagonists
Lipid-Derived Autacoids: Eicosanoids & Platelet-Activating Factor
Analgesic-Antipyretic & Anti-Inflammatory Agents & Drugs for Gout
Drugs for Asthma

Drugs Affecting the Renal and Cardiovascular Function
Diuretics
Vasopressin & Other Agents Affecting the Renal Conservation of Water
Drugs for Myocardial Ischemia
Antihypertensive Agents
Antiarrhythmic Drugs
Drugs for Hypercholesterolemia & Dyslipidemia

Drugs Affecting Gastrointestinal Function
Agents for Gastric Acidity & Peptic Ulcers & Gastroesophageal Reflux Disease
Prokinetic Agents, Antiemetics, & Agents for Irritable Bowel Syndrome
Agents for Diarrhea, Constipation, & Inflammatory Bowel Disease; Agents for Biliary & Pancreatic Disease

Chemotherapy of Parasitic Infections
Drugs for Protozoal Infections: Malaria
Drugs for Protozoal Infections: Amebiasis, Giardiasis, Trichomoniasis, Leishmaniasis, & Other Protozoal Infections
Drugs for Helminthiasis

TABLE 9-1 GOODMAN & GILMAN'S
MAJOR CATEGORIES OF DRUGS
The Pharmacological Basis of Therapeutics

Chemotherapy of Microbial Diseases
Antimicrobial Agents: Sulfonamides, Trimethoprim-Sulfamethoxazole, Quinolones, and Agents for Urinary Tract Infections
Antimicrobial Agents: Penicillins, Cephalosporins, & Other ß-Lactam Antibiotics
Antimicrobial Agents: The Aminoglycosides
Antimicrobial Agents: Protein Synthesis Inhibitors & Miscellaneous Antibacterial Agents
Antimicrobial Agents: Drugs for Tuberculosis, *Mycobacterium avium*
Complex
Disease, & Leprosy
Antimicrobial Agents: Antifungal Agents
Antimicrobial Agents: Antiviral Agents (Nonretroviral)
Antimicrobial Agents: Antiretroviral Agents
Chemotherapy of Neoplastic Diseases
Antineoplastic Agents
Drugs Used for Immunomodulation
Immunomodulators: Immunosuppressive Agents, Tolerogens, & Immunostimulants
Drugs Acting on the Blood & the Blood-Forming Organs
Hematopoietic Agents: Growth Factors, Minerals, & Vitamins
Anticoagulant, Thrombolytic, & Antiplatelet Drugs

TABLE 9-1 GOODMAN & GILMAN'S
MAJOR CATEGORIES OF DRUGS
The Pharmacological Basis of Therapeutics

Hormones & Hormone Antagonists

Pituitary Hormones & Their Hypothalamic Releasing Factors

Thyroid & Antithyroid Drugs

Estrogens & Progestins

Androgens

Adrenocorticotropic Hormone; Adrenocortical Steroids & Their Synthetic Analogues; Inhibitors of the Synthesis & Action of Adrenocortical Hormones

Insulin, & Oral Hypoglycemic Agents

Agents Affecting Calcification & Bone Turnover: Calcium, Phosphate, Parathyroid Hormone, Vitamin D, Calcitonin, & Other Compounds

---

The Vitamins

Water-Soluble Vitamins: The Vitamin B Complex & Ascorbic Acid

---

Dermatology

Antihistamines; Glucocorticoids; Immunosuppressive Agents; Retinoids;

Agents for Pruritus; Agents for Psoriasis; Agents for Acne; Anti-Infective

Agents: Antibacterials, Antifungals, Antivirals, Antiectoparasitics; Antineoplastic Agents; Drugs for Androgenetic Alopecia (Pattern Baldness)

TABLE 9-1 GOODMAN & GILMAN'S MAJOR CATEGORIES OF DRUGS
The Pharmacological Basis of Therapeutics

Ophthalmology
Antimicrobial Agents: Antibacterials, Antivirals, Antifungals, Antiprotozoals
Autonomic Agents: Cholinergic Agonists, Anticholinesterase Agents, Muscarinic Antagonists, Sympathomimetic Agents, α-& β-Adrenergic Antagonists
Immunomodulatory Drugs: Glucocorticoids, NSAIDS, Antihistamines & Mast
Cell Stabilizers, Immunosuppressive & Antimitotic Agents
Vitreous Substitutes & Other Biological Agents Used in Ophthalmic Surgery
Anesthetics for Ophthalmic Procedures
Vitamins, Trace Elements, & Other Ophthalmic Agents
Anti-Poisoning Agents
Heavy-Metal Antagonists (Chelating Agents)
Agents for Nonmetallic Environmental Toxicants: Agents for Air Pollutants, Agents for Solvents & Vapors, Agents for Pesticides (Insecticides, Fumigants, Fungicides, Rodenticides), Agents for Herbicides

Another excellent source of information on pharmaceuticals is the *Physician's Desk Reference*. The Product Category Index is presented in Section 3 of that reference. Table 9-2 below is taken from the 56th edition of the *Physicians' Desk Reference* (Scrips, 2002).

TABLE 9-2 SCRIP'S THERAPEUTIC CATEGORIES
1. Cardiovascular
2. Alimentary/Metabolism
3. Central Nervous System
4. Anti-infectives
5. Respiratory
6. Genito-urinary
7. Musculo-skeletal
8. Cytostatics
9. Dermatologicals
10. Blood Agents

Another good source of pharmaceutical information is the World Health Organization (WHO). Table 9-3 presents the WHO Model List of Essential Drugs that should be available everywhere on earth.

TABLE 9-3 WORLD HEALTH ORGANIZATION MODEL LIST OF ESSENTIAL DRUGS

1. Anesthetics [3]
2. Analgesics, Antipyretics, Nonsteroidal Anti-Inflammatory Drugs (NSAIDs), Drugs Used to Treat Gout and Disease-Modifying Agents used in Rheumatic Disorders (DMARDs) [4]
3. Antiallergics and Drugs Used in Anaphylaxis [0]
4. Antidotes and Other Substances Used in Poisonings [2]
5. Anticonvulsants/Antiepileptics [0]
6. Anti-Infective Drugs [6]
7. Antimigraine Drugs [2]
8. Antineoplastic and Immunosuppressive Drugs and Drugs Used in Palliative Care [4]
9. Antiparkinsonism Drugs [0]
10. Drugs affecting the Blood [2]
11. Blood Products and Plasma Substitutes [2]
12. Cardiovascular Drugs [6]
13. Dermatological Drugs (topical) [7]
14. Diagnostic Agents [2]
15. Disinfectants and Antiseptics [2]
16. Diuretics [0]
17. Gastrointestinal Drugs [7]
18. Hormones, other Endocrine Drugs and Contraceptives [8]
19. Immunologicals [3]
20. Muscle Relaxants (peripherally acting) and Cholinesterase Inhibitors [0]
21. Ophthalmological Preparations [5]
22. Oxytocics and Antioxytocics [2]
23. Peritoneal Dialysis Solution [0]
24. Psychotherapeutic Drugs [4]
25. Drugs Acting on the Respiratory Tract [2]
26. Solutions Correcting Water, Electrolyte and Acid-base Disturbances [3]
27. Vitamins and Minerals [0]

Again, in this part of the book, these Tables (Table 9-1 through Table 9-7) are primarily intended to demonstrate the differences and inconsistencies across the various accepted sources of pharmaceutical information. Table 9-4 is a partial listing of the Product Category Index taken from the earlier referenced Physician's Desk Reference.

TABLE 9-4 PHYSICIAN'S DESK REFERENCE
Product Category Index (PARTIAL)
"A"
ACROMEGALY AGENTS
AIDS ADJUNCT AGENTS
ALCOHOL ABUSE PREPARATIONS
ALZHEIMER'S DISEASE MANAGEMENT
AMYOTROPHIC LATERAL SCLEROSIS THERAPEUTIC AGENTS
ANALGESICS
ANESTHETICS
ANTICONVULSANTS
ANTIDIABETIC AGENTS
ANTIDOTES
ANTIFIBROSIS THERAPY, SYSTEMIC
ANTIHISTAMINES & COMBINATIONS
ANTI-INFECTIVE AGENTS, SYSTEMIC
ANTI-INFECTIVES, NON-SYSTEMIC
ANTINEOPLASTICS
ANTIPARKINSONIAN AGENTS
ANTIRHEUMATIC AGENTS
APPETITE STIMULANTS

Note now that a very valuable source of pharmaceutical information is the company IMS Health, Inc. Here in Table 9-5 is a partial listing of the IMS Master Class Index.

TABLE 9-5 IMS HEALTH INC.	
Master Class Index (PARTIAL)	
Uniform System of Classification	
01000 Amebacide/Trichomonacide/ Antibacterial	
	01100 Amebacide
	01200 Trichomonacide/ Antibacterial
02000 Analgesics	
03000 Analgesics, Proprietary	
04000 Anesthetics	
05000 Antacids/Antiflatulents	
06000 Antacids, Proprietary	
07000 Anthelminthics, Ethical	
08000 Anthelminthics, Proprietary	
09000 Antiarthritics, Ethical	
10000 Antiarthritics, Proprietary	
11000 Hemostatic Modifiers	
12000 Reserved	
13000 Antidiarrheals	
14000 Antihistamines Systemic	
15000 Anti-Infectives Systemic	
16000 Antimalarials	
17000 Antinauseants	
18000 Anti-Obesity, Ethical	
19000 Proprietary Anti-Obesity	
20000 Neurological Disorder Misc.	
21000 Antiseptic/Periodontitis	
22000 Proprietary Antiseptics	
23000 Gastrointestinal	
24000 Genitourinary	
25000 Baby Care Products, Proprietary	
26000 Bile Therapy	
27000 Biologicals	
	27110 Rubella Vaccine
	27120 Rubeola Vaccine

TABLE 9-5 IMS HEALTH INC.

Master Class Index (PARTIAL)

Uniform System of Classification

	27130 Polio Vaccine
	27140 Mumps Vaccine
	27150 DPT Vaccine & Toxoid
	27160 Tetanus Toxoid
28000 Respiratory Therapy	
29000 Cardiac Agents	
30000 Cancer Therapy	
31000 Vascular Agents	
32000 Cholesterol/Lipotropics	
	32100 Cholesterol Reducers
	32110 Cholesterol Reducers, Rx
	32120 Cholesterol Reducers, Rx, Statins
33000 Contraceptives	
34000 Cough/Cold Preparations, Rx	
35000 Cough/Cold Preparations, OTC	
36000 Denture Prep., Proprietary	
37000 Dermatology	
38000 Anti-fungal Agents	
39000 Diabetes Therapy	
40000 Diagnostic Aids	
	40100 Diagnostic X-ray Media
	40200 Blood Testing Aids
	40300 Diagnostic Urine Tests

TABLE 9-5 IMS HEALTH INC.

Master Class Index (PARTIAL)

Uniform System of Classification

	40400 Other Diagnostics
41000 Diuretics, Ethical	
42000 Diuretics, Proprietary	
43000 Enzymes	
44000 Digestants, Proprietary	
45000 Fem. Hygiene, Ethical	
46000 Fem. Hygiene, Proprietary	
47000 Foot Prep., Proprietary	
48000 Blood Growth Factors	
49000 Hemorrhoid Prep., Ethical	
50000 Hemorrhoid Prep., Proprietary	
51000 Reserved	
52000 Hormones	
53000 Hospital Solutions	
54000 Infant Formulas	
55000 Repellants, Proprietary	
56000 Laxatives, Ethical	
57000 Laxatives, Proprietary	
58000 Lip Protectors, Proprietary	
59000 Musculoskeletal	
	59100 Muscle Relaxants
	59200 Bone Density Regulators
60000 Nutrients & Supplements	
61000 Ophthalmic Preparations	
62000 Otics, Ethical	
63000 Parasympathetics	
64000 Psychotherapeutics	
	64100 Antipsychotics
	64200 Reserved
	64300 Antidepressants
	64400 Anti-mania

TABLE 9-5 IMS HEALTH INC.

Master Class Index (PARTIAL)

Uniform System of Classification

	64500 Analeptics
	64600 Antianxiety
	64700 Reserved
	64800 Reserved
	64900 Psychotherapy, Other
65000 Respiratory Stimulants	
66000 Rubbing Alcohol	
67000 Sedatives	
68000 Sedatives, Proprietary	
69000 Smoking Deterrents	
70000 Suntan Prep., Proprietary	
71000 Sweetening Agents	
72000 Thyroid Therapy	
73000 Tonics, Proprietary	
74000 Tuberculosis Prep.	
75000 Reserved	
76000 Vitamins, Ethical	
77000 Vitamins, Proprietary	
78000 Misc. Drugs, Ethical	
79000 Misc. Remedies, Proprietary	
80000 Non-drug Preparation	
81000 Lit. A/V AIDS, etc.	
82000 Antiviral	
83000 Interferon	
84000 Natural Medicine	
85000 Sexual Function Disorder	
86000 Transplant / Immunosuppressant	
87000 Burn Remedies	

The giant pharmaceutical company, Merck, is another great source of pharmaceutical information. Table 9-6 presents the Merck Therapeutic Category and Biological Activity Index. Again, look for distinctive features between this Categorization Scheme and this Index and the other sources of pharmaceutical information presented in the other tables.

TABLE 9-6 THE MERCK INDEX

Therapeutic Category and Biological Activity Index (PARTIAL)

ABORTIFACIENT / INTERCEPTIVE
ACE-INHIBITOR *see also* Antihypertensive
I-ADRENERGIC AGONIST *see also* Antihypotensive; Antihypertensive; Antiulcerative; Decongestant; Mydriatic
J-ADRENERGIC AGONIST *see also* Bronchodilator; Cardiotonic; Tocolytic
I-ADRENERGIC BLOCKER *see also* Antihypertensive
J-ADRENERGIC BLOCKER *see also* Antianginal; Antiarrhythmic; Antiglaucoma; Antihypertensive
ADRENOCORTICAL STEROID *see also* Glucocorticoid; Mineralocorticoid
ADRENOCORTICAL SUPPRESSANT
ADRENOCORTICOTHROPIC HORMONE
ALCOHOL DETERRENT
ALDOSE REDUCTASE INHIBITOR
ALDOSTERONE ANTAGONIST *see also* Diuretic
5-ALPHA REDUCTASE INHIBITOR *see* 5α-Reductase Inhibitor
AMPA RECEPTOR ANTAGONIST
ANABOLIC
ANALEPTIC *see* CNS Stimulant
ANALGESIC (DENTAL)
ANALGESIC (NARCOTIC)
ANALGESIC (NON-NARCOTIC)
ANDROGEN
ANESTHETIC (INHALATION)
ANESTHETIC (INTRAVENOUS)

TABLE 9-6 THE MERCK INDEX

Therapeutic Category and Biological Activity Index (PARTIAL)

ANESTHETIC (LOCAL)
ANGIOTENSIN CONVERTING ENZYME *SEE* ACE-INHIBITOR
ANGIOTENSIN II RECEPTOR ANTAGONIST *SEE ALSO* ANTIHYPERTENSIVE
ANOREXIC
antacid
anthelmintic (cestodes)
anthelmintic (nematodes)
anthelmintic (schistosoma)
anthlemintic (trematodes)
antiacne *see also* Keratolytic
antiallergic *see also* Antihistaminic; Decongestant; Glucocorticoid
antiallergic (hyposensitization therapy)
antiallergic (steroidal, nasal) *SEE ALSO* GLUCOCORTICOID
antialopecia agent
antiamebic
antiandrogen *see also* Antiacne; Antialopecia Agent; Antineoplastic (Hormonal); Antiprostatic Hypertrophy
antianginal *see also* Vasodilator (Coronary)
antiarrythmic
antiarteriosclerotic *see also* Antihyperlipoproteinemic
antiarthritic/antirheumatic *see also* Anti-inflammatory (Nonsteroidal); Glucocorticoid
antiasthmatic (nonbronchodilator) *see also* Bronchodilator; Glucocorticoid
antiasthmatic (steroidal, inhalant) *SEE ALSO* GLUCOCORTICOID

TABLE 9-6 THE MERCK INDEX

Therapeutic Category and Biological Activity Index (PARTIAL)

antibacterial (antibiotics)
antibacterial (synthetic)
antibacterial (leprostatic)
antibacterial (Rickettsia) *SEE* ANTIRICKETTSIAL
antibacterial (tuberculostatic)
antibacterial adjuncts
antibiotic *see* Antibacterial (Antibiotics); Antifungal (Antibiotics); Antineoplastic
anticancer *see* Antineoplastic
anticholelithogenic *see* Cholelitholytic Agent
anticholesteremic *see* Antihyperlipoproteinemic
anticholinergic *SEE* ANTIMUSCARINIC
anticoagulant *see* also Antithrombotic; Thrombolytic
anticonvulsant
antidepressant *see also* Antimanic
antidiabetic
antidiarrheal
antidiuretic
antidote (acetaminophen poisoning)
antidote (curare)
antidote (cyanide)
antidote (folic acid antagonistS)
ANTIDOTE (HEAVY METAL POISONING)
ANTIDOTE (METHANOL AND ETHYLENE GLYCOL POISONING)
ANTIDOTE (ORGANOPHOSPHATE POISONING)
ANTIDYSKINETIC see **Antiparkinsonian**
ANTIECZEMATIC
ANTIEMETIC
ANTIEPILEPTIC see **Anticonvulsant**

TABLE 9-6 THE MERCK INDEX

Therapeutic Category and Biological Activity Index (PARTIAL)

ANTIESTROGEN
ANTIFIBROTIC
ANTIFLATULENT
ANTIFUNGAL (ANTIBIOTICS)
ANTIFUNGAL (sYNTHETICS)
ANTIGLAUCOMA
ANTIGONADOTROPIN
ANTIGOUT
ANTIHEMOPHILIC FACTOR
ANTIHEMORRHAGIC *SEE HEMOSTATIC*
ANTIHISTAMINIS see also **Antiallergic**
ANTIHYPERCHOLESTEROLEMIC *SEE*
ANTILIPOPROTEINEMIC
ANTIHYPERLIPPOPROTEINEMIC
ANTIHYPERPRATHYROID
ANTIHYPERPHOSPHATEMIC
ANIHYPERTENSIVE see also **Diuretic**
antihyperthyroid
antihypotensive
antihypothyroid
anti-infective see Antiseptic/Disinfectant
anti-inflammatory (nonsteroidal) see also **Antiarthritic/**
Antirheumatic
anti-inflammatory (steroidal) *SEE ALSO GLUCOCORTICOID*
antileprotic see Antibacterial (Leprostatic)
antileukemic see **Antineoplastic**
antilipemic see Antihyperlipoproteinemic
antilipidemic see Antihyperlipoproteinemic
antimalarial
antimanic

TABLE 9-6 THE MERCK INDEX

Therapeutic Category and Biological Activity Index (PARTIAL)

antimethemoglobinemic
antimigraine
antimuscarinic see also Antiparkinsonian; Antispasmodic; Mydriatic
antimycotic *see also* Antifungal (Antibiootics); Antifungal (Synthetics)
antinauseant *see* Antiemetic
antineoplastic
antineoplastic (hormone)
antineoplastic (photosensitizer)
antineoplastic (radiation source)
antineoplastic adjunct
antineutropenic
antiobesity agent *SEE ALSO* ANOREXIC
antiobsessional
antiosteoporotic *see also* Bone Resorption Inhibitor; Calcium Regulator
antipagetic *see also* Bone Resorption Inhibitor; Calcium Regulator
antiparkinsonian
antiperistaltic *SEE* ANTIDIARRHEAL
antipheochromocytoma
antipneumocystic
antiprogestin
antiprostatic hypertrophy
antiprotozoal (ameba) *SEE* ANTIAMEBIC
antiprotozoal (cryptosporidium)
antiprotozoal l(giardia)
antiprotozoal (leishmania)
ANTIPROTOZOAL (MALARIA) *see* Antimalarial

TABLE 9-6 THE MERCK INDEX

Therapeutic Category and Biological Activity Index (PARTIAL)

antiprotozoal (pneumocystic) *SEE ANTIPNEUMOCYSTIC*
antiprotozoal (toxoplasma)
antiprotozoal (trichomonnas)
antiprotozoal (trypanosoma)
antipruritic
antipsoriatic
antipsychotic
antipyretic
antirheumatic see Antiarthritic/Antirheumatic
antirickettsial
antiseborrheic
antisepsis
antiseptic/disinfectant
antispasmodic see also **Antimuscarinic**
antisyphilitic see also **Antibacterial**
antithrombocythemic
antithrombotic see also Anticoagulant; Thrombolytic
antitubercular see Antibacterial (Tuberculostatic)
antitumor see **Antineoplastic**
antitussive
antiulcerative see also **Antacid**
antiurolithic
antivenin
antivertigo *SEE* ANTIEMETIC
antiviral
anxiolytic
aromatase inhibitors *see also* Antineoplastic (Hormonal)
astringent
atriopeptidase inhibitor
benzodiazepine antagonist

TABLE 9-6 THE MERCK INDEX

Therapeutic Category and Biological Activity Index (PARTIAL)

beta-blocker *see* J-Adrenergic Blocker
blood substitute
bone resorption inhibitor ***SEE ALSO*** CALCIUM REGULATOR
bradycardic agent ***SEE ALSO*** ANTIANGINAL
bradykinin antagonist
bronchodilator *see also* Antiasthmatic; Glucocorticoid
calcium channel blocker *see also* Antianginal; Antihypertensive; Vasodilator (Coronary)
calcium regulator
calcium supplement *see* Replenishers/Supplements
cancer chemotherapy ***SEE*** ANTINEOPLASTIC
capillary protectant ***SEE*** VASOPROTECTANT
carbonic anhydrase inhibitor ***SEE ALSO*** ANTIGLAUCOMA; DIURETIC
cardiac depressant (anitarrhythmic) ***SEE*** ANTIARRHYTHMIC
carioprotective
cardiotonic
cathartic *see* Laxative/Cathartic
cation-exchange resin ***SEE*** ION-EXCHANGE RESIN
cck antagonist
central stimulant ***SEE*** CNS STIMULANT
central vasodilator *see* Vasodilator (Cerebral)
chelating agent
cholecystokinin antagonist ***SEE*** CCK ANTAGONIST
cholelitholytic agent
choleretic
cholinergic
cholinesterase inhibitor
cholinesterase reactivator
cns stimulant

TABLE 9-6 THE MERCK INDEX

Therapeutic Category and Biological Activity Index (PARTIAL)

cognition activator
comt inhibitor
contraceptive (implantable)
contraceptive (injectable)
contraceptive (oral)
control of intraocular pressure *SEE ALSO* ANTIGLAUCOMA
converting enzyme inhibitor *SEE* ACE-INHIBITOR
coronary vasodilator *see* Vasodilator (Coronary)
CYCLOOXYGENASE-2 INHIBITOR *see also* Anti-inflammatory (Nonsteroidal)
CYTOPROTECTANT (GASTRIC) *see also* Antiulcerative
debriding agent
decongestant
dental plaque inhibitor
depigmentor
dermatitis herpetiformis suppressant
diagnostic aid
diagnostic aid (MRI contrast agent)
diagnostic aid (radioactive imaging agent)
DIAGNOSTIC AID (RADIOPAQUE MEDIUM)
DIAGNOSTIC AID (ULTRASOUND CONTRAST AGENT)
DIGESTIVE AID
DISINFECTANT see Antiseptic/Disinfectant
DIURETIC
DOPAMINE RECEPTOR AGONIST see also Antihypertensive; Animigraine; Antiparkinsonian; Prolactin Inhibitor
dopamine receptor antagonist see also **Antiemetic; Antipsychotic**
ectoparasiticide
electrolyte replenisher see **Replenishers/Supplements**

TABLE 9-6 THE MERCK INDEX

Therapeutic Category and Biological Activity Index (PARTIAL)

emetic
endothelin receptor antagonist see also **Vasodilator (Peripheral)**
enkephalinase inhibitor see Neutral Endopeptidase Inhibitor
enzyme
enzyme cofactor *SEE VITAMIN*
enzyme inducer (hepatic)
enzyme replacement therapy
estrogen
estrogen antagonist *SEE ANTIESTROGEN*
expectorant
fibrinogen receptor antagonist *SEE ALSO ANTITHROMBOTIC*
gastric and pancreatic secretion stimulant
gastric proton pump inhibitor *SEE ALSO ANTIULCERATIVE*
gastric secretion inhibitor
gastroprokinetic
glucocorticoid
I-glucosidase inhibitor *SEE ALSO ANTIDIABETIC*
gonad-stimulating principle
gout suppressant *SEE ANTIGOUT*
growth hormone antagonist inhibitor
growth hormone releasing factor
growth stimulant
hematinic
hematopoietic
hemolytic
hemorheologic agent
hemostatic
heparin antagonist
hepatoprotectant
histamine H_2-Receptor antagonist *SEE ANTIHISTAMINIC*

TABLE 9-6 THE MERCK INDEX

Therapeutic Category and Biological Activity Index (PARTIAL)

histamine H_2-Receptor antagonist *SEE ALSO* ***ANTIULCERATIVE***
hiv fusion inhibitor *SEE ALSO* ***ANTIVIRAL***
hiv protease inhibitor *SEE ALSO* ***ANTIVIRAL***
HMG Coa reductase inhibitor see also **Antihyperlipoproteinemic**
hypnotic
hypocholesteremic see Antihyperlipoproteinemic
hypolipidemic see Antihyperlipoproteinemic
hypotensive see **Antihypertensive**
immunomodulator
immunosuppressant
insulin sensitizer see also **Antidiabetic**
ion-exchange resin
keratolytic *see also* Antiacne
lactation stimulating hormone
laxative/cathartic
leukotriene antagonist *SEE ALSO* ***ANTIASTHMATIC***
lh-rh agonist see also Antineoplastic; Gonad-Stimulating Principle
lipotropic
5-lipoxygenase inhibitor see also Antiallergic; Antiasthmatic; Anti-inflammatory; Antipsoriatic
local anesthetic see **Anesthetic (Local)**
lupus erythematosus suppressant
major tranquilizer *SEE **ANTIPSYCHOTIC***
matrix metalloproteinase inhibitor
mineralocorticoid
minor tranquilizer *SEE **ANXIOLYTIC***
miotic

TABLE 9-6 THE MERCK INDEX

Therapeutic Category and Biological Activity Index (PARTIAL)

monoamine oxidase inhibitor see also Antidepressant; Antihypertensive; Antiparkinsonian
mucolytic
muscle relaxant (skeletal) see also **Neuromuscular Blocking Agent**
muscle relaxant (smooth) *SEE ANTIMUSCARINIC*
mydriatic
narcotic analgesic see **Analgesic (Narcotic)**
NARCOTIC ANTAGONIST
NASAL DECONGESTANT *SEE DECONGESTANT*
NEURAMINIDASE INHIBITOR *SEE ALSO ANTIVIRAL*
NEUROLEPTIC see *Antipsychotic*
NEUROMUSCULAR BLOCKING AGENT
NEUTRAL ENDOPEPTIDASE INHIBITOR see also **Antihypertensive; Antidiarrheal**
NEUROPROTECTIVE
NMDA RECEPTOR ANTAGONIST *SEE ALSO NEUROPROTECTIVE*
NOOTROPIC
NSAID see Anti-inflammatory (Nonsteroidal)
OPIOID ANALGESIC *see* Analgesic (Narcotic)
ORAL CONTRACEPTIVE *see* Contraceptive (Oral)
OVARIAN HORMONE
OXYTOCIC
PARASYMPATHOMIMETIC *SEE* CHOLINERGIC
PEDICULICIDE *see* Ectoparasiticide
PEPSIN INHIBITOR
PERIPHER AL VASODILATOR *see* Vasodilator (Peripheral)
PERISTALTIC STIMULANT *SEE* GASTROPROKINETIC

TABLE 9-6 THE MERCK INDEX

Therapeutic Category and Biological Activity Index (PARTIAL)

PHOSPHODIESTERASE INHIBITOR *see also* Antiasthmatic; Antithrombotic
PIGMENTATION AGENT
PLASMA VOLUME EXPANDER
PLATELET ACTIVATING FACTOR ANTAGONIST
POTASSIUM CHANNEL ACTIVATOR/OPENER *see also* Antihypertensive; Antianginal
POTASSIUM CHANNEL BLOCKER *SEE ALSO* ANTIARRHYTHMIC
PRESSOR AGENT *see* Antihypotensive
PROGESTOGEN
PROLACTIN INHIBITOR
prostaglandin/prostaglandin analog *see also* Abortifacient/Interceptive; Antiglaucoma; Antithrombotic; Antiulcerative; Oxytocic
protease inhibitor *see also* HIV Protease Inhibitor
proton pump inhibitor see Gastric Proton Pump Inhibitor
pulmonary surfactant
5I-reductase inhibitor *see also* Antiprostatic Hypertrophy
replenishers/supplements
respiratory stimulant
retroviral protease inhibitor *SEE* HIV PROTEASE INHIBITOR
reverse transcriptase inhibitor *SEE ALSO* ANTIVIRAL
scabicide *see* Ectoparasiticide
sclerosing agent
sedative/hypnotic *SEE ALSO* ANXIOLYTIC
serotonin noradrenaline reuptake inhibitor (SNRI) *SEE ALSO* ANTIDEPRESSANT; ANTIOBESITY AGENT

TABLE 9-6 THE MERCK INDEX
Therapeutic Category and Biological Activity Index (PARTIAL)
serotonin receptor agonist *see also* Anxiolytic; Antidepressant; Antimigraine; Neuroprotective; Serenic
serotonin receptor antagonist *see also* Antidepressant; Antiemetic; Antihypertensive; Antimigraine
Serotonin Uptake Inhibitor *see also* Antidepressant; Antiobsessional
sialagogue
skeletal muscle relaxant *see* Muscle Relaxant (Skeletal)
SNRI *see* Serotonin Noradrenaline Reuptake Inhibitor (SNRI)
somatostatin analog
spasmolytic *see* Antispasmodic
stool softener *see* Laxative/Cathartic
succinylcholine synergist
sympathomimetic *see* I-Adrenergic Agonist; J-Adrenergic Agonist
Thrombolytic *see also* Anticoagulant; Antithrombotic
Thromboxane A_2-Receptor Antagonist *see also* Antithrombotic; Antiasthmatic
Thrombooxane A_2-Synthetase Inhibitor *SEE ALSO* ANTITHROMBOTIC
Thyroid Hormone *see also* Antihypothyroid
thyroid inhibitor *see* Antihyperthyroid
thyrotropic hormone
tocolytic
topical protectant
topoisomerase I inhibitor *SEE ALSO* ANTINEOPLASTIC
Topoisomerase II Inhibitor *SEE ALSO* ANTINEOPLASTIC
tranquilizer *see* Antipsychotic; Anxiolytic
Ultraviolet screen
uricosuric *see also* Antigout
vasodilator (cerebral)
vasodilator (Coronary)

TABLE 9-6 THE MERCK INDEX
Therapeutic Category and Biological Activity Index (PARTIAL)
VASODILATOR (PERIPHERAL)
VASOPEPTIDASE INHIBITOR *see* Neutral Endopeptidase Inhibitor
VASOPRESSOR *see* Antihypotensive
VASOPROTECTANT
VITAMIN/VITAMIN SOURSEs *SEE ALSO* ENZYME COFACTOR
VULNERary
wilson's disease treatment
zanthine oxidase inhibitor *SEE ALSO* ANTIGOUT

The American Food and Drug Administration (FDA) also publishes Indices of pharmaceutical products. Here is the final table in this part of the book, Table 9-7. Table 9-7 is a partial listing of the FDA Index to Over-the-Counter (OTC) drugs as well as the associated codes necessary to find and read FDA's OTC Reports.

TABLE 9-7 FDA INDEX OF OTC DRUGS

Codes to Review OTC Reports

Code	Description	Code	Description
AA	Antacid	EP	Exocrine Pancreatic Insufficiency
AB	Antibiotic	FB	Oral Drugs for Fever Blister
AC	Anticaries	FE	Fever Blister/Cold Sore (External)
AD	Antidiarrheal	HG	Hair Grower /Loss
AE	Antiemetic	HO	Hormone
AF	Antifungal	HY	Hypophosphatemia/ Hyperphosphatemia
AH	Anthelmintic	IA	Internal Analgesic
AK	Acne	IB	Insect Bite & Sting
AL	Alcohols (Topical)	IO	Oral Insect Repellant
AM	Antimicrobial	IR	Insect Repellant
AN	Antiflatulent	IT	Ingrown Toenail
AP	Antiperspirant	LC	Leg Muscle Cramps
AR	Anorectal	LX	Laxative
AS	Astringent	MD	Menstrual /Diuretic
AT	Acute Toxic Ingestion	ME	Mercury
AX	Aphrodisiac	MG	Male Genital Desensitizer
BT	Boil Treatment	NS	Nighttime Sleep Aid
BP	Benign Prostatic Hypertrophy	NT	Nailbiting/Thumbsucking
CA	Cough Cold (Anticholinergic)	OD	Relief of Oral Discomfort
CB	Cough Cold (Bronchodilator)	OH	Oral Health Care
CC	Cough Cold (Combinations)	OI	Oral Muscosal Injury

TABLE 9-7 FDA INDEX OF OTC DRUGS

Codes to Review OTC Reports

CE	Cough Cold (Expectorant)	O	Ophthalmic
CG	Cough Cold (General)	OR	Overindulgence in Alcohol and Food
CH	Cough Cold (Antihistamine)	OT	Otic
CK	Cholecystokinetic	PE	Pediculicide
CN	Cough Cold (Nasal Decongestant)	PI	Poison Ivy /Oak /Sumac Prevention
CO	Camphorated Oil	PT	Poison Treatment
CR	Corn/Callus Remover	PW	Pregnancy Warning
CS	Camphor Statement	SA	Stomach Acidifier
CT	Cough Cold (Antitussive)	SB	Skin Bleaching
CV	Contraceptive (Vaginal)	SD	Smoking Deterrent
DA	Digestive Aid	SK	Skin Protectant
DE	Deodorants for Internal Use	SN	Sweet Spirits of Niter
DH	Diphenhydramine Notice	ST	Stimulant
DP	Dandruff/Seborrheic Dermatitis /Psoriasis	SU	Sunscreen
DR	Diaper Rash	TR	Triclosan
DS	Daytime Sedative	VG	Vaginal
EA	External Analgesic	WC	Weight Control
EM	Emetic	WR	Wart Remover

"NATURAL" VS. "ORGANIC" & "SYNTHETIC"

In recent years, it has become popular among significant numbers of people to use the word "organic" as if it were synonymous with the word "natural." Its use in this manner occurs particularly with respect to fruits, vegetables, and other foods that are produced without the use of industrial fertilizers, herbicides, preservatives, etc. During the final two or three decades of the twentieth century, certain agricultural interests developed the means of producing and marketing relatively large and consistent quantities of such foods to these consumer segments more-or-less directly (without middlemen). These agricultural interests began to realize substantially higher profits than conventional producers and marketers of food. Thus, a competitive situation arose in which many foods began to be marketed using terminology such as fresh, pure, no artificial ingredients, vine-ripe, hand-picked, all-natural, organic, etc.

Agricultural interests focused largely on the use of the word "organic" and responded with standards for certifying "organic" foods and lobbying governments to legislate and enforce these standards. Over a period of time, their sustained efforts led to proposed legislation clarifying what is meant by terms such as "certified organic." Nevertheless, recent marketing research has shown that a significant percentage of the population perceives the words "natural" and "organic," among others, but these especially to mean essentially the same thing. Certain segments of consumers with clearly identifiable profiles are willing to pay substantially higher prices for *attractive* fresh fruits and vegetables that are grown, harvested, stored, transported, and marketed without the use of artificial chemicals of any kind. Other segments of consumers are willing to pay slightly higher prices for such foods even if they are not well–formed, bruised and unattractive.

It should be made clear that henceforth whenever the word "organic" is used in this book, unless otherwise specifically stated, it will mean chemicals comprised of carbon, primarily in combination with hydrogen, oxygen, and nitrogen (which together comprise the building blocks of life) regardless of their source, natural or synthetic. Life as we know it is based on the chemistry of carbon (principally in combination with hydrogen, oxygen, and nitrogen), although as we have already discussed, certain other elements are also required for life to exist, albeit in smaller quantities than carbon, hydrogen, oxygen, and nitrogen. Historically, the chemistry of carbon with these three other elements has been referred to within the sciences as "organic chemistry," and this will be its meaning within this book.

HYDROCARBONS

There are many different kinds of organic chemicals such as alkaloids, carbohydrates, hydrocarbons, nucleic acids, proteins, etc. "Hydrocarbons" are by far the most important to modern civilization. Hydrocarbons consist of practically innumerable combinations of carbon atoms together with only hydrogen, and anything else appearing solely as contaminants. Hydrocarbons are sources of energy, heat, fuel, and as an essential feedstock material for the chemical process industries, including pharmaceuticals and related products.

PHARMACEUTICAL PRODUCTS

ETHICAL PHARMACEUTICALS

Ethical pharmaceuticals have active ingredients that are manufactured according to ultra-high pure, exacting standards such as those published in an official pharmacopeia, or patent application. Use of the term "ethical" is derived from the fact that previously they were not advertised to the general public, only to physicians and other health care professionals. (Note: this practice has changed dramatically with the advent of Direct-to-Consumer or DTC advertising.) Ethicals may be synthetic, semi-synthetic, or derived from natural products or extracts. The key to their definition is ultra-high purity of active ingredients according to published procedures.

Prior to marketing, ethical pharmaceuticals must pass through a series of rigorous, carefully controlled trials in animals and humans to demonstrate both safety and efficacy at stated dosages. For this reason, they are sometimes referred to as "legend pharmaceuticals." The **"legend"** is the body of empirical data compiled and presented to regulatory authorities in support of the drug's safety and efficacy. In early years, when an ethical brand has an enforceable patent, usually in defense of demonstrated superior performance, it will, typically, command premium prices in the marketplace and high profit margins for manufacturers.

GENERIC PHARMACEUTICALS

While also being ethical pharmaceuticals, these medicines are non-patented, non-branded, and available by prescription only. Generic pharmaceuticals are marketed by their generic names, rather than brand names. A generic name is nonproprietary, indicating that the drug is not protected by a brand name or trademark. Different from brand names, which are marketing artifacts, generic names are usually indicative of a drug's chemical structure. Generics may be synthetic, semi-synthetic, or derived from natural products or extracts. Typically, they represent drugs whose patents have expired and are being manufactured by companies other than the original or "legend" manufacturer. In the United States, generic pharmaceuticals are required to demonstrate "bioequivalence" with their legend counterparts. The process of demonstrating bioequivalence is significantly less tedious and less time-consuming than the processes of demonstrating safety and efficacy. Drug products demonstrating such bioequivalence that have been approved by the U.S. Food and Drug Administration (FDA) are listed in the current edition of the *Orange Book* published by the FDA.

BIOLOGICS (BIOLOGICAL PRODUCTS)

A "biological" or "biological product" is a medicinal preparation made from living organisms and their products, including serums, vaccines, antigens, antitoxins, etc. In general, when used in the context of pharmaceuticals or medicinal preparations, the term "biologics" tends to have the same meaning as the terms "biologicals" or "biological products," except for the legal definition in the United States, presented below (i.e., it includes trivalent arsenic compounds).

TABLE 10-1 DEFINITIONS OF REPRESENTATIVE BIOLOGICS
Serum – the clear portion of any body fluid, such as the clear fluid that separates from the blood on clotting or via a centrifuge. Blood serums from recuperating patients have been used to treat measles, scarlet fever, and whooping cough. An "immune serum" (also called an antiserum) is from an immunized animal and is used for passive immunization. Serums do not necessarily have to come from the same species as the recipient. Equine antiserums are used as powerful immunosuppressive agents to destroy circulating human lymphocytes. Horse and rabbit antiserums were used to treat pneumococcal pneumonia before the advent of modern antibiotics. Some serums are capable of bacterium lyses (destruction). Equine antiserums are also used for rabies if "rabies immune globulin is unavailable." Sometimes, antiserums are referred to as "antivenins" or "antitoxins" (such as tetanus antitoxin).
Vaccine – a suspension of attenuated or killed microorganisms (e.g., bacteria, viruses, or rickettsiae). "Vaccine" also refers to antigenic proteins, which induce an immune response; (see Antigen below) that are derived from such microorganisms and administered for the prevention, amelioration, or treatment of infectious diseases. The word vaccine usually refers to cows for historical reasons (e.g., cowpox virus used to cure smallpox) and there are many bovine vaccines. However, vaccines like "anthrax vaccine" are cell-free protein extracts of *Bacillus anthracis*. "Cholera vaccine" is a mixture of equal portions of killed bacteria of the Inaba and Ogawa strains of *Vibrio cholerae*.

TABLE 10-1 DEFINITIONS OF
REPRESENTATIVE BIOLOGICS

Antigen – an antigen is any substance capable of inducing a specific immune response and of interacting with the products of that immune response, i.e., specific antibodies, specially sensitized T-lymphocytes, or both. Antigens may be soluble like toxins, or particulate matter such as bacteria and tissue cells. Nevertheless, it is only the "antigenic determinant" that combines with the antibody or specific receptor on a lymphocyte. Antigenic determinants are specific portions of specific protein or polysaccharide molecules. Some antigens are used as specific *"markers"* to distinguish cell lineages, developmental stages, and functional subsets. Such *markers* can be distinguished by specific monoclonal antibodies. Antigens are used in the treatment of hepatitis with some success. They also play an important role in the potential for rejection of organ transplants.

TABLE 10-1 DEFINITIONS OF REPRESENTATIVE BIOLOGICS

Toxins – poisons, frequently specific proteins produced by some higher plants, certain animals, and pathogenic bacteria, which are capable of producing a powerful immune response in other life forms, causing for example: acute food poisoning, severe diarrhea, paralysis of the central nervous system, gangrene, intestinal necrosis, cardiac arrest, and many other causes of death. Toxins are different from plant alkaloids because of their high molecular weight and antigenicity. Bacterial toxins include: "exotoxins," "endotoxins," "enterotoxins," and "neurotoxins." Examples of toxins include the Type A exotoxin produced by *Clostridium botulinum*, which is **one of the most powerful poisons known to man**. There are seven distinct toxins produced by this bacterium (Types A-G), but **Type A is the worst**. It blocks the release of acetylcholine by binding to the presynaptic terminals of the CNS, leading to paralysis. Toxins are responsible for conditions related to anthrax, botulism, cholera, diphtheria, gas gangrene, scarlet fever, tetanus, and whooping cough, among other diseases.

Antitoxins – antibodies against toxins. Usually a purified antiserum from horses that have been immunized by injections of toxins or toxoids. There are antitoxins for botulism, diphtheria, gas gangrene, tetanus, etc.

TABLE 10-1 DEFINITIONS OF REPRESENTATIVE BIOLOGICS
Immunoglobulins – any of a large number of structurally related glycoproteins that function as antibodies. There are many classes and subclasses of immunoglobulins. Some can appear on the surface of B cells as antigen receptors. B cells that are activated by antigens differentiate into plasma cells and secrete a variety of immunoglobulins through gene rearrangement. However, regardless of the class of the secreted immunoglobulin, it will have the same antigenic specificity as the antigen receptors of the parent B cell, which is rather amazing. The IgG class of immunoglobulins is the only class transferred across the placenta, and is thus responsible for the health of the growing fetus, protecting it from infection.
Toxoids – modified or inactivated bacterial exotoxins that has lost its toxicity, but retains the ability to combine with or stimulate the production of antitoxin. Two common toxoids are tetanus toxoid and diphtheria toxoid.

A LOOK AT THE U.S. DEFINITION FOR BIOLOGICS

As another introduction to what a legal definition can look like, let's consider the meaning of the term "biologic," as it is defined in the U.S. Code of Federal Regulations, Title 21, Chapter 1, Subchapter F, Part 600, Subpart A, Section 600.3

In this section, the term "biologic" or "biologic products" includes the same basic idea of a biological or biological product given in the above paragraphs, *plus* **it also includes trivalent organic arsenical compounds** (see paragraph "g" of Section 600.3).

Paragraph "h" of Section 600.3 defines the meaning of the term "Biological product" as "any virus, therapeutic serum, toxin, antitoxin, or analogous product applicable to the prevention, treatment or cure of diseases or injuries of man":

(1) A virus is interpreted to be a product containing the minute living cause of an infectious disease and includes but is not limited to filterable viruses, bacteria, rickettsia, fungi, and protozoa.

(2) A therapeutic serum is a product obtained from blood by removing the clot or clot components and the blood cells.

(3) A toxin is a product containing a soluble substance poisonous to laboratory animals or to man in doses of 1 milliliter or less (or equivalent in weight) of the product, and having the property, following the injection of non-fatal doses into an animal, of causing to be produced therein another soluble substance which specifically neutralizes the poisonous substance and which is demonstrable in the serum of the animal thus immunized.

(4) An antitoxin is a product containing the soluble substance in serum or other body fluid of an immunized animal, which specifically neutralizes the toxin against which the animal is immune.

(5) A product is analogous:

(i) To a virus, if prepared from or with a virus or agent actually or potentially infectious, without regard to the degree of virulence or toxicogenicity of the specific strain used.

(ii) To a therapeutic serum, if composed of whole blood or plasma or containing some organic constituent or product other than a hormone or an amino acid, derived from whole blood, plasma, or serum.

(iii) To a toxin or antitoxin, if intended, irrespective of its source of origin, to be applicable to the prevention, treatment, or cure of disease or injuries of man through a specific immune process."

Paragraph "i" of Section 600.3 defines the meaning of the term "Trivalent organic arsenicals" as: "arsphenamine and its derivatives (or any other trivalent organic arsenic compound) applicable to the prevention, treatment, or cure of diseases or injuries of man."

OVER-THE-COUNTER MEDICATIONS

In general, OTC medications refer to nonprescription drugs. In this general sense, OTC medications subsume all of the remaining sectors of pharmaceutical products: homeopathic medicines, vitamins and minerals, medicinal botanicals & herbal medicines, botanical extracts & phytochemicals, dietary supplements, and nutraceuticals. However, there are too many differences across these remaining sectors to think of them all as simply OTC medications. Furthermore, it is becoming increasingly common for prescription pharmaceuticals, i.e., "ethicals," to be switched from Rx to OTC status, albeit at a lower dosage. For example, the anti-ulcer drugs: Tagamet, Zantac, Pepcid, and Axid all began as prescription pharmaceuticals and were then switched to OTC status. Thus, in this "switched" context, OTC medications contain the identical ingredients as the prescription drugs, just at a lower dosage and are considered as a result to be much safer than their prescription counterparts. Most importantly, OTC medications are often branded and, therefore, are also often referred to as "proprietary" medications, although there are also generic and store-brand OTC medications. Thus, the key ideas in defining an OTC medication for our purposes are that OTC medications are typically compounded medicines, using similar or identical ingredients as existing or previous prescription drugs, but in lower dosages. They also have well-established therapeutic profiles, and are regarded as efficacious and safe. Finally, there usually must be published data establishing the **general** or **widespread** recognition of the drug's safety and efficacy, including the results of well-controlled clinical trials.

HOMEOPATHIC MEDICINES

Homeopathic medicine is a system of therapeutics based on drugs that are administered in very small doses. Furthermore, the drugs that are used in homeopathy, when administered to healthy persons, produce symptoms like those of the disease they are intended to treat. In other words, a homeopathic drug is similar to but not the same as the causative agent of the disease. The general idea is that with the induced symptoms being similar, the body will react to the drug in a manner that will cure the disease.

Ever since the beginnings of homeopathy, in the late eighteenth century, practitioners have sought substances that mimic diseases, and have applied this "likenesses" principle "similia similibus curentur," or "let likes be cured by likes," in their treatment of the sick. Today, homeopathy is popular in many countries of the world, particularly France and Germany, and is frequently associated with self-medication in the United States, where it has been experiencing a substantial resurgence in popularity.

VITAMINS & MINERALS

A British naval physician by the name of Dr. James Lind was severely ridiculed by the medical community when he proposed in 1747 that scurvy, a disease characterized by weakness, bruising, bleeding gums, and anemia, could be cured with limes, oranges, and green vegetables. It wasn't for another half-century that the British navy decided to make limes part of a sailor's daily rations. Vitamin C, the essential ingredient that prevents scurvy, was not isolated until 1928.

Kanehiro Takaki was similarly ridiculed when he suggested in 1877 that diet could also cure beriberi, a disease of the nervous system. It wasn't until 1912 that an extract of rice hulls was obtained containing the vitamin we now call **thiamine**, which does indeed cure beriberi.

The term "vitamins" refers to a group of unrelated organic substances that are necessary in very small amounts for the normal metabolic functioning of the body. Vitamins are either fat-soluble (A, D, E, and K), which can be stored in the body, or water-soluble (the B vitamins and vitamin C), which are excreted in the urine and not appreciably stored in the body.

Vitamins are present in exceedingly small quantities and function as catalysts. Most play the role of either enzymes or coenzymes. The human body has over 1,000 types of enzymes, but only 13 so-called essential vitamins, although this number seems to be growing all the time. Enzymes are proteins, but many, if not most enzymes require metals in order to function. For example, vitamin B_{12}, which is required for DNA synthesis, contains cobalt. Most such metals are referred to as *trace elements*, because like the vitamins themselves, and most enzymes, they are present in the body in minute quantities. In order for a substance to be classified as a vitamin, a deficiency of the substance must result in a specific disease.

The human body requires a number of minerals, both metallic and nonmetallic in order to sustain life. Such minerals are usually divided into three categories, those that are generally required in **gram quantities** per day by adult humans, those that are generally required in **milligram quantities** per day by adult humans, and those that are generally required in **microgram quantities** per day by adult humans. The so-called macrominerals (gram quantities per day) include calcium, chloride, potassium, phosphorous, and sodium. The milligram level minerals include copper, fluoride, iron, magnesium, manganese, and zinc. Those minerals that are required in microgram quantities include chromium, iodine, molybdenum, and selenium. Of the milligram and microgram-level minerals, all except fluoride and chromium are incorporated into various enzymes or hormones that are required in metabolism. Other minerals thought to be important to human genetics and/or nutrition, most of which have been implicated in animal nutrition models, include aluminum, arsenic, boron, cobalt (as mentioned, a necessary component of vitamin B_{12}), nickel, silicon, and vanadium.

MEDICINAL BOTANICALS & HERBAL MEDICINES

Medicine from plants or medical botany, including medicines from bacteria, algae, and fungi, has been practiced around the world since the earliest of times. It seems that the preferred term for medicinal plants today is "botanicals," although many people continue to refer to them as "medicinal botanicals" and both terms are in common usage.

The term "botanicals" as we will use it here includes plant materials, algae, macroscopic fungi, and combinations thereof. It does not include fermentation products such as products fermented with yeast, bacteria, and other microscopic organisms, nor does it include highly purified or chemically modified substances derived from botanical sources, such as Paclitaxel.

Botanical raw materials may sometimes be dispensed at clinics as needed or by prescription basis and subsequently prepared by patients themselves at home. There is usually some type of manufacturing process (e.g., pulverization, decoction, expression, aqueous extraction, or ethanolic extraction) at the home, which may render the raw material a botanical substance under the law if it were to be resold.

Medicinal botanicals and herbal medicines are typically consumed as whole parts of plants: roots, stems, leaves, flowers, etc. A "botanical drug substance," on the other hand, is obtained from such raw materials by a manufacturing process, such as decoction or extraction. "Botanical products" are derived further by adding one or more excipients to raw plant materials, and then mixing, blending, granulating, tableting, encapsulating, or performing other dosage form-specific procedures, followed by packaging.

Plant-based medicine is preferred today within many cultures (e.g., China and India), and among clearly identifiable segments of consumers in almost all cultures. Up until the time of Paracelsus (1493–1542), who advocated the use of minerals and metals in treating the sick, medicine in Europe was still based upon the teachings and practices of the Roman physician, Claudius Galen (A.D. 129–216). Galen's teachings were largely based on Aristotle's (384–322 B.C.) ideas of the four bodily humors (black bile, yellow bile, phlegm, and blood) and medicinal botany. One of Aristotle's most famous sayings in this regard was "let food be your medicine and medicine be your food." It is still very good advice. Additionally, many of today's most effective medicines have their roots in plant-based medicines (discussed below), if not directly consisting of various extracts of the plants themselves.

BOTANICAL DRUG PRODUCTS, EXTRACTS & PHYTOCHEMICALS

Botanical products are finished, labeled products that contain vegetable matter as ingredients. Botanical drug products have certain unique characteristics that should be taken into account in categorizing them. Plant materials used in the production of botanical drug products often are not completely characterized and defined or are prone to contamination, deterioration, and variation in composition and properties. In many cases, the active constituent(s) in a botanical drug is (are) not identified, nor is it's (their) biological activity well–characterized. Therefore, unlike synthetic or highly purified drug products, it may be difficult to ensure the quality of a botanical drug by controlling only the corresponding drug substance and drug product.

Botanical drugs are derived from vegetable matter and are usually prepared as complex mixtures via a manufacturing process. Their chemical constituents are not always well-defined. Therefore, documentation that should be provided for botanical drugs will be different from that for synthetic or highly purified drugs, whose active constituents can be more readily chemically identified and quantified. In such circumstances, regulatory authorities will most probably rely on controls (e.g., strict quality controls of the botanical raw materials and adequate in-process controls), and process validation (especially for the drug substance) to ensure the identity, purity, quality, strength, potency, and consistency of the botanical drug.

A botanical product that has been marketed in the United States for a material time and to a material extent for a specific OTC indication may be eligible for consideration in the OTC drug monograph system. Currently, there are several botanical drugs, including Cascara, Psyllium, and Senna, that are included in the OTC drug review. For a botanical drug substance to be included in an OTC Monograph, there must be published data establishing general recognition of safety and effectiveness, including results of adequate and well-controlled clinical studies.

Traditional herbal medicines or currently marketed botanical products, because of their extensive, though uncontrolled use in humans, may require less preclinical information to support initial clinical trials than would be expected for synthetic or highly purified drugs. When early clinical studies are to be conducted with a botanical product that is not currently lawfully marketed in the United States, but is prepared, processed, and used according to methodologies for which there is prior human experience outside the United States, sufficient information may be available to support such studies without standard preclinical testing.

The sponsor should be prepared to include information found in historical sources (e.g., books of medical practice in Ayurveda, traditional Chinese medicine, Unani, and Sida) and scientific literature about the prior human use of the botanical product, and each of its ingredients, in traditional foods and drugs. The literature should be provided in the language of the regulatory agency (and in its original language, if other than that of the regulatory agency).

The type of manufacturing process (e.g., pulverization, decoction, expression, aqueous extraction, or ethanolic extraction) should be provided, if available. This is especially important where more than one process exists in the literature on which the safety of the botanical drug substance is based.

A botanical drug product is manufactured from a botanical drug substance by adding one or more excipients, mixing, blending, granulating, tableting, encapsulating, or performing other dosage form-specific procedures, followed by packaging. When packaged without further processing, a botanical drug substance is considered the drug product.

DIETARY SUPPLEMENTS

Legal Definition (U.S.): 1. A product (other than tobacco) intended to supplement the diet that bears or contains one or more of the following dietary ingredients: (A) a vitamin; (B) a mineral; (C) an herb or other botanical; (D) an amino acid; (E) a dietary substance for use by man to supplement the diet by increasing the total dietary intake; or (F) a concentrate, metabolite, constituent, extract, or combination of any ingredient described in clause (A), (B), (C), (D), or (E); (2) A product that (A) is intended for ingestion in a form described in section 411(c)(1)(B)(i) [of the FD&C Act]; or complies with section 411(c)(1)(B)(ii); is not represented for use as a conventional food or as a sole item of a meal or the diet; and is labeled as a dietary supplement; and (3) does (A) include an article that is approved as a new drug under section 505 or licensed as a biologic under section 351 of the Public Health Service Act (42 U.S.C. 262) and was, prior to such approval, certification, or license, marketed as a dietary supplement or as a food unless [FDA] has issued a regulation, after notice and comment, finding that the article, when used as or in a dietary supplement under the conditions of use and dosages set forth in the labeling for such dietary supplement, is unlawful under section 402(f); and (B) not include (i) an article that is approved as a new drug under section 505, certified as an antibiotic under section 507, or licensed as a biologic under section 351 of the Public Health Service Act (42 U.S.C. 262), or (ii) an article authorized for investigation as a new drug, antibiotic, or biological for which substantial clinical investigations have been instituted and for which the existence of such investigations has been made public, which was not before such approval, certification, licensing, or authorization marketed as a dietary supplement or as a food unless [FDA], in [its] discretion, has issued a regulation, after notice and comment, finding that the article would be lawful under this Act@ (21 U.S.C. 321(ff)).

This definition of Dietary Supplements is exceeding broad, and is not very useful as an aid to understanding the structure of the pharmaceutical industry. Notice in particular that vitamins, minerals, herbs and botanicals, as well as amino acids are included in the definition. The Dietary Health Supplement and Education act (DSHEA) of 1994 was the response of congress to a public backlash against FDA proposed regulations. For our purposes, a dietary supplement consists of essential nutrients that have been associated with a specific disease when absent (much like the definition of vitamins we gave earlier). However, we would like to explicitly exclude vitamins and minerals, herbs, and botanicals from our definition, realizing fully well that they are included in the official U.S. definition of a Dietary Supplement.

Our definition of a dietary supplement consists of such nutrients as the **essential amino acids** (histidine, isoleucine, leucine, lysine, methionine, cystine, phenylalanine, tyrosine, threonine, tryptophan, and valine). Plus the **essential fatty acids** (arachidonic acid, docosahexaenoic acid, eicosapentaenoic acid, linoleic acid, and linolenic acid) are also included.

Also included in our definition of dietary supplements are various antioxidants, such as cartenoids, flavonoids, and phenolic compounds. Supplemental sources of fiber are included, as are some forms of complex carbohydrates.

Dr. Michael Colgan,[15] who runs his own clinic in New Zealand and also works in clinics and hospitals there and elsewhere, has pointed to some extraordinary empirical data. His researchers purchased a wide variety of common foods from many different suppliers and found the nutrients they contained to vary widely, almost unbelievably so. (For example, when analyzing carrots for content of Provitamin A, he found the content to vary from 70 IU to 18,500 IU.) With samples of wheat germ, he found the Vitamin E content to vary from 3.2 IU to 21 IU. And with stone ground wheat flour, the content of Pantothenic acid ranged from 0.3 mg to 3.3 mg per hundred grams of flour, an eleven-fold increase!

The point of all this is that we cannot count on food, fruits, vegetables, nuts, berries, meats, whatever, to supply our daily nutrient requirements. The conventional processing of foods by heat causes the denaturation of proteins between 60°–90° C, which is a relatively mild heat. Similarly, oxidation and "leaching" (aqueous extraction) cause

---

[15]   Colgan, Michael (1982).

vitamin loss and enzyme deactivation. Most oxidative and hydrolytic enzymes (e.g., proteases, lipases, lipoxygenases, amylases, and polyphenoloxidase) are also deactivated by moderate heat 70°–105° in the process called "blanching." Enzyme denaturation also occurs in asceptically prepared foods, which involves continuous heating and then continuous cooling prior to packaging, but some vitamins do not deteriorate during this process. So, clearly a trade-off exists, but one that does not detract from our central thesis concerning the nutrient values of conventional foods. Radiation, Ultrasonics, Oscillating Magnetic Fields, High-density Pulsed Electric Fields (PEF), and other modern methods of food processing have similar effects on a range of nutrients.[16]

NUTRACEUTICALS

Useful Definitions according to the United States FDA:

Active Constituent: The chemical constituent in a botanical raw material, drug substance, or drug product that is responsible for the intended pharmacological activity or therapeutic effect.

Botanical Product; Botanical: A finished labeled product that contains vegetable matter, which may include plant materials, algae, macroscopic fungi, or combinations of these. Depending in part on its intended use, a botanical product may be a food, drug, medical device, or cosmetic.

Botanical Drug Product; Botanical Drug: A botanical product that is intended for use as a drug; a drug product that is prepared from a botanical drug substance. Botanical drug products are available

---

[16]   Schmidl, Mary K. and Theodore P. Labuza (2000).

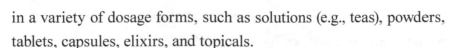

in a variety of dosage forms, such as solutions (e.g., teas), powders, tablets, capsules, elixirs, and topicals.

Botanical Drug Substance: A drug substance derived from one or more plants, algae, or macroscopic fungi. It is prepared from botanical raw materials by one or more of the following processes: pulverization, decoction, expression, aqueous extraction, ethanolic extraction, or other similar process. It may be available in a variety of physical forms, such as powder, paste, concentrated liquid, juice, gum, syrup, or oil. A botanical drug substance can be made from one or more botanical raw materials. A botanical drug substance does not include a highly purified or chemically modified substance derived from natural sources.

Botanical Ingredient: A component of a botanical drug substance or product that originates from a botanical raw material.

Botanical Raw Material: Fresh or processed (e.g., cleaned, frozen, dried, or sliced) part of a single species of plant or a fresh or processed alga or macroscopic fungus.

Cosmetic: An article intended to be rubbed, poured, sprinkled, or sprayed on, introduced into, or otherwise applied to the human body or any part thereof for cleansing, beautifying, promoting attractiveness, or altering the appearance, or an article intended for use as a component of any such article, except that such term does not include soap (21 U.S.C. 321(i)).

Dosage Form: A pharmaceutical product type, for example, tablet, capsule, solution, or cream that contains a drug ingredient (substance) generally, but not necessarily, in association with excipients.

Drug: Means (A) articles recognized in the official United States Pharmacopeia, official Homeopathic Pharmacopeia of the United States, or official National Formulary, or any supplement to any of them; and (B) articles intended for use in the diagnosis, cure, mitigation, treatment, or prevention of disease in man or other animals; and (C) articles (other than food) intended to affect the structure or any function of the body of man or other animals; and (D) articles intended for use as a <u>component</u> of any articles specified in clause (A), (B), or (C). A food or dietary supplement for which a claim, subject to sections 403(r)(1)(B) and 403(r)(3) [of the FD&C Act] or sections 403(r)(1)(B) and (r)(5)(D), is made in accordance with the requirements of section 403(r) is <u>not</u> a drug solely because the label or the labeling contains such a claim. A food, dietary ingredient, or dietary supplement for which a truthful and not misleading statement is made in accordance with section 403(r)(6) is <u>not</u> a drug under clause (C) <u>solely</u> because the label or the labeling contains such a statement (21 U.S.C. 321(g)(1)).

Drug Substance: An active ingredient that is intended to furnish pharmacological activity or other direct effect in the diagnosis, cure, mitigation, treatment, or prevention of disease or to affect the structure or ordinary function of the human body (21 CFR 314.3(b)).

Drug Product: The dosage form in the final immediate packaging intended for marketing.

Food: The term *food* means (1) articles used for food or drink, (2) chewing gum, and (3) articles used for components of such articles (21 U.S.C. 321(f)).

Formulation: A formula that lists the components (or ingredients) and composition of the dosage form. The <u>components</u> and <u>composition</u> of a multi-herb botanical drug substance should be part of the total formulation.

Multi-Herb (Botanical Drug) Substance or Product: A botanical drug substance or drug product that is derived from more than one botanical raw material, each of which is considered a botanical ingredient. A multi-herb botanical drug substance may be prepared by processing together two or more botanical raw materials, or by combining two or more single-herb botanical drug substances that have been individually processed from their corresponding raw materials. In the latter case, the individual single-herb botanical drug substances may be introduced simultaneously or at different stages during the manufacturing process of the dosage form.

Plant Material: A plant or plant part (e.g., bark, wood, leaves, stems, roots, flowers, fruits, seeds, berries, or parts thereof), as well as exudates.

Single-Herb (Botanical Drug) Substance or Product: A botanical drug substance or drug product that is derived from one botanical raw material. Therefore, a single-herb substance or product generally contains only one botanical ingredient.

INDUSTRY ISSUES AND IDEAS

There are a number of important issues facing the pharmaceutical industry today, yet far from being "timely" issues, they are rather "timeless" issues. In other words, they have been around for quite some time, and they show every sign of staying with us for the foreseeable future.

It seems like, a good way to build upon the conceptual basis of the "global challenge" that was developed earlier is to remain within the realm of lofty ideas just long enough to gain a sense of the stage and principal actors who are really making themselves heard at the present time, and could, if they were to gain political power, substantially alter the environment currently faced by the industry.

PERCEPTIONS OF THE PHARMACEUTICAL INDUSTRY

How do you think most objective observers would characterize and define the pharmaceutical industry? Is it a part of the chemical industry? Is it part of the health care industry? Is it a "life sciences" industry? Does it include medicinal plants, vitamins and minerals, or the products of biotechnology? These questions have been debated endlessly, particularly in recent years, when there was an emphasis on life sciences. While there is no doubt that the modern pharmaceutical industry had its roots in the chemical industry (primarily in Germany in the late nineteenth and early twentieth centuries), most people think of it today as either a health care or life sciences industry, which includes agricultural interests such as plant breeding. Health care is the more common classification, but among some companies, there is a clear emphasis on the more composite picture known as "life sciences." Referring to the pharmaceutical industry as a health care industry seems the most appropriate designation at this time.

The importance of the ties between the chemical industry and the pharmaceutical industry should not be minimized or discounted because the discovery of modern drugs began with chemistry and biology. The major pharmaceutical companies employ thousands of chemists for this purpose, and there are thousands more in universities, and government laboratories studying and researching problems peculiar to the industry. There are also thousands of chemical companies around the world who are engaged in the manufacture of the varied ingredients of modern drugs. While the finished products might be packaged and marketed by large pharmaceutical companies, the feedstock ingredients, precursor compounds, and other raw materials are often manufactured by other companies. In large measure, these other companies are better thought of as *chemical* companies, rather than pharmaceutical companies per se, but they are closely related and definitely a part of the pharmaceutical industry as a whole.

The pharmaceutical industry is popularly thought to be a manufacturing industry. While the industry is indeed engaged in manufacturing, it is much more than manufacturing alone. The industry is engaged in very significant research and marketing activities. In fact, much more money is spent by the industry on research and marketing than is spent on manufacturing. This is not to downplay the role of manufacturing in the pharmaceutical industry, but it is to say that, from an economic viewpoint research and marketing are much more important.

Most people recognize that the pharmaceutical industry is an innovative, high technology, research-based industry, but they tend to think that manufacturing takes a bigger slice of the pie than it actually does because they fail to recognize the relatively large sums of money required to develop and market medicines on a worldwide basis.

THE ROLE OF GOVERNMENT

The pharmaceutical industry is one of the most regulated industries in the world. For decades, governments have viewed the industry as crucial to public health and welfare with availability, accessibility, good quality, and the rational use of drugs as consistent goals.

Both liberal and conservative governments have sought public favor through actions to improve health care and restrain prices. In the United States, for example, federal drug legislation began in earnest over concerns about medical quackery. A perceived need to protect an unsuspecting public was the impetus that led to passage of the Federal Food and Drug Act in 1906. This law remained on the books until it was replaced in 1938 by the more comprehensive, Federal Food, Drug, and Cosmetic Act, which remains in force today. As the result of significant amendments to the 1938 law (particularly the 1962 Kefauver-Harris Amendments), there are now complex and detailed application and review procedures (generally referred to under the rubric of Clinical Trials) that pharmaceutical companies must respect in their development of new drugs.

MAJOR MARKETS & REGULATORY AGENCIES

Perhaps because the United States is the largest market for pharmaceutical products in the world, the largest regulatory agency in the world is also in the United States: the U.S. Food and Drug Administration (FDA). There are similar, though smaller regulatory agencies in other countries. Although there are no direct corollaries to the FDA in the other large markets of the world for pharmaceuticals (Japan and the European Union), there are analogous administrative systems, which will be discussed in detail later. For the moment, however, in the European Union, it is the Enterprise Directorate-General (DG), which is responsible for the regulation of chemicals, pharmaceuticals, and cosmetics throughout the EU; in addition, there are individual government regulatory bodies within each of the member states of the EU and the jurisdiction of each depends upon the circumstances involved.

REGULATION IN THE UNITED STATES

"DRUGS" VS. "PHARMACEUTICALS"

In general, the word "drug" implies a greater sense of danger than the word "pharmaceutical," although both imply danger as a matter of degree. In many jurisdictions, the essence of the word "drug" consists of two primary ideas: 1) an intention to prevent or treat disease (which can be dangerous in the sense that most drugs are toxic at higher doses and may, in this context, be considered dangerous, poisons-of-sorts), and 2) an intention to affect the structure or function of the body, which is by its definition dangerous because it is the structure and the function of the body which sustain life. We will be using the word "pharmaceutical" in this book to include the ideas of health <u>maintenance</u>, and health <u>enhancement</u> or <u>improvement</u>, without necessarily implying a disease-based, prevention, treatment; or structure-function intent. The distinction may seem somewhat obscure at this juncture, but it is extremely important at law and, as already indicated, will be discussed in greater detail later.

However, for the time being, let us point out that the issue primarily concerns the "labeling" that is allowed to accompany a pharmaceutical product, and thereby what the brand may say in its advertising and promotion campaigns. There are basically three types of claims: 1) a health claim, 2) a disease claim, and 3) a structure-function claim.

The definitions of these three types of claims have evolved in the United States over time in the legal contexts of several different pieces of legislation, each with a different intent. Therefore, the issues raised are far from settled, but some uniformity and consistency in meaning does seem to be evolving.

Health, Disease, and Structure-Function Claims

The Nutrition Labeling and Education Act of 1990 (NLEA) legislated requirements for:

1. Health claims
2. Nutrient content claims
3. Nutrition labeling

The requirements for health claims are of **most importance** to us here. In particular, health claims require *prior* regulatory approval, that is, regulatory approval prior to the use of the claim.

"Health claims" are defined in regulations resulting from the NLEA as: "any claim made on the label or in labeling of a food, including a dietary supplement, that expressly or by implication, including 'third party' references, written statements (e.g., a brand name including a term such as 'heart'), symbols (e.g., a heart symbol), or vignettes, **characterizes the relationship of any substance to a disease or health-related condition**. Implied health claims include those statements, symbols, vignettes, or other forms of communication that suggest, within the context in which they are presented, that a relationship exists between the presence or level of a substance in food and a disease or health-related condition."

A claim is a **"disease claim"** and causes a product to be **regulated as a drug** if it claims to "diagnose, mitigate, treat, cure, or prevent disease." Thus, a "disease claim" is, in a sense, a subset of a "health claim." But realize that "health claims" only apply to food and dietary supplements. However, the Dietary Supplement, Health and Education Act of 1994 (DSHEA), made the definition of dietary supplements very broad, with equally broad implications.

DSHEA was the result of a huge public outcry in response to FDA's attempt to remove dietary supplements from the market, and/or regulate them as drugs. DSHEA defined dietary supplements using the following criteria:

1. Is "a product, other than tobacco, intended to supplement the diet that contains at least one of the following ingredients: a vitamin, a mineral, an herb, an amino acid, or a dietary substance for use to supplement the diet by increasing total dietary intake; or a concentrate, metabolite, constituent, or extract of any of these ingredients."
2. Is "intended for ingestion in pill, capsule, tablet, or liquid form."
3. Is "not represented as a conventional food or as the sole item of a meal or diet."
4. Is **"labeled as a "dietary supplement."**
5. Includes "products such as an approved new drug, certified antibiotic, or licensed biologic that was marketed as a dietary supplement or food before approval, certification, or license (unless the Secretary of Health and Human Services waives this provision).

In summary, DSHEA permits companies, *without prior approval*, to make claims on dietary supplements **regarding structure-function, mechanisms of action, well-being, and classic deficiencies.** However, DSHEA prohibits claims regarding the diagnosis, treatment, mitigation, cure, and prevention of disease; e.g., if a company produced capsules of cranberry extract that "prevented" the recurrence of urinary tract infections, it would be *unable* to make this claim without the extract being considered a misbranded drug. It could say, "Our cranberry extract provides dietary support for a healthy urinary tract." which is a half-truth, instead of saying, "Our cranberry extract prevents urinary tract infections," which would make it a drug.

The DSHEA restricts the FDA's authority over these products so that FDA can only remove them from the market if they are either:

1. Proven to be unsafe through clinical evidence *obtained by the agency* or
2. Misbranded

The removal of cholestin and the herbal fenphen from the market demonstrates clearly that the FDA is able to take such drastic action based on misbranding. The FDA considered both products to be unapproved drugs. This is why the issues raised above with respect to labeling and claims, i.e., "branding," and perhaps more importantly "misbranding," are so very important.

Health claims differ from structure-function claims, because health claims include the idea of disease. Health claims, as legislated by the NLEA, concern the risk reduction of a health problem. Structure-function claims are legislated by DSHEA, and refer to the structure or processes (function) of the body. Structure-function claims do not require FDA approval. Health claims, and especially disease claims do require prior approval. Manufacturers of dietary supplements under DSHEA, are only required to notify FDA of the claims they are making **within 30 days of the commencement of marketing** dietary supplements. It is up to FDA to challenge such claims. In other words, the burden is on the FDA. Under DSHEA, manufacturers must include a very specific disclaimer, however, that dietary supplements *are not drugs and receive no FDA pre-market approval.*

As already mentioned, the ingredients of dietary supplements include: vitamins, minerals, amino acids, herbs or botanicals, mixtures of these materials, concentrates, or extracts. Therefore, as we get into the next section on sectors of pharmaceutical products, please bear in mind that our purpose is to understand the structure of the industry, which bears little relationship to the U.S. FDA definitions discussed above. You should remain aware, however, that several of our "sectors" are subsumed under the heading of dietary supplements under U.S. law. Further, virtually everything other than the prescription drugs (Ethicals, Biologics, and Generics) is subsumed under the even broader heading of OTC medications. It is expected that these discrepancies and the many problems they create *will be resolved* in the coming years through court actions and other dispute resolution procedures. It is my belief that these changes will take place along the lines outlined below.

In the United States, the Food and Drug Administration (FDA) is responsible for enforcement of the Federal Food, Drug, and Cosmetic Act, which is the primary legislation regulating the pharmaceutical industry. The FDA is the largest such regulatory agency in the world. While the Federal Food, Drug, and Cosmetic Act is, by far, the centerpiece legislation of FDA responsibility and authority, there are several other pieces of federal legislation that have been used to grant additional powers to the FDA over the years by the Congress, and

President of the United States. Of particular importance, especially with respect to biologics, is the Public Health Service Act, which was enacted in **1944** and became Public Law 78-410.

U.S. PUBLIC HEALTH SERVICE ACT

Authority for the regulation of biologics was granted to the FDA in Section 351 of the Public Health Service Act. As with all federal laws of the United States, the Public Health Service Act has been codified, or made a part of the official United States Code (USC). Today, it can be found in Chapter 6A of Title 42 USC. The specific language that grants authority for the regulation of biologics to the FDA is found under Subchapter II – General Powers and Duties, Part F – Licensing of Biological Products and Clinical Laboratories, Subpart I: Biological Products, Section 262 – Regulation of Biological Products. Because various references to the Public Health Service Act (and other pieces of federal legislation) can sometimes be confusing, it is important to recognize that 42 USC Sec. 262 is exactly the same thing as Section 351 of the original Act. Although the law is generally more accessible today as part of the United States Code, it is still common for the FDA to reference its authority for the regulation of biologics as Section 351 of the Public Health Service Act.

As stated earlier, biologics are derived from living sources and are frequently complex mixtures that are not easily identified or characterized. They include such products as: viruses, therapeutic serums, toxins, antitoxins, vaccines, blood and blood components or derivatives, allergenics, etc. This last category, allergenics, consists of products manufactured from natural substances, such as molds, pollens, insect venoms, animal hair, and foods, which are known to elicit allergic reactions in susceptible individuals. They are frequently used in the diagnosis of specific types of allergies.

In addition to the types of biologics listed above, all of which are specifically mentioned, or itemized, in 42 USC Sec. 262, the Public Health Service Act also lists *arsphenamine* or its derivatives (or any other trivalent organic arsenic compound) as products to be regulated similarly to biologics. Arsphenamine is a drug that was used in the treatment of syphilis and other spirillum infections. It was later replaced by *oxophenarsene* (another arsenic-based compound), and then by *penicillin*. Arsphenamine has also been marketed under the trade name *Salvarsan*.

THE ORGANIZATION OF THE FDA

The FDA is a large, bureaucratic institution, organized as part of the U.S. Department of Health and Human Services. The Secretary of the Department of Health and Human Services reports directly to the President of the United States and the Commissioner of the Food and Drug Administration reports directly to the Secretary of the Department of Health and Human Services.

The FDA is organized into various centers, offices, and divisions. Three centers are of particular importance to the pharmaceutical industry. The Center for Drug Evaluation and Research (**CDER**) regulates prescription and over-the-counter drugs that are intended for human consumption, while the Center for Veterinary Medicine (**CVM**) regulates drugs that will be given to animals. Biologics are regulated by the Center for Biologics Evaluation and Research (**CBER**).

APPLICATIONS FOR MARKETING APPROVAL IN THE UNITED STATES

The Federal Food, Drug, and Cosmetic Act requires that before a new drug can be introduced or delivered for introduction into interstate commerce, an effective, approved application must be on file with the Secretary of Health and Human Services, i.e., the FDA. There are two types of such applications. The first is known as a "new drug application" or **NDA**. The second is known as an "abbreviated new drug application" or **ANDA**. The NDA is used for "novel," new drugs and the ANDA is used for "generic," new drugs. A generic new drug is one for which the active ingredients are the same as a previously approved novel, new drug, typically whose patent has expired. Novel new drugs are typically patented new drugs, containing active ingredients that have never before been approved. Regulations require that applications for new drugs intended for use in humans be filed with CDER, veterinary drugs with CVM, and biologics with CBER.

It is important to understand that the powers of the federal government in such matters derive from the idea of interstate commerce. This is the realm of federal authority conceived by the framers of the United States Constitution. A new drug may be introduced or delivered for introduction into interstate commerce without an effective, approved NDA or ANDA on file *only if* with an exemption from the Secretary of Health and Human Services, i.e., the FDA. Exemptions are allowed, according to the Federal Food, Drug, and Cosmetic Act, if:

The drug is intended solely for investigational use by experts qualified by scientific training and experience to investigate the safety and effectiveness of drugs.

An application for such an exemption is known as an "investigational new drug application" or **IND**.

REQUIREMENTS FOR BOTH DRUG SAFETY AND EFFECTIVENESS

The approval of an NDA is contingent upon submission of extensive data on the new drug's safety and effectiveness. These data must be the result of strictly controlled investigations by qualified experts. An effective, approved IND must be on file with the FDA prior to distributing a new drug to investigators for clinical testing. Data resulting from such clinical tests form the basis of any FDA action on an NDA.

U.S. FEDERAL LAW

The United States federal government is the largest provider of high-quality business and economics information in the world, including information on foreign markets and international trade. It is therefore important to become familiar with the various agencies of the U.S. federal government that collect and report information related to the global pharmaceutical industry and the various types of information they make available.

As with all federal laws of the United States, the Public Health Service Act has been codified, or made a part of the official United

States Code (USC). Today, it can be found in Chapter 6A of Title 42 USC.

According to Article I, Section 2 (3) of the Constitution of the United States, Congress must direct that the people of the United States be counted (a census) every ten years, to begin within three years after the first meeting of the first United States Congress. Thereafter, the census that was taken in 1810 (the third census) was directed by an act of Congress to include a number of questions concerning manufacturing along with those that concerned population. Thus, the census of 1810 marks the historical beginning of what is today known as the **Economic Census of the United States**, a vast reservoir of information that is the focus of our attention here. Federal laws relating to the Economic Census are contained in Title 13 of the United States Code. The United States Code following Title 7 is arranged alphabetically.

TABLE 13-1 THE UNITED STATES CODE
(50 Titles)
Title 1, General Provisions
Title 2, The Congress
Title 3, The President
Title 4, Flag and Seal, Seat of Government, and the States
Title 5, Government Organization and Employees; and Appendix
Title 6, Surety Bonds (Repealed)
Title 7, Agriculture
Title 8, Aliens and Nationality
Title 9, Arbitration
Title 10, Armed Forces; and Appendix
Title 11, Bankruptcy; and Appendix

TABLE 13-1 THE UNITED STATES CODE

(50 Titles)

Title 12, Banks and Banking
Title 13, Census
Title 14, Coast Guard
Title 15, Commerce and Trade
Title 16, Conservation
Title 17, Copyrights
Title 18, Crimes and Criminal Procedure; and Appendix
Title 19, Customs Duties
Title 20, Education
Title 21, Food and Drugs
Title 22, Foreign Relations and Intercourse
Title 23, Highways
Title 24, Hospitals and Asylums
Title 25, Indians
Title 26, Internal Revenue Code; and Appendix
Title 27, Intoxicating Liquors
Title 28, Judiciary and Judicial Procedure; and Appendix
Title 29, Labor
Title 30, Mineral Lands and Mining
Title 31, Money and Finance
Title 32, National Guard
Title 33, Navigation and Navigable Waters
Title 34, Navy (Repealed)
Title 35, Patents
Title 36, Patriotic Societies and Observances
Title 37, Pay and Allowances of the Uniformed Services
Title 38, Veterans' Benefits; and Appendix
Title 39, Postal Service

TABLE 13-1 THE UNITED STATES CODE

(50 Titles)

Title 40, Public Buildings, Property, and Works; and Appendix
Title 41, Public Contracts
Title 42, The Public Health and Welfare
Title 43, Public Lands
Title 44, Public Printing and Documents
Title 45, Railroads
Title 46, Shipping; and Appendix
Title 47, Telegraphs, Telephones, and Radiotelegraphs
Title 48, Territories and Insular Possessions
Title 49, Transportation
Title 50, War and National Defense; and Appendix

TABLE 13-2 TITLE 21 USC – FOOD AND DRUGS

(Chapters 1 – 24)

CHAPTER 1	ADULTERATED OR MISBRANDED FOODS OR DRUGS
CHAPTER 2	TEAS
CHAPTER 3	FILLED MILK
CHAPTER 4	ANIMALS, MEATS, AND MEAT AND DAIRY PRODUCTS
CHAPTER 5	VIRUSES, SERUMS, TOXINS, ANTITOXINS, AND ANALOGOUS PRODUCTS
CHAPTER 5A	BUREAU OF NARCOTICS
CHAPTER 6	NARCOTIC DRUGS
CHAPTER 7	PRACTICE OF PHARMACY AND SALE OF POISONS IN CONSULAR DISTRICTS IN CHINA

TABLE 13-2 TITLE 21 USC – FOOD AND DRUGS

(Chapters 1 – 24)

CHAPTER 8	NARCOTIC FARMS
CHAPTER 9	FEDERAL FOOD, DRUG, AND COSMETIC ACT
CHAPTER 10	POULTRY AND POULTRY PRODUCTS INSPECTION
CHAPTER 11	MANUFACTURE OF NARCOTIC DRUGS
CHAPTER 12	MEAT INSPECTION
CHAPTER 13	DRUG ABUSE PREVENTION AND CONTROL
CHAPTER 14	AlCOHOL AND DRUG ABUSE EDUCATIONAL PROGRAMS AND ACTIVITIES
CHAPTER 15	EGG PRODUCTS INSPECTION
CHAPTER 16	DRUG ABUSE PREVENTION, TREATMENT, AND REHABILITATION
CHAPTER 17	NATIONAL DRUG ENFORCEMENT POLICY
CHAPTER 18	PRESIDENT'S MEDIA COMMISSION ON ALCOHOL AND DRUG ABUSE PREVENTION
CHAPTER 19	PESTICIDE MONITORING IMPROVEMENTS
CHAPTER 20	NATIONAL DRUG CONTROL PROGRAM
CHAPTER 21	BIOMATERIALS ACCESS ASSURANCE
CHAPTER 22	NATIONAL DRUG CONTROL POLICY
CHAPTER 23	NATIONAL YOUTH ANTI-DRUG MEDIA CAMPAIGN
CHAPTER 24	INTERNATIONAL NARCOTICS TRAFFICKING

TABLE 3-3 21 USC CHAPTER 9
The Federal Food, Drug, and Cosmetic Act

SUBCHAPTER I - SHORT TITLE

    Sec.

    301. Short title.

SUBCHAPTER II - DEFINITIONS

    321. Definitions; generally.

    321a. "Butter" defined.

    321b. "Package" defined.

    321c. Nonfat dry milk; "milk" defined.

SUBCHAPTER III - PROHIBITED ACTS AND PENALTIES

    331 Prohibited acts.

    332. Injunction proceedings.

    333. Penalties

    333a. Repealed.

    334. Seizure.

    335. Hearing before report of criminal violation.

    335a. Debarment, temporary denial of approval, and suspension.

    335b. Civil penalties.

    335c. Authority to withdraw approval of abbreviated drug applications.

    336. Report of minor violations.

    337. Proceedings in name of United States; provision as to subpoenas.

SUBCHAPTER IV - FOOD

    341. Definitions and standards for food.

    342. Adulterated food.

    343. Misbranded food.

    343-1. National uniform nutrition labeling.

    343-2. Dietary supplement labeling exemptions.

    343-3. Disclosure.

    343a. Repealed.

    344. Emergency permit control.

    345. Regulations making exemptions.

TABLE 3-3 21 USC CHAPTER 9

The Federal Food, Drug, and Cosmetic Act

346. Tolerances for poisonous or deleterious substances in food; regulations.

346a. Tolerances and exemptions for pesticide chemical residues.

346b. Authorization of appropriations.

347. Intrastate sales of colored oleomargarine.

347a. Congressional declaration of policy regarding oleomargarine sales.

347b. Contravention of State laws.

348. Food additives.

349. Bottled drinking water standards; publication in Federal Register.

350. Vitamins and minerals.

350a. Infant formulas.

350b. New dietary ingredients.

SUBCHAPTER V - DRUGS AND DEVICES

PART A - DRUGS AND DEVICES

351. Adulterated drugs and devices.

352. Misbranded drugs and devices.

353. Exemptions and consideration for certain drugs, devices, and biological products.

353a. Pharmacy compounding.

354. Veterinary feed directive drugs.

355. New drugs.

355a. Pediatric studies of drugs.

356. Fast track products.

356a. Manufacturing changes.

356b. Reports of post-marketing studies.

356c. Discontinuance of life saving product.

357. Repealed.

358. Authority to designate official names.

359. Non-applicability of subchapter to cosmetics.

TABLE 3-3 21 USC CHAPTER 9

The Federal Food, Drug, and Cosmetic Act

360. Registration of producers of drugs or devices.

360a. Repealed.

360b. New animal drugs.

360c. Classification of devices intended for human use.

360d. Performance standards.

360e. Pre-market approval.

360f. Banned devices.

360g. Judicial review.

360h. Notification and other remedies.

360i. Records and reports on devices.

360j. General provisions respecting control of devices intended for human use.

360k. State and local requirements respecting devices.

360l. Post-market surveillance.

360m. Accredited persons.

PART B - DRUGS FOR RARE DISEASES OR CONDITIONS

360aa. Recommendations for investigations of drugs for rare diseases or conditions.

360bb. Designation of drugs for rare diseases or conditions.

360cc. Protection for drugs for rare diseases or conditions.

360dd. Open protocols for investigations of drugs for rare diseases or conditions.

360ee. Grants and contracts for development of drugs for rare diseases and conditions.

PART C - ELECTRONIC PRODUCT RADIATION CONTROL

360hh. Definitions.

360ii. Program of control.

360jj. Studies by the Secretary.

360kk. Performance standards for electronic products.

360ll. Notification of defects in and repair or replacement of electronic products.

TABLE 3-3 21 USC CHAPTER 9

The Federal Food, Drug, and Cosmetic Act

360mm. Imports.

360nn. Inspection, records, and reports.

360oo. Prohibited acts.

360pp. Enforcement.

360qq. Repealed.

360rr. Federal-State cooperation.

360ss. State standards.

PART D - DISSEMINATION OF TREATMENT

INFORMATION

360aaa. Requirements for dissemination of treatment information on drugs or devices.

360aaa-1. Information authorized to be disseminated.

360aaa-2. Establishment of list of articles and publications disseminated and list of providers that receive articles and reference publications.

360aaa-3. Requirement regarding submission of supplemental application for new use; exemption from requirement.

360aaa-4. Corrective actions; cessation of dissemination.

360aaa-5. Definitions.

360aaa-6. Rules of construction.

PART E - GENERAL PROVISIONS RELATING TO DRUGS

AND DEVICES

360bbb. Expanded access to unapproved therapies and diagnostics.

360bbb-1. Dispute resolution.

360bbb-2. Classification of products.

SUBCHAPTER VI - COSMETICS

361. Adulterated cosmetics.

362. Misbranded cosmetics.

363. Regulations making exemptions.

TABLE 3-3 21 USC CHAPTER 9

The Federal Food, Drug, and Cosmetic Act

SUBCHAPTER VII - GENERAL AUTHORITY

PART A - GENERAL ADMINISTRATIVE PROVISIONS

371. Regulations and hearings.
372. Examinations and investigations.
372a. Transferred.
373. Records of interstate shipment.
374. Inspection.
375. Publicity.
376. Examination of sea food on request of packer; marking food with results; fees; penalties.
377. Revision of United States Pharmacopoeia; development of analysis and mechanical and physical tests.
378. Advertising of foods.
379. Confidential information.
379a. Presumption of existence of jurisdiction.
379b. Consolidated administrative and laboratory facility.
379c. Transferred.
379d. Automation of Food and Drug Administration.

PART B - COLORS

379e. Listing and certification of color additives for foods, drugs, sevices, and cosmetics.

PART C – FEES

SUBPART 1 - FREEDOM OF INFORMATION FEES

379f. Recovery and retention of fees for freedom of information requests.

SUBPART 2 - FEES RELATING TO DRUGS

379g. Definitions
379h. Authority to assess and. use drug fees.

PART D - INFORMATION AND EDUCATION

379k. Information system.
379l. Education.

REGULATION IN THE UNITED STATES

TABLE 3-3 21 USC CHAPTER 9
The Federal Food, Drug, and Cosmetic Act

PART E - ENVIRONMENTAL IMPACT REVIEW
  379o. Environmental impact.
PART F - NATIONAL UNIFORMITY FOR
NONPRESCRIPTION DRUGS AND PREEMPTION FOR
LABELING OR PACKAGING OF COSMETICS
  379r. National uniformity for nonprescription drugs.
  379s. Preemption for labeling or packaging of cosmetics.
PART G - SAFETY REPORTS
  379v. Safety report disclaimer
SUBCHAPTER VIII - IMPORTS AND EXPORTS
  381. Imports and exports.
  382. Exports of certain unapproved products.
  383. Office of International Relations.
  384. Importation of covered products.
SUBCHAPTER IX - MISCELLANEOUS
  391. Separability clause.
  392. Exemption of meats and meat food products.
  393. Food and Drug Administration.
  394. Scientific review groups.
  395. Loan repayment program.
  396. Practice of medicine.
  397. Contracts for expert review.

U.S. LEGAL DEFINITIONS

Large integrated drug companies are not the only firms involved in the pharmaceutical industry. Many different types of companies and other organizations are involved, including chemical companies of various sizes, specialized forms of research organizations, trade associations, professional societies, foundations, etc. All of these together, and others everywhere in the world, constitute what is known as the pharmaceutical industry, but one formal definition describes it as: *"all companies, public and private, foreign and domestic, that perform or substantially contribute to the performance of any of the following functions: the discovery, development, manufacturing, and/or marketing of drugs for human use."*

Some people argue that this definition does not explicitly include veterinary drugs and should be modified, but not all types of products need to be explicitly mentioned for a definition to be complete. Veterinary drugs are not intended for human consumption; they are intended for human use. The above definition includes veterinary drugs in this way, and with a little reflection, you should come to see that this is a good and full description of the pharmaceutical industry.

The general population tends to equate the meaning of the term "drug" with the meaning of the term "medicine." The term "medicine" refers to *the art, science, or practice of the diagnosis, treatment, and prevention of disease, particularly as distinct from surgical methods.* The burgeoning field of alternative medicine is widely practiced in order to avoid the use of drugs. Examples of alternative medicines include such therapies as acupuncture, aromatherapy, biofeedback, chiropractic, hypnosis, magnetism, humor, music, light, etc.

Legal Definitions within the United States

Title 21 of the United States Code contains the Federal Food, Drug, and Cosmetic Act. This legislation was enacted in 1938 and, with amendments, has remained the law of the land in the United

States since that time. It defines a "drug" as any one of four types of articles: (A), (B), (C), and (D), as follows:

The term "drug" means
(A) articles recognized in the official United States Pharmacopeia, official Homeopathic Pharmacopeia of the United States, or the official National Formulary, or any supplement to any of them; and
(B) articles intended for use in the diagnosis, cure, mitigation, treatment, or prevention of disease in man or other animals; and
(C) articles (other than food) intended to affect the structure or any function of the body of man or other animals; and
(D) articles intended for use as a component of any articles specified in clause (A), (B), or (C). A food or dietary supplement for which a [disease or health-related] claim is made... is not a drug solely because the label or the labeling contains such a claim. A food, dietary ingredient, or dietary supplement for which a truthful and not misleading statement is made in accordance with [this Act] is not a drug under clause (C) solely because the label or labeling contains such a statement.

Several key ideas are contained in this legal language. First, a drug is defined as any one of four types of "articles." In common usage of the English language, the word "article" means solely an item or commodity that is not further distinguished and therefore lacks specificity. It is a very general word. Thus, the term "drug" would take on a very general meaning if defined solely as an article. Its exact form, size, weight, method of preparation, administration, etc., would be left ambiguous at this point. A great deal of specificity is added, however, by the additional language in clause (A) above, which makes the identification of a "drug" much more precise. If an article appears on any one of these three lists, or their supplements, then it is a drug! For practical purposes, the official United States Pharmacopeia is the most important of these three lists.

There is a considerable disparity among the classification systems employed by the available sources of information on the pharmaceutical industry, and for this reason, it is not a good idea to become too closely tied to any one system.

TABLE 13-3 GENERAL CATEGORIES OF DRUGS	
Analgesics	Cardiovasculars
Narcotics	Antianginals
NSAIDs	Antihypertensives
Anesthetics	Diuretics
Anticonvulsants	Hypolipemics
Antidiabetics	Vasodilators
Antihistamines	Contraceptives
Anti-Infectives	Dietary Supplements
Antibacterials	Amino Acids
Antibiotics	Minerals
Antifungals	Vitamins
Antimalarials	Gastrointestinals
Antituberculars	Hormones
Antivirals	Migraine Preparations
Anti-Inflammatory Agents	Psychotherapeutics
Antineoplastics	Antianxieties
Antiparkinsonians	Antidepressants
Biologicals	Antipsychotics
Antitoxins	Hypnotics
Antivenins	Sedatives
Vaccines	Respiratory Agents

Serums	Antitussives
Toxoids	Bronchodilators
Blood Modifiers	Decongestants
Anticoagulants	Expectorants
Hematinics	Skin & Mucous Membrane Agents
Hemostatics	Urinary Tract Agents
Bone Metabolism Regulators	Vaginal Preparations

The term "drug" commonly refers to a chemical or biological substance that is used in medicine. However, most countries have adopted official lists of drugs known as "pharmacopeias," or "national formularies" (for example, the official United States Pharmacopeia,), and a "drug" is, therefore, frequently defined as any substance appearing on one of these official lists. Of course, such lists must be regularly revised and updated as new drugs are discovered and developed by the industry.

The United States Pharmacopeia

The first United States Pharmacopeia (USP) was published in the United States on December 15, 1820 in both English and Latin and included 217 drugs. Today, after the discovery and development of many new drugs, it includes approximately 3,700 entries! The USP is the property of The United States Pharmacopeial Convention Inc., and is a *legally recognized* compendium, consisting of standards for drugs. It contains assays and tests for the determination of their strength, quality, and purity. It generally contains a description of their method of preparation and also a statement of their average dosage.

The United States National Formulary

The term "drug," that is defined in the Federal Food, Drug, and Cosmetic Act, also means any article recognized in the official National Formulary. The National Formulary (NF) includes standards similar to the USP, but for vitamins, minerals, botanicals, and excipients (Excipients are more or less inert substances added to a drug formulation for suitable consistency, etc.). The NF originated in 1888 by the American Pharmaceutical Association. In 1975, however, The United States Pharmacopeial Convention purchased the National Formulary, combining the USP and the NF into a single publication known as the USP-NF. The USP-NF is available for purchase from The United States Pharmacopeial Convention via their web site at http://www.usp.org for prices that range between roughly $500.00 and $1000.00 depending on format.

The United States Homeopathic Pharmacopeia

The Federal Food, Drug, and Cosmetic Act also defines the term "drug" to include articles recognized in the official Homeopathic Pharmacopeia of the United States, which contains information on approximately 1,300 homeopathic medicines. It is available for approximately $900.00 from the Homeopathic Pharmacopeia Convention. The official Homeopathic Pharmacopeia of the United States web site is located at http://www.hpus.com.

Drugs and Disease, Structure or Function of the Body

Having to refer to an official pharmacopeia or national formulary to determine whether or not a particular chemical or biological substance is considered a drug is not a very concise method of definition. The additional meanings of the term "drug" (contained in clauses B and C, are conceptual and therefore far more useful as a practical matter. They add breadth to the meaning contained in clause (A) alone and make the legal definition more inclusive than what might be contained in the pharmacopeias and/or formulary.

Given this conceptual nature, it is important to note that the idea of "disease" is central to the meaning of the term "drug" contained in clause (B); yet, the term "disease" is not defined within the Act itself and is, therefore, somewhat ambiguous in this context. An authoritative reference, *Dorland's Medical Dictionary*, defines the term "disease" as any deviation from or interruption of the normal structure or function of the body. Not surprisingly then, this "structure or function" concept is also a central aspect of the additional meaning of the term "drug" contained in clause (C) of the Act. Any inconsistency or diminution of meaning which results from the failure of the Act to define the term "disease" in clause (B), is resolved by the structure or function language contained in clause (C).

The meaning of the term "drug," as defined in the Federal Food, Drug, and Cosmetic Act, is related not only to our conventional notion of disease in clause (B), but also to its more technical, medical conceptualization, which relates directly to the structure or function of the body in clause (C). It is important that by separating out the notion of disease per se, in clause (B), from the notion of structure or function in clause (C), the Act also encompasses those articles (drugs) associated with recreational use that affect the structure or function of the body without a disease being involved.

The Special Nature of Biologics

The worldwide pharmaceutical industry includes all those individuals and organizations working to discover, develop, manufacture and/or market a special group of products known collectively as "biologics," or simply "biological products," which are derived from living sources and are frequently complex mixtures that are not easily identified or characterized. They include such products as: viruses, therapeutic serums, toxins, antitoxins, vaccines, blood and blood components or derivatives, allergenics, etc. This last category, allergenics, consists of products manufactured from natural substances, such as molds, pollens, insect venoms, animal hair, and foods, which are known to elicit allergic reactions in susceptible individuals. They are frequently used in the diagnosis of specific types of allergies.

Many biologics are manufactured using biotechnology and are often discussed and regulated differently. Most of them meet the definition of the term "drug" in the Federal Food, Drug, and Cosmetic Act and are included in the definition of the pharmaceutical industry that was presented earlier.

Antibiotics vs. Antibacterials

The term "antibiotic" is used to differentiate drugs that are produced from living cells, as opposed to an "antibacterial" which is produced using synthetic organic chemistry. Important antibiotics such as penicillin, streptomycin, and erythromycin have been produced using fermentation techniques. Modern genetic engineering modifies living organisms to produce antibiotics in commercial quantities.

Over-the-Counter Drugs

The legal difference between prescription drugs and drugs that do not require a prescription is made in the Federal Food, Drug, and Cosmetic Act, found in Section 353 of Title 21 of the United States Code, under the heading: "Exemptions and Considerations for Certain Drugs, Devices, and Biological Products. The Act stipulates that a drug intended for use by man shall be dispensed only upon a written prescription of a practitioner licensed by law to administer such drug if:

(A) It is a habit-forming drug, containing any quantity of the narcotic or hypnotic substance alpha-eucaine, barbituric acid, beta-eucaine, bromal, cannabis, carbromal, chloral, coca, cocaine, codeine, heroin, marijuana, morphine, opium, paraldehyde, peyote, or sulfonmethane; or any chemical derivative of such substance found by the Secretary of Health and Human Services to be, and by regulations designated as, habit-forming;

(B) Because of its toxicity or other potentiality for harmful effect, or the method of its use, or the collateral measures necessary to its use, is not safe; or

(C) It is so limited by an approved new drug application.

It was not until 1972 that the FDA mandated a retrospective review of OTC medications for safety and efficacy. At that time, approximately 700 active ingredients were being used in OTC medicines marketed in the United States.

Dietary Supplements

The Dietary Supplement, Health, and Education Act, DSHEA (1994), defined a dietary supplement using the following criteria:

1. Is "a product, other than tobacco, intended to supplement the diet that contains at least one of the following ingredients: a vitamin, a mineral, an herb, an amino acid, or a dietary substance for use to supplement the diet by increasing total dietary intake; or a concentrate, metabolite, constituent, or extract of any of these ingredients."
2. Is intended for ingestion in pill, capsule, tablet, or liquid form.
3. Is not represented as a conventional food or as the sole item of a meal or diet.
4. Is labeled as a "dietary supplement."
5. Includes products such as an approved new drug, certified antibiotic, or licensed biologic that was marketed as a dietary supplement or food before approval, certification, or license (unless the Secretary of Health and Human Services waives this provision).

DSHEA permits companies, without prior approval, to make claims on dietary supplements regarding structure-function, mechanisms-of-action, well-being, or classic deficiencies. However, DSHEA prohibits claims regarding the diagnosis, treatment, mitigation, cure, and prevention of disease. For example, as described earlier, if a company produced capsules of cranberry extract that prevented the recurrence of urinary tract infections, it would be unable to make this claim. It could say, "Our cranberry extract provides dietary support for a healthy urinary tract," which is a half-truth of: "Our cranberry extract prevents urinary tract infections."

Health claims differ from structure-function claims. Structure-function claims are legislated by DSHEA and refer to the structure or processes of the body. Health claims concern the risk reduction of a health problem. Structure-function claims do not require FDA approval. Manufacturers are only required to notify FDA of the claims they are making within 30 days of initiating marketing of dietary supplements. It is up to FDA to challenge such claims. Under DSHEA manufacturers must include a disclaimer, however, that dietary supplements are not drugs and receive no FDA pre-market approval. Ingredients in dietary supplements can include vitamins, minerals, amino acids, herbs or botanicals, mixtures of these materials, concentrates, or extracts.

REGULATION IN JAPAN

Japan represents the second-largest, single-country market for pharmaceuticals in the world, and even has a higher per capita consumption than the United States. The Japanese Ministry of Health, Labor and Welfare is, perhaps, the most analogous regulatory authority to the U.S. Food and Drug Administration, but the Ministry of Agriculture, Forestry and Fisheries also has a major role to play in the regulation of pharmaceuticals in Japan. Furthermore, Japan's local, Prefectural governments also play a significant role, being responsible for the regulation of most over-the-counter products in Japan. This decentralization of the pharmaceutical regulatory authority in Japan is stipulated in the Japanese Pharmaceutical Affairs Law (PAL). Thus, while the Ministry of Health, Labor and Welfare does serve in a coordinating capacity for the entire structure of pharmaceutical administration in Japan, the extent of analogy between it and the FDA does not go much beyond that point. The Central Pharmaceutical Affairs Council, which consists of 19 committees and 60 subcommittees, is responsible for setting standards for medicinal products in Japan and revisions of the Japanese Pharmacopeia, available in version XIII at the time of this writing.

REGULATION BY JAPANESE PREFECTS

There are Prefectural Pharmaceutical Affairs Councils in each of the 47 Prefects of Japan, as well as Prefectural Health Centers where applications for marketing approval are to be filed by all companies domiciled in that Prefect. The process by which an application is then routed from the respective Prefectural Health Center, through the entire pharmaceutical administrative structure of Japan, is complex, but eventually, applicants are notified by their Prefectural Health Center of the outcome. For obvious reasons, most marketing applications are filed in Tokyo.

The Japanese Ministry of Agriculture, Forestry and Fisheries is the sole authority for marketing applications for medicines intended exclusively for use in animals. Drugs that are intended for use in both man and animals must be approved by the process described above, and now is coordinated by the Ministry of Health, Labor and Welfare in consultation with the Ministry of Agriculture, Forestry and Fisheries.

REGULATION IN EUROPE

With the exception of the United States, which, as already mentioned, is the largest market for pharmaceuticals in the world, no other country in the world has a pharmaceutical market even half the size of Japan's. In fact, the Japanese market is roughly the size of the next five countries combined (Germany, France, Italy, United Kingdom, Spain). However, the combined countries of the European Union (EU) now represent a larger, overall pharmaceuticals market than the single-country market of Japan. The simultaneous existence of the EU administrative structure, together with the administrative structures of the individual member states of the EU, can make pharmaceutical regulation in Europe seem even more complex than what exists in Japan.

INDIVIDUAL MEMBER STATES AND THE EMEA

Each of the member states of the EU still retains its own national regulatory authority for pharmaceuticals while, at the same time, the EU has created the European Medicines Evaluation Agency (EMEA) to approve applications for the marketing of pharmaceuticals throughout the EU. It is possible, therefore, and perfectly legal, for a pharmaceutical company to apply for marketing authorization of a particular drug to any of the individual member states or to the EMEA for the entire EU (all member states). Applications approved

Hank Laskey

by an individual member state permit the marketing of the drug only within its national borders. Applications approved by the EMEA lead to marketing authorization in every member state. There are advantages to both types of applications; however, biotechnology-derived products must apply to the EMEA.

ADMINISTRATIVE STRUCTURE OF THE EUROPEAN UNION

According to the Treaty of Amsterdam, which entered into force in May of 1999, consolidating the meaning and intent of previous treaties, legislation enacted by the Council of Ministers of the European Union and the European Parliament (as a co-legislator) is binding on all member states. (Previously, only the Council of Ministers could enact binding legislation.) However, legislation is generally proposed and brought forth in draft form by the European Commission, frequently in consultation with the Parliament. The commission is also responsible for administration of the law, upon enactment. The commission is the initiator, administrator, mediator, negotiator and guardian of all the relevant international treaties pertaining to the EU. It is also empowered to grant authorization for pharmaceutical marketing throughout the EU, upon applications that are first approved by the EMEA.

THE EUROPEAN COMMISSION

The European Commission consists of 20 commissioners, selected from across Europe, who serve in various capacities, including a president, two vice-presidents, and 17 other commissioners responsible for the various operating divisions of the European Commission, known as Directorates-General.

THE ENTERPRISE DIRECTORATE GENERAL

The Enterprise Directorate-General, or Enterprise DG, is the division of the European Commission responsible for, among other things, supervising the regulation of chemicals, pharmaceuticals, and cosmetics in the EU. Administratively, the Enterprise DG is organized into units. The pharmaceuticals unit, sometimes referred to as the "F2 Unit," as its name implies, **is responsible for supervising the regulation of pharmaceuticals in the EU**.

THE EUROPEAN MEDICINES EVALUATION AGENCY

The European Council of Ministers created the EMEA as an independent agency of the European Union in July 1993, to take effect in January 1995. While the pharmaceuticals unit of the Enterprise DG is headquartered in Brussels, the EMEA is headquartered in London. The main task of the EMEA is to provide the European Commission (through the pharmaceuticals unit), other EU institutions, and the member states of the EU, with the best possible scientific advice on questions about the quality, safety, and efficacy of medicinal products for human and veterinary use.

The legislation that created the EMEA stipulates that the opinions of the EMEA, on all matters relating to medicinal products, shall be exclusively formulated by one of two committees: the Committee for Proprietary Medicinal Products in matters relating to products for human use, and the Committee for Veterinary Medicinal Products in matters relating to products for animal use. Furthermore, the membership of each of these two committees shall consist of two members from each of the member states. An interesting responsibility of the EMEA is that, as part of the marketing approval process, it must forward its opinion and all supporting documents to the pharmaceuticals unit of the Enterprise DG in each of the eleven languages of the EU.

STANDING COMMITTEES OF THE EUROPEAN UNION

To complicate matters even further, there are two additional committees involved in the marketing authorization process having names similar to the two committees of the EMEA mentioned above. These two additional committees are referred to as "Standing Committees," however, and were created by the Council of Ministers of the European Union to assist the European Commission in the marketing approval process.

The Standing Committee on Medicinal Products for Human Use and the Standing Committee on Veterinary Medicinal Products each consists of one representative from each member state of the European Union. After the European Commission receives the opinion of the EMEA (in eleven languages), it prepares a draft decision on the marketing application. This draft decision is then forwarded to the appropriate Standing Committee, whose members then consult with their respective member states for <u>linguistic</u>, <u>scientific</u>, and <u>technical</u> comments.

This procedure must be conducted in writing. Duly justified objections raised by any one or more of the member states are discussed in a plenary meeting of the Standing Committee. Only if the decision of the Standing Committee (taken by a special, "weighted" vote) is in agreement with the draft decision of the European Commission can the commission proceed with the marketing authorization process; the final decision being issued by the commissioner responsible for the Enterprise DG. If, however, the decision of the Standing Committee is in disagreement with the draft decision of the European Commission, then the commission must forward the matter to the Council of Ministers of the European Union, whose decision is binding on all member states. However, if the Council of Ministers takes no action on the matter, within a prescribed period of time, then, by default, the European Commission is allowed to proceed with the marketing authorization process and the Commissioner for the Enterprise DG issues the final decision. This decision is then published in the *Official Journal of the European Communities.*

THE EUROPEAN PHARMACOPOEIA

One of the original problems faced by European pharmaceutical policy makers was finding ways to harmonize the diverse pharmaceutical manufacturing and control standards of the member states. The European Pharmacopoeia was founded in1964 by eight countries: Belgium, France, Germany, Italy, Luxembourg, The Netherlands, Switzerland, and the United Kingdom. By 1999, the European Pharmacopoeia had 26 signatories (the EU itself, all 15 member states of the EU, and ten other countries. The European Pharmacopoeia is the responsibility of the European Pharmacopoeia Commission, located in Strasbourg, with its website located at http://www.pheur.org). The European Pharmacopeia is, at the time of this writing, in its fourth edition and can be purchased from outside the EU, in English, in either book or CD-ROM form, for about 500 euros.

NATIONAL PHARMACEUTICAL INDUSTRIES

THE AMERICAN INDUSTRY

The American Civil War (1861–1865) began just five years after Perkin's discovery of mauve in England, and ended just as Louis Pasteur was beginning his landmark study of the silkworm disease in southern France. BASF (1861), Hoechst (1862), and Bayer (1863) all began just prior and during the American Civil War. The smallpox vaccine that Edward Jenner had invented in 1796 was available to protect soldiers from the deadly smallpox disease, but the combined effects of dysentery, malaria, typhoid, yellow fever, and venereal disease killed more men than all of those who died in battle during the entire four years of the war. There was a desperate need for drugs such as quinine, morphine, camphor, chloroform, ether, iodine, and mercurial compounds.

The typical American drug company of the nineteenth century was a small-scale, family-owned firm, but several American pharmaceutical giants of today trace their roots back to the period prior to the American Civil War. These include such companies as American Home Products, Bristol-Myers Squibb, Pfizer, and SmithKline (the American-born portion of today's British-owned pharmaceutical giant Glaxo SmithKline). In addition to the four firms mentioned above, which were all founded before the Civil War,

Abbott Laboratories, Eli Lilly, and the Upjohn Company all began as family operations shortly after the Civil War.

American Folk Medicine

Folk medicine was widely practiced in the American colonies, and the medicinal herbs and plants used by the indigenous or native Indians were quickly adopted by the American colonists in addition to those medicines they obtained from Europe. A religious sect named the United Society of Believers in Christ's Second Appearing ("Shakers") began arriving in New York from England about 1774, and by 1850 had established communities from Maine to Kentucky. They gathered and sold bulk quantities of herbs, roots, barks and other natural products to support their communities. Even after the Civil War, in 1876, when Civil War veteran Colonel Eli Lilly in Indianapolis founded Eli Lilly & Co., his first products were entirely preparations including extracts from Bear's Foot, Black Haw, Cramp Bark, Hardhack, Life Root, Skullcap, Sea Wrack, Squaw Vine, Wahoo, and Wormseed.

In order to supply drugs to George Washington's army during the American Revolutionary War (1775–1783), the chief pharmacist of the American army, Dr. Andrew Craigie, had set up a medical laboratory in Carlisle, Pennsylvania. (Carlisle is about 100 miles northwest of Philadelphia, and north of Gettysburg, near the site of what is now the Army War College, "Carlisle Barracks"). After the war, Dr. Craigie began his own drug wholesale business, selling to area pharmacies. During this period, many medical practitioners still diagnosed illness in terms of the four body humors: blood, phlegm, and both black and yellow bile.

The Philadelphia College of Pharmacy

In 1821, a group of 68 pharmacists from throughout the Delaware Valley (between Pennsylvania and New Jersey) met in Philadelphia and in 1822 incorporated the Philadelphia College of Pharmacy, the first college of pharmacy in the Western Hemisphere. Over the years, a number of the students of this institution graduated and were to become major U.S. pharmaceutical giants. They include:

- Josiah and Eli Lilly (Eli Lilly & Co.)
- Mahlon Kline (Smith, Kline & Co.; now part of Glaxo SmithKline)
- Silas Burroughs and Henry Wellcome (Burroughs Wellcome & Co.; now also a part of Glaxo SmithKline)
- John Wyeth (Wyeth is the current name for American Home Products)
- Gerald Rorer (Rhone-Poulenc Rorer, now part of Aventis)
- Robert McNeil (McNeil division of Johnson & Johnson)
- William Warner (Warner-Lambert, now a part of Pfizer)

WILLIAM S. MERRELL

William S. Merrell was an early sales representative of Medicinal Botanicals and their extracts when America was expanding westward along the Ohio River. He is credited with being the first pharmaceutical manufacturer in the United States, first to prepare and sell commercial quantities of *salts of sanguinarine* from the sanguinaria plant, also called *bloodroot*, which was known both to American Indians and to Europeans. He was also the first to prepare and market the oleoresin *Eupurpurin*, from the plant known as *queen of the meadow*.

Merrell founded William S. Merrell & Company in Cincinnati, Ohio sometime around 1824. Running what was a successful pharmaceutical company ever since that time, he later became part of Merrell Dow, and then Marion Merrell Dow, Hoechst Marion Roussel, and today, as a result of the merger between German-owned Hoechst Marion Roussel and French-owned Rhone-Poulenc Rorer in December 1999, is part of the giant Aventis. Unfortunately, Merrell became notorious in the mid-1950s and early 1960s as the manufacturer of the drug thalidomide, which was found in Europe and elsewhere to cause serious birth defects. This led to the famous confrontation with Dr. Francis Kelsey at the U.S. Food and Drug Administration and, ultimately, the passage of the Kefauver-Harris amendments to the Food, Drug, and Cosmetic Act in 1962.

SMITH, KLINE & CO

John K. Smith and his partner John Gilbert opened a pharmacy in Philadelphia in 1830. They manufactured extracts, elixirs, syrups, tablets and pills. George K. Smith joined his brother John in 1841 and was one of the earliest advocates of high product quality and treatment reliability. The Smiths were one of the first firms to market drugs directly to physicians, and they supplied quinine and other pharmaceuticals to U.S. troops during the Mexican-American War (1846–1848). They also supplied the Union army during the American Civil War (1861–1865).

Mahlon Kline, who started as a bookkeeper for the Smiths in 1865, and attended the Philadelphia College of Pharmacy, became a full partner in the firm in 1875 when they changed the name of the company to Smith, Kline & Co. By that time, the Smith brothers

Hank Laskey

had already become successful drug wholesalers. Kline later became president of the Philadelphia Drug Exchange and had a strong influence on the early development of the drug industry in America. In 1891, Smith, Kline & Co. absorbed another drug wholesaler, French Richards & Co, to become what was one of America's most highly respected drug houses for many years into the future: Smith, Kline and French. SK&F was the largest drug wholesaler in Philadelphia and sold hundreds of products from medicines to perfumes.

AMERICAN CHICLE

American Chicle resulted from a suggestion by Mexican General Antonio Lopez de Santa Ana, the victor in the Battle of the Alamo in 1836, and commander of the Mexican army in the Mexican-American War (1846–1848). He was exiled from Mexico in 1855 and fled to New York City and was living there in 1869, when he commented to Thomas Adams (later the Adams Division of Warner-Lambert) that there might be a use for inexpensive Mexican chicle in the United States. Santa Ana supplied Adams with a ton of chicle for research and Adams, having failed to combine it with rubber in the manufacture of cheap carriage tires, rolled what chicle remained into small pellets and packaged them as the first chewing gum. Thus was formed the American Chicle Company that went on to produce such well-known chewing gums as Adam's Black Jack, Beeman's, and Dentyne, Rolaids antacid mints, Clorets gum and mints, and Certs candy breath mints before becoming a part of Warner-Lambert in 1962 and, ultimately, Pfizer in 2000.

E.R. SQUIBB & CO.

Before the Civil War, the U.S. Army accepted and inventoried its medical supplies at its purveying depot in New York City. Medicines were then shipped from New York to regional depots in the south and west, and finally circulated to individual army posts. In response to erratic imports of quality pharmaceuticals from Europe, Dr. Edward Robinson Squibb, a U.S. Navy medical officer and surgeon, persuaded the Surgeon General of the United States, William Hammond, to establish army laboratories to test and manufacture drugs, similar to the one Squibb had helped establish for the navy in 1852 at the Naval Hospital in Brooklyn. Two army laboratories were established: one in Astoria, New York, and the other in Philadelphia.

By this time, ether had gained wide acceptance as a surgical anesthetic, having first been used by the U.S. Army in 1847, during the Mexican-American War, and was produced by distillation of a mixture of alcohol and sulphuric acid, much as it had been since medieval times. However, its manufacture was complicated by its flammability and toxic by-products. Chloroform was also used as an anesthetic, having been discovered in the 1830s, and was produced by distilling alcohol with bleaching powder. Among other things, problems with product quality caused E.R. Squibb to leave the navy and establish his own drug manufacturing company in Brooklyn in 1857. Whereas, variations in the potency of chloroform had resulted in dozens of deaths when it was first used, E.R. Squibb & Co. soon gained a reputation for a most consistent product.

This major manufacturing base for ether and chloroform provided a distinct advantage for the Union during the Civil War and, together with the Federal naval blockade of the South, soon reduced the

availability of anesthetics in the Confederacy to blockade runners from Europe and raids on Union supply lines. Early in the war, however, when Stonewall Jackson lost his arm, chloroform was readily available to southern surgeons. General Jackson described its effects as "an infinite blessing" before he lost consciousness. More than a million ounces each of chloroform and ether were purchased by the Union during the course of the war.

Nevertheless, in the beginning, the Union was not prepared for a lengthy war against the Confederacy, and it was not until the Federal defeat at First Manassas that the U.S. Quartermaster began the practice of purchasing standard medicines for the army. Shortly thereafter, Squibb entered into a contract to supply the Federal army with standardized, sturdy and protected, bound medicine chests suitable for field use, with each chest containing 52 standard medicines packaged in unbreakable, varnished tin containers for $100.00 per medicine chest. By 1883, Squibb manufactured more than 320 medicinal preparations, which he sold internationally. He remained a powerful voice for high-quality, safe medicines and was an influential force that led to the eventual passage, six years after his death, of the U.S. Pure Food and Drug Act in 1906.

CHARLES PFIZER & COMPANY

A philosopher and doctor of theology, Johannes Jacob Pfizer was born in 1684 and lived in Ludwigsburg, Germany, just north of the city of Stuttgart on the Necker River (southeast of where it enters the Rhine at Ludwigshafen). Ludwigshafen is the place where, 200 years later, BASF (1861) established its headquarters. A little south of the Pfizer homestead, Stuttgart is where the forerunner of today's pharmaceutical giant Boehringer Ingelheim was established in 1817 by German entrepreneurs Christian Boehringer and Christian Engelmann (two years after the defeat of Napoleon at Waterloo).

Charles Pfizer was born in Germany in 1823, the great-great-grandson of Johannes Jacob Pfizer, doctor of theology, and the son of Karl Frederick Pfizer, who was involved in the grocery and confectionary trades. In 1848, at the age of 25, Charles and his cousin, Charles Erhart, age 28, traveled to America with $2,500 that Pfizer had borrowed from his father Karl. Pfizer had trained as a chemist and served as a pharmacist's apprentice in Germany. Erhart had apprenticed under Pfizer's father.

In 1849, the two cousins established Charles Pfizer & Company in Brooklyn, to manufacture chemicals that were not then produced in America. Their first product was a flavored candy blend of the drug santonin, an anthelmintic obtained as an extract of the Middle Eastern *wormseed* plant and used as a treatment for intestinal worms. The product combined Pfizer's knowledge of chemistry with Erhart's knowledge of confections.

Pfizer imported raw materials from all over the world and the two cousins traveled frequently to Europe to meet with and buy from their suppliers. During the American Civil War, the company supplied the Union Army with large quantities of borax, camphor, chloroform, cream of tartar, iodine, morphine, tartaric acid, and mercurial compounds. After the war, in 1880, Pfizer began producing what would become its most successful product: citric acid, used extensively in the flavoring of foods and soft drinks. When Charles Erhart died in 1891, Charles Pfizer acquired his cousin's share of the business and became sole owner.

JOHN WYETH & BROTHER

On the eve of the American Civil War, John Wyeth and his brother Frank founded in Philadelphia what would ultimately become the Wyeth-Ayerst division of pharmaceutical giant American Home Products, which changed its name from AHP (in 2002) to Wyeth. John Wyeth & Brother began as a Philadelphia pharmacy in 1860. Wyeth & Brother instituted a practice that was relatively novel in the nineteenth century: dispensing premeasured doses of medicines. The company then established the first ever mail-order catalog of pharmaceutical products in 1862, focusing on elixirs and tonics. Eventually, John Wyeth's son, Stuart Wyeth, bequeathed the company to the trustees of his alma mater, Harvard University, who sold it to American Home Products in 1931.

THE FRENCH INDUSTRY

France represents a fascinating study of a social structure and set of relationships between the government and private enterprise that does not so obviously exist in any other of the major industrialized countries.

ROUSSEL-UCLAF

Jean-Claude Roussel's father, Dr. Gaston Roussel, in the Institute de Serotherapie Hemopoietique, a small laboratory producing Hemostyl, a drug to counteract anemia and certain other blood diseases, began the Roussel Company in 1922. In 1962, Gaston's son, Jean-Claude Roussel, at the age of 39, became president and director general of the second-largest French pharmaceutical company, Roussel-Uclaf.

Roussel-Uclaf was formed in 1961, when Jean-Claude Roussel, age 39, became head of the company founded by his father and subsequently formed a new pharmaceuticals subsidiary, Laboratoires Roussel, to represent the company's pharmaceutical products throughout the world.

The eventual merger of Roussel-Uclaf and Hoechst AG began as a partnership agreement whereby Hoechst would acquire a minority ownership in Roussel-Uclaf shares that was signed on September 30, 1968. Following the death of Jean-Claude Roussel as the result of a crash while piloting his personal helicopter in 1972, the various factions of the widely branched Roussel family offered a majority of Roussel-Uclaf shares to Hoechst, which were accepted.

In 1928, the Laboratoires Francais de Chimiotherapic and the Usines Chimiques des Laboratoires Francais (Uclaf) was formed. The first Uclaf factory was built in Romainville, near Paris, on the site of the former Serum Institute.

In 1946, Gaston Roussel formed the Societe Francaise de la Penicilline (SOFRAPEN) which began the Roussel group's involvement in antibiotics.

Dr. Gaston Roussel died in 1947, when Jean-Claude Roussel was 25 years old.

In 1962, Roussel-Uclaf acquired Procida, the second-largest producer of agrochemicals in France. The combined company synthesized a group of natural products, nontoxic to warm-blooded animals, called pyrethrenoids, which had been used for many years in household insecticides, and which the company now expanded into a wide range of agricultural products.

By the mid- to late 1960s, Roussel-Uclaf had become the second-largest French pharmaceuticals manufacturer after Rhone-Poulenc.

The president of Rhone-Poulenc, the largest chemical company in France at the time of the original partnership agreement between Roussel-Uclaf and Hoechst AG in 1968, was Wilfrid Baumgartner, honorary governor of the Bank of France, and French finance minister from 1960 to 1962.

During the five-year period following the formation of Roussel-Uclaf, and its acquisition of Procida, total group sales more than doubled.

An executive board that had only four members managed Roussel-Uclaf.

In May 1968, there was widespread rioting and social unrest in France as the country came close to a civil war. The upheaval included radical left and anarchist students and intellectual elements in industry, research institutes, and civil administration. Ultimately, president Charles DeGaulle, who was strongly supported by Georges Pompidou, called upon the army to put an end to the crisis. Remarkably in retrospect, the communists and left-wing socialist elements in France, like the working population generally, did not support the insurrection by the students and intellectuals.

The French government had spent billions of francs for many years following World War II on chemical research and the expansion of the chemical industry, particularly on R&D in petroleum and natural gas. In the late 1950s, French chemical industries were focused on relatively inexpensive and plentiful supplies of oil and gas from the Sahara region of North Africa. These sources of raw materials were sharply cut back, however, when Algeria won its independence from France in 1962.

As a result, many chemical companies turned to the more expensive development of natural gas deposits in southwestern France, around Lacq, in the Pyrenean foothills. Societe Nationale des Petroles d'Aquitaine, S.A. (SNPA) in particular constructed a major chemical complex near Lacq. Major pipelines running from Lacq to industrial centers throughout France were constructed.

Perhaps as at least a partial result of these and other factors, the national social insurance system in France has experienced rising health care costs and large deficits and, as in other countries, the pharmaceutical industry has frequently been criticized in France as a major contributing factor. Such criticisms are typical of ill-informed or politically motivated groups in general. For example, it is typically not mentioned that during the 1970s Roussel-Uclaf spent an average of 200 million francs per year on research activities alone.

Nevertheless, the pharmaceutical price structure for finished products and imported raw materials is rigidly controlled in France. Furthermore, finished pharmaceutical products cannot be imported into France. Therefore, foreign pharmaceutical companies doing business in France have no choice except domestic manufacture, which they have tended to accomplish through partnerships with French "laboratories."

Hank Laskey

In the upper Rhone valley, refineries in St. Etienne and Grenoble are supplied raw materials by a pipeline that was originally constructed to deliver oil and gas from the Sahara, which would arrive by ship at the port of Marseilles. The St. Etienne and Grenoble refineries in turn supply the industrial areas of Lyon and Alsace.

Lyon is an ancient Roman city at the confluence of the Rhone and Saone rivers. Roussel-Uclaf has a large factory there with complex facilities capable of producing various categories of fine synthetic organic chemicals, in Neuville, a suburb near Lyon. The production of fine chemicals is a specialized and therefore expensive activity.

Five of the seven largest chemical companies in France have been wholly or partially nationalized.

After World War II, all of the many coal mining areas of France were nationalized for economic or political reasons.

The northern French and Lorraine coal mining groups operated under the umbrella of the Charbonnages de France (CdF). Chemical plants, leading eventually to the formation of CdF-Chimie, soon joined them.

State-promoted concentration of the postwar chemical industry was characteristic of French government undertakings in both the private and public sectors of the French economy.

Concentration, in general, is accelerated by the rising costs of research and technology. It has strengthened the position of the French chemical industry in international competition.

RHONE-POULENC

Rhone-Poulenc is the sixth-largest industrial company in France, and has approximately 300,000 shareholders. Rhone-Poulenc S.A. is an excellent example of the concentration of production potential and capital.

Marcel Poulenc in 1801 initially founded Poulenc. Rhone-Poulenc produced basic organic and inorganic products, especially dyestuffs and pharmaceuticals.

Poulenc combined with Societe Chimiques des Usines du Rhone in 1928.

In the early 1960s, Rhone-Poulenc acquired the Celtex group (Gillet), controlling approximately 80% of French synthetic fiber production.

In 1969, under Wilfred Baumgartner, Rhone-Poulenc acquired majority holdings in Pechiney-Saint-Gobain and Progil. These acquisitions boosted total sales to 14 billion francs.

In the boom year of 1974, Rhone-Poulenc achieved record sales of over 20 billion francs, thus matching the three largest German companies.

Renaud Gillet succeeded Wilfred Baumgartner. He divided Rhone-Poulenc into several new operating divisions and subsidiary companies. Fiber production went to Rhone-Poulenc Textile, and organics went to Naphtachimie S.A in Levera, in which the French arm of British Petroleum has a substantial minority holding. Together with Naphtachimie S.A. and Ruhrchemie AG, Hoechst operates an oxo-synthesis plant in Levera (Oxochimie S.A.).

The Gillet family still holds a considerable number of shares in the company.

PUK was formed in a merger between Ugine Kuhlmann and the part of Pechiney that was not absorbed by Rhone-Poulenc. After Rhone-Poulenc, it is the second-largest private concern in France. The holding company Produits Chimiques Ugine-Kuhlmann accounted for two-thirds of 4.6 billion francs in 1975.

Nationalized companies such as Enterprise Miniere ET Chimique (EMC), the largest producer of fertilizer in France, are expanding their activities.

CdF-Chimie acquired Ripolin-Georget-Freitag S.A. and now operates in the paint sector.

The largely nationalized oil groups, Societe Nationale des Petroles d'Aquitaine S.A. (SNPA) and Companies Francais des Petroles S.A., are expanding into processing. In 1971, their interests in neurochemistry were consolidated into Oxochimie, and their polymer interests into Ato-Emballage.

The nationalized oil company, Elf-Erap was fused with SNP to form Elf-Aquitaine.

As a condition of the Roussel-Uclaf merger with Hoechst AG, Hoechst was required to reduce its interest in Nobel-Bozel, which was part of the Roussel holdings, to less than 20% of the shares outstanding.

During World War II, I.G. Farben forced Kuhlman to form a partnership in Francolor. Similarly, Rhone-Poulenc was forced to yield its pharmaceutical production to Theraplix, a joint venture with Bayer.

With the help of an offspring of I.G. Farben, Solytec, a new dyestuffs business was built up based on the products of the three major I.G. successors. This dyestuffs business became part of Peralta, which was later changed in 1969 to Hoechst France, when the company had a staff of 800 people.

The small Mowilith stains factory near Paris became Nobel-Hoechst-Chimie, in Lamotte, south of Orleans, and manufactured surfactants or tenicides (kills tapeworms), and auxiliary products.

Only Pharmaceuticals remained separate as Laboratories Hoechst. Today it is united with Roussel-Uclaf, and both the production and administration of the gleaming plant in L'Aigle, in Normany, (which produces Hoechst pharmaceuticals) operate autonomously.

Hoechst also acquired a plastics plant near the mouth of the Seine at Lillebonde in a temporary partnership with several French companies, which was later dissolved by mutual consent. Since then Hoechst has increased the plant's capacity to 70,000 tons per year, and has also added an aldehyde plant at the same site.

There is a dramatic difference in the social climates of Germany and France. Differences among social strata in France are much greater than in Germany where class distinctions have been largely eroded by defeat in World War II, and also inflation.

The French trade unions are all politically committed. The Confederation Generales des Travailleurs (CGT), which represents approximately 60% of the trade unions in France, is largely an organ of the French Communist party. The Confederation Francais Democratique des Travailleurs (CFDT), which was originally a right-wing trade union, has tried to bolster its essentially weaker position by attempting to surpass the CGT on the left. The trade unions generally seek confrontation rather than cooperation with the wealth owning classes. There is a large degree of trade union influence among academically trained employees.

THE GERMAN INDUSTRY

Beginning in the late 1800s and continuing for over half a century, German chemical/pharmaceutical companies completely dominated world markets for dyestuffs, chemical intermediates, and pharmaceuticals. The most important German companies that began during this period are still in existence today, including Bayer, Boehringer Ingelheim, BASF, and Hoechst. Although Hoechst is now part of the German-French conglomerate Aventis, it is the dominant element of the combined company.

HOECHST

Researchers at Hoechst focused on the development of an antipyretic that would not have the side effects associated with Antifebrin. Toward this end, they studied various ketone derivatives of pyrazole, having anti-inflammatory, analgesic, and antipyretic effects, which are known today as *pyrazolones*. In the late 1800s,

Hoechst marketed several such products, including *antipyrin* in 1884, *antipyrine* in 1888, and *pyramidon* in1893.

At about this same time, Robert Koch's assistant, Paul Erlich, came up with the idea that dyestuffs could also be used to *kill* bacteria. He demonstrated the action of *methylene blue* on the malaria parasite in 1891. Erlich also found, in 1905, that *atoxyl*, an organic derivative of arsenic, was effective against Trypanosoma, a genus of protozoa consisting of many pathogenic species, including those that cause sleeping sickness.

Erlich began working for Hoechst in 1907, and in 1909 discovered an arsenobenzene compound that was effective against syphilis. Hoechst marketed the product under the trade name *Salvarsan*. Paul Erlich also worked with Emil von Behring, who had discovered the diphtheria antitoxin. Together they prepared the first commercial antidiphtheria serum, which was also marketed by Hoechst as the first tetanus antitoxin (1894–1897). In 1905, Alfred Einhorn, another Hoechst researcher, discovered the anesthetic *Novocaine*, which is still used today.

BAYER

Bayer researchers also worked to develop a commercial antipyretic that would not have the side effects associated with *Antifebrin*. Unlike researchersat Hoechst, theyfocusedonderivativesofphenol, compounds similar to Hermann Kolbe's salicylic acid. They first developed phenacetin in 1888, and in 1898 they developed *acetylsalicylic acid*, which became the most popular pain reliever in the world as *Bayer Aspirin*. In 1899, Bayer obtained a patent on acetylsalicylic acid.

This period around the turn of the century was a remarkable time of pharmacological innovation at Bayer. The company regularly tested dyestuffs compounds for their effectiveness against bacteria. In 1908, the basic compound for the powerful class of *sulfa* drugs was first synthesized as a reddish orange dye at Bayer Laboratories, and was later found to be effective against pneumonia.

On the eve of World War I, Bayer was Germany's third-largest chemical company, having over 10,000 employees worldwide. During the war, and despite the many lives that could have been saved, Bayer and other German chemical companies tried to deprive the Allies of the many drugs they controlled. While other countries were now awakened to the vital relationship between dyestuffs manufacturing and national health, French chemists duplicated the basic sulfa compound and made it available to the world market.

I.G. FARBEN

Interessen Gemeinschaft Farbenwerke (I.G. Farben) was a "conglomerate" of chemical companies in Germany. It was organized as a series of progressively more powerful trusts that completely dominated world markets by setting quotas and pooling profits, until being dismantled by the Allies in the interests of "peace and democracy" in 1951. The integration occurred in two separate "mega-mergers," the first in 1904 and the second in 1925. The first collaboration was the brainchild of a Bayer chemist, Dr. Carl Duisberg, who had joined Bayer in 1884 and went on to become its president. By joining BASF and AGFA, Bayer hoped to more effectively compete against Hoechst and its affiliates, who were generating higher profits as a result of their concentration on pharmaceuticals. (They later became known as the "Little I.G.")

Following World War I, although Bayer's Carl Duisberg opposed it for a time, Dr. Carl Bosch, of BASF, pushed through the final integration of the "Big I.G." to include Hoechst and its partners. The final merger involved approximately 100,000 employees, including over 1,000 chemists.

According to the terms of the Treaty of Versailles that ended World War I, the French were allowed to occupy the Ruhr Valley, which they did in 1923. Realizing that the French occupation was imminent, Bosch succeeded in dismantling and relocating all of BASF's proprietary synthetic ammonia equipment out of Ludwigshafen to Leuna, which was far to the east of the Rhine. The Leuna facility, near Leipzig, expanded to produce huge quantities of synthetic ammonia, synthetic rubber, and synthetic gasoline, each of which was of major strategic importance in Germany's drive for resource independence. It is therefore possible that Carl Bosch's primary motivation for forming the "Big I.G." was his need for an increased base of capital with which to finance the completion of the Luna facilities.

After World War II, when the Allies divided Germany into four sectors, the French sector included the existing BASF works at Ludwigshafen, while the enormous Leuna facilities fell within the Russian sector. The primary Bayer facilities at Leverkusen fell within the British sector and, in Frankfurt, Hoechst's operations fell to the Americans.

The I.G. Farben cartel strongly supported the Nazi party and was given possession of foreign chemical companies immediately following their capture by German armed forces during World War II. Its factories were also supplied with slave labor. I.G. Farben employed slave labor to build many new factories in remote areas, covered by camouflage. As a result, at the end of the war, only **15%** of I.G. Farben's productive capacity had been destroyed, according to testimony given by I.G. Farben executives when they appeared before the War Crimes Tribunal at Nuremburg after the war.

THE DOMINANCE OF GERMAN DYESTUFFS

Now a part of Aventis, the German pharmaceutical giant, Hoechst (1862), began as a dyestuff manufacturer, as did Bayer (1863), AGFA, and BASF. Unlike AGFA, however, Bayer, Hoechst and BASF settled in what was known as the Rhineland-Westphalia region and the Lower Palatinate ("palatinate" referring to a German emperor's castle), along the Rhine River. Here also were the very important specialty manufacturers, Kalle (1864) and Cassella (1807), among others. Boehringer Ingelheim, for example, which is also one of the world's largest pharmaceutical companies today, originated in Stuttgart in 1817, and then moved to Mannheim on the river Rhine in 1872, shortly after the Franco-Prussian War. This is also the area where Pfizer has its large pharmaceutical facility today, in Karlsruhe. (The Pfizer family originated in nearby Ludwigsburg, just north of Stuttgart and the Boehringer Ingelheim homestead.)

The Rhineland-Westphalia region became a part of Prussia in 1815 after having been taken by the French during the Napoleonic Wars, which had ended Austria's rule over the Holy Roman Empire that

included most of Germany. The Rhine River, which flows through this region, is the most important inland waterway in Europe. The Rhine provided these chemical plants with easy access to the Ruhr Valley coal-mining district downstream and the coking ovens that produced the essential coal tar for synthetic dyestuffs manufacturing. Furthermore, Basel, Switzerland, was just upstream with CIBA, Geigy, and Sandoz who also all began as dyestuffs companies and are all part of pharmaceutical powerhouse Novartis today.

THE BRITISH INDUSTRY

THE BIRTH OF IMPERIAL CHEMICAL INDUSTRIES

The three leading British dyestuffs firms in 1914 were Ivan Levinstein, Read Holliday, and British Alizarine. Together they produced about 4,000 tons of dyestuffs, whereas the major German firms produced 140,000. Germany at this time was supplying over 80% of Britain's artificial color.

By losing their dominance in synthetic dyestuffs to Germany, the British had put their entire chemical industry in jeopardy. By this time, the Germans had also succeeded in producing their own feedstock materials, thereby eliminating their dependence on imported British coal tar derivatives. BASF had developed an improved process for recovering benzene from Ruhr Valley coking ovens that were associated with Germany's massive increase in steel production since the end of the Franco-Prussian War. Thus, the British had essentially forfeited all of the downstream demand their former dyestuffs industry had represented to British coal tar refiners. Other British industries that had come to rely on imported German colors and synthetic intermediates were also negatively affected by the outbreak of the war. The availability of medicines in both Britain and the United States was sharply curtailed. Furthermore, the manufacture of explosives and other munitions required basic materials similar to those employed in dyestuffs; i.e., benzol, toluol, nitric and sulphuric acids. Swiss firms CIBA, Geigy, and Sandoz supplied the majority of British imports during the war.

British Alizarine was a London-based company that had bought the remaining patents and inventory of Perkin and Sons, following the sale of the company founded by the discoverer of mauve. W.H. Perkin had sold his company when he was only thirty-six years old and the company was still profitable, claiming he could foresee the demise of the British dyestuffs industry. Following a dramatic transformation during World War I, when dyestuffs chemists were in very high demand and highly paid, several British dyestuffs companies, including Read Holliday, Bradford Dyers, and Calico Printers, merged to form British Dyes Ltd., and then promptly laid off over fifty of the chemists that had helped win the war.

In 1919, British Dyes merged with Ivan Levinstein and several smaller British dyestuffs companies to form the British Dyestuffs Corporation, in which the British government also remained a partner until 1925. Then, in 1926, the British Dyestuffs Corporation merged with Brunner, Mond & Co., Nobel Industries, Ltd., United Alkalai Co. Ltd., and the British Alizarine Company to form the powerhouse *Imperial Chemical Industries (ICI)*, which could thus trace its roots all the way back to Perkin's wonderful discovery and, by the time of World War II, could ensure that Britain was self-sufficient in dyestuffs and *related* products. It seems that the British had finally learned their lesson. During World War I when the *Manchester*

Guardian newspaper published a telltale article explaining to its readers that from now on **"dyes and drugs must be thought of together. Whatever serves the modern dyemaker directly serves national health."** As big as ICI was, however, it was no match for I.G. Farben, which controlled over 100 industrial plants and mines, and employed approximately 120,000 workers. Thus, in 1932, the British Parliament passed the "Safeguarding Industries Act," which placed a heavy customs duty (33.3%) on all synthetic organic derivatives imported from abroad.

ICI'S PHARMACEUTICALS DIVISION

ICI was a highly diversified conglomerate, and by far the dominant chemical company in Britain, with a monopoly in the key areas of alkalais, chlorine, hydrochloric and nitric acids, sodium, synthetic ammonia and nitrate explosives. In 1936, the company's dyestuffs division set up a department for special therapeutics research, which later became ICI's pharmaceuticals division in 1957.

During World War II, in 1942, ICI researchers discovered *sulfamethazine*, a sulfonamide, or sulfa drug, used as an antibacterial in a variety of infections. Then after the war, in 1946, they discovered *paludrin*, or proguanil hydrochloride, an antimalarial used in the prophylaxis (prevention) and treatment of malaria; *chlorhexidine* in 1954, an antibiotic and derivative of paludrin, which they marketed as *Hibitane*; the potent inhalational anesthetic *halothane* in 1957, which is widely used for the induction and maintenance of general anesthesia, and which they marketed as *Fluothane*; and *propranolol hydrochloride* in 1964, a beta-adrenergic blocking agent, used for a variety of cardiovascular diseases and marketed as *Inderal*.

Hank Laskey

THE SWISS INDUSTRY

Rather than follow a policy of market expansion, Renard Freres, the French holder of the fuchsine patent, implemented a high-price policy for the dye. This led to its production by competing firms in Switzerland, who were not affected by French patent laws. Twentieth-century Swiss pharmaceutical giants like CIBA, Geigy, and Sandoz (all three of whom ultimately merged to form Novartis) began as dye manufacturers in Basel, Switzerland, near the border with Germany and France on the Rhine River. Hoffman-La Roche, another Swiss pharmaceutical giant, was founded in 1894 in Basel.

The Swiss dyestuffs manufacturers could not hope to compete with the much-larger German companies created in the 1860s in the big alizarin and indigo markets, so they cleverly formed alliances with them and focused on specialty niche markets around the world instead. The Swiss firms arranged to buy their feedstock materials from the Germans as bulk intermediate compounds, which they then modified into high value-added, technically complex finished products. The Swiss have maintained this strategy of specialization up to the present day.

OTHER NATIONAL INDUSTRIES

Some industry observers have referred to the rest of the world as a "throw away" for most pharmaceutical companies because of the high percentage of worldwide pharmaceutical sales represented by the combined U.S., Japanese, and European markets. This is a rather callous perspective. There is a strong emphasis on preventive health maintenance in the U.S., Japan, and the EU that does not exist in other parts of the world; and it is a difficult problem for which there appears to be no easy answer. Other areas of the world have a much higher incidence of disease than the U.S., Japan, and the EU; consequently the needs for effective medication are much greater in these other countries. Unfortunately, they also have little ability to pay for the drugs they need. This situation has been the cause of enormous confrontation and debate throughout the world. Nevertheless, the primary focus of health care in the <u>developed</u> world is on health maintenance and the prevention of disease, whereas in the <u>developing</u> world the focus is on crisis intervention.

STRUCTURE OF THE PHARMACEUTICAL INDUSTRY

INDUSTRY TRENDS AND CORPORATE PERFORMANCE

In recent years, advances in combinatorial chemistry, molecular biology, rational drug design, and genomics have had a significant influence on the development of medicine. There has been spectacular growth in the industry and significant industry consolidation has followed through corporate mergers and acquisitions. At the end of the twentieth century, there was a general slowdown in world economies following a collapse of valuations in the U.S. equities markets and a number of other factors related to the global monetary and financial system. The restructuring of the global pharmaceutical industry that began gradually in the first decades following World War II, and then accelerated sharply in the closing decades of the century, is expected to continue into the future.

Because of the complexity of the financial transactions involved, fluctuations in international exchange rates, intra-firm transfers of assets and materials across national borders, and differences in accounting standards and practices it is common to find inconsistencies in the data that are published by various sources of economic and financial information. For these reasons and others related to the timeliness of statistics and their publication dates,

Hank Laskey

the sales figures for the world's largest pharmaceutical companies presented in table 17-1 for the final period of the twentieth century do not include the results of certain mergers and acquisitions, including the merger between Glaxo Wellcome and SmithKline Beecham, the acquisition of Alza by Johnson & Johnson, and the acquisition of DuPont Pharmaceuticals by Bristol-Myers Squibb, as well as several others, including the name change of American Home Products to Wyeth. Nevertheless, the information contained in Table 17-1 gives a fairly accurate representation of the corporate identities of the major players and their relative levels of pharmaceutical sales at the time. For comparative purposes, all sales figures have been converted to **millions** of U.S. dollars.

TABLE 17-1 TOP DRUG COMPANIES

Ranked by Worldwide Pharmaceutical Sales

In **Millions** of U.S. Dollars ($USD)

	Company	Sales		Company	Sales
1	Pfizer	20,500.00	21	Shionogi	3,319.60
2	Merck	17,481.60	22	Merck KGaA	3,044.80
3	AstraZeneca	14,834.00	23	Amgen	3,042.80
4	Aventis	14,808.50	24	Yamanouchi	3,039.30
5	Bristol-Myers Squibb	14,309.00	25	Knoll	2,645.10
6	Glaxo Wellcome	13,732.30	26	Schering AG	2,451.20
7	Novartis	12,679.70	27	Eisai	2,431.60
8	Pharmacia	11,177.00	28	Novo Nordisk	2,352.90
9	Hoffman LaRoche	10,973.80	29	Fujisawa	2,293.20
10	Johnson & Johnson	10,694.00	30	Taisho	2,252.00
11	American Home Products	9,505.90	31	Akzo Nobel	1,821.60

12	Eli Lilly	9,375.10	32	Servier	1,639.40
13	SmithKline Beecham	8,477.20	33	Dupont Pharmaceuticals	1,630.00
14	Schering Plough	7,956.00	34	Chugai	1,579.50
15	Takeda	6,102.50	35	Welfide Corporation	1,524.30
16	Abbott	5,648.00	36	Otsuka	1,454.20
17	Sanofi Synthelabo	5,347.70	37	Solvay	1,437.10
18	Bayer	5,329.60	38	Tanabe Seiyaku	1,402.90
19	Boehringer Ingelheim	4,966.80	39	Kyowa Hakko	1,256.70
20	Sankyo	4,095.70	40	Kaneka	1,214.30
Source: Scrip's League Tables (1999-2000)					

Because of their potency and high degree of therapeutic activity, modern pharmaceuticals in most countries of the world require a written prescription by a licensed physician or medical doctor in order to be dispensed to patients by licensed pharmacists. To serve their customers' needs, pharmacists typically obtain necessary quantities of medicines from specialized pharmaceutical wholesalers or drug distributors who, in turn, obtain them in bulk quantities directly from pharmaceutical manufacturers. Wholesalers and distributors thereby incur the costs associated with holding large diverse inventories of pharmaceuticals and related products over time, as well as the costs associated with combining assortments of these and transporting them to local or regional pharmacies. Physicians and pharmacists are therefore the primary and often *only* points of contact between consumers (patients) and the pharmaceutical industry.

At the end of the twentieth century, total worldwide sales of all pharmaceutical products were valued at over $335 billion U.S.

dollars, and there were more than 15 drugs that were each worth over a billion dollars in worldwide sales per year. Table 17-2 lists the brands with worldwide annual sales of over one billion U.S. dollars at the end of the century and their manufacturers. Given such large dollar volume or economic impact, the industry is frequently criticized on grounds ranging from high prices and monopoly power to restricted distribution and an artificially elevated cost structure.

TABLE 17-2 MEGA-BRANDS		
Brand	Manufacturer	Sales
Prilosec	AZN	3,894,541 bln USD
Lipitor	PFE	3,464,817
Prevacid	TAP	2,635,633
Prozac	LLY	2,381,911
Zocor	MRK	2,100,834
Celebrex	SRL	1,870,971
Zoloft	PFE	1,724,152
Paxil	SKB	1,644,054
Claritin	SGP	1,523,425
Norvasc	PFE	1,474,556
Glucophage	BMS	1,470,703
Augmentin	SKB	1,410,993
Vioxx	MRK	1,385,129
Zyprexa	LLY	1,363,507
Pravachol	BMS	1,140,407
Neurontin	PD	1,050,792
Oxycontin	PUR	1,005,851

Also in terms of U.S. dollars, over 125 companies in the world each accounted for pharmaceutical sales in excess of $100 million during the final year of the twentieth century. All together, these 125 companies had pharmaceutical sales that totaled approximately $290 billion. As shown in Table 17-3, the ten largest companies represented over 48% of this amount. Yet figures that are aggregated in this way do not reveal the complete picture of the industry. Within individual countries and therapeutic categories or classes of drugs, a different picture emerges. It is important to examine disaggregated data that are broken down in this way as well as long-term trends in aggregate statistics.

TABLE 17-3 INDUSTRY CONCENTRATION

Level of Annual Pharmaceutical Sales	Number of Companies	Combined Sales	Percent of Total
Greater than $10 billion	10	141,189.9	48.83%
$5 billion: $10 billion	8	57,742.0	19.97%
$4 billion: $5 billion	2	9,062.5	3.13%
$3 billion: $4 billion	4	12,446.5	4.30%
$2 billion: $3 billion	6	14,426.0	4.99%
$1 billion: $2 billion	15	20,301.2	7.02%
$500 million: $1 billion	27	18,913.5	6.54%
$100 million: $500 million	54	15,064.3	5.21%
TOTAL	126	289,145.9	100.00%

In the context of costs and pricing, and within the realm of the effects of market forces, or market-derived regulation, managed care organizations (MCOs), pharmacy benefit managers (PBMs), and other entities have come into existence and rapidly expanded their influence on the industry's ability to raise or control prices. Pharmaceutical marketing and distribution have dramatically changed as a result of these organizations and the social forces that created them. A stronger focus on costs has resulted within the industry, and pharmaceutical companies have turned to quality-of-life, disease management, cost-effectiveness, and other "pharmacoeconomic" concepts and practices in order to justify prices. These trends are likely to continue and grow in importance in the future, but they will also likely continue to be critically evaluated and restrained by the forces of managed care, etc. (market governance forces).

GLOBAL INDUSTRY STRUCTURE

Industry structure relates to the pattern of ownership, intensity of competition, and the economic power of industry participants. It largely concerns the perceptions of companies, their products and services, by various elements of society, including customers, consumers, other businesses and government agencies. In the context of competition, economists frequently talk about "barriers to entry" that might exist against new companies coming into an industry, which tend to perpetuate the power of existing firms, and provide them with de-facto control over supplies and prices. Beyond this, the notion of industry structure also involves the internal organizations of participating firms and their relationships to one another, their strategic competitive advantages, relative market shares, sustainable rates of growth, costs and profitability, pricing power and marketing activities that tend to either inhibit or promote competition.

RESEARCH VS. MARKETING

To a large extent, understanding the structure of the worldwide pharmaceutical industry lies in understanding the fundamental differences between the research and marketing functions that occur within the industry. The large, integrated pharmaceutical companies have thousands of sales representatives. The importance of the sales representative in generating and maintaining market share for all categories of patented, generic, over-the-counter, and biological products should never be underestimated. Nor should the contributions of extremely talented, individual research scientists be underestimated. However, the two fields (marketing and research) tend to attract very different types of people, having very different views of the world, different educational training and experiences. The ability to manage an integrated organization, consisting of huge research and marketing operations, while maintaining above-average levels of profit, and a sustainable competitive advantage, therefore, requires extraordinary vision and industry know-how. It is important to closely examine the marketing-research interface wherever it exists, not only within a single organization (or quasi-organization employing a high degree of outsourcing), but also across companies, such as the small drug development firm and it's much larger or specialized marketing partner.

When considering the structure of the global pharmaceutical industry, it is important to differentiate among different types of product categories; for example, prescription pharmaceuticals and over-the-counter products. Such broad-based product categories frequently represent very different markets and competitive situations among various groups of companies. The prescription and over-the-counter markets are so different, in fact, that the major companies have set up entirely different operating divisions and, in some cases, different subsidiary companies for each one.

MAJOR SECTORS OF PHARMACEUTICAL PRODUCTS

There are six major sectors of pharmaceutical products:

(1) **Ethical, patented (usually branded), synthetic or semi-synthetic, pharmaceuticals (usually requiring a prescription)**

(2) **Generic, non-patented (usually non-branded), synthetic or semi-synthetic pharmaceuticals (usually requiring a prescription)**

(3) **Biologics**

(4) **Homeopathic medicines**

(5) **Over-the-counter or "proprietary" medications (usually branded)**

(6) **Dietary supplements such as vitamins, minerals, botanicals, etc.**

There are important, structure-related differences between patented and generic pharmaceuticals, as well as between those drugs that are the product of traditional synthetic chemistry and those that are produced through biotechnology, recombinant DNA and genetic engineering. The biotech firms, with a few notable exceptions, such as Amgen, Biogen, etc., tend to be much smaller than the large, integrated pharmaceutical companies. The biotech firms also tend to be more dynamic, flexible, and innovative than the large firms. Increasingly, the large companies are outsourcing their activities to such smaller, specialized firms who tend to be aggressive and hungry for the opportunities that outsourcing represents.

THERAPEUTIC CATEGORIES OF MEDICINES

Companies tend to specialize in various therapeutic categories; and the industry, therefore, tends to be structured around the different therapeutic categories of drugs. Pfizer, at present for example, specializes in (and is formally organized around) four therapeutic categories: (1) cardiovascular, (2) central nervous system, (3) anti-infectives, and (4) men's and women's health (which includes drugs such as *Viagra*).

A therapeutic category is a general grouping of drugs according to their intended use or function on various parts of the body and the diseases that tend to affect that part of the body. For example, cardiovascular drugs, central nervous system drugs, respiratory drugs, and dermatologicals are intended for use on different parts of the body and the different types of diseases that tend to occur there.

A minor problem within the industry is that there is sometimes a lack of uniformity in the formation and use of therapeutic categories. For example, "men's and women's health" is a special category designated by Pfizer. Furthermore, usually for historical reasons, there are differences between, and even unique aspects to, various important sources of data on drugs and the drug industry, such as the World Health Organization, IMS, and Scrip's.

Because of the important role played by the World Health Organization in promoting the uniformity of world drug regulations, and the very significant progress that has been made in this area, and the promise of additional progress, it seems advantageous to examine the World Health Organization's system of drug therapeutic categories as a basis for studying the structure of the worldwide pharmaceutical industry.

THE WHO LIST OF ESSENTIAL DRUGS

The World Health Organization's Model List of **Essential** Drugs contains 27 major therapeutic categories of drugs. Most of these have sub-categories, and some are further divided into specific drug types. For example, the Anti-infective Drugs category contains six sub-categories, including Anthelminthics, Antibacterials, and Antifungal Drugs. Furthermore, the Anthelminthics sub-category contains three specific drug types: (1) Intestinal Anthelminthics, (2) Antifilarials, and (3) Antischistosomals and Other Antitrematode Drugs.

While the WHO Model List is indeed useful as an orienting device toward understanding the structure of the pharmaceutical industry, it does have its limitations. For example, it does not include a category to neatly accommodate drugs like *Viagra*, which some sources categorize as a "lifestyle" drug. The WHO Model List contains useful basic categories of drugs and should be memorized by anyone seeking to understand the structure of the worldwide pharmaceutical industry.

Using the alternative categorization scheme employed by Scrip (an important supplier of data on the pharmaceutical industry), Table 17-4 contains worldwide annual sales figures, in **billions** of U.S. dollars, for each of the top ten selling therapeutic "categories" in 1999 to 2000.

TABLE 17-4 SCRIP'S THERAPEUTIC CATEGORIES	
Annual Sales	
1. Cardiovascular	$41.4
2. Alimentary/Metabolism	32.9
3. Central Nervous System	32.1
4. Anti-infectives	21.5
5. Respiratory	19.5
6. Genito-urinary	11.8
7. Musculo-skeletal	11.7
8. Cytostatics	8.0
9. Dermatologicals	7.8
10. Blood Agents	6.6
Source: Scrip's, 1999-2000	

THERAPEUTIC CLASSES

A therapeutic class, in contrast to a therapeutic category, is a much more precise, sub-category of drugs that are intended for a more specific use, relative to a particular disease or condition that affects a particular part of the body. For example, antidepressants and antipsychotics are therapeutic classes of central nervous system drugs. Furthermore, calcium channel blockers and ACE inhibitors (Angiotensin Converting Enzyme) are classes of cardiovascular drugs. Antipruritics and antifungals are classes of dermatological drugs.

Unfortunately, there is a lack of consistency here too among various references. Sometimes, classes of drugs that have a broadly similar function or use within a category are grouped together under other category sub-headings, such as grouping antidepressants and antipsychotics together with drugs for anxiety and panic under the subheading of "psychotherapeutic drugs." This is done in order to differentiate them in a meaningful way from other so-called "classes" of central nervous system drugs, such as stimulants, hypnotics, or anticonvulsants.

It is also common for drugs with a similar mechanism of action to be referred to as a therapeutic "class". For example, within the antidepressant class of drugs, there are the monoamine oxidase inhibitors, the selective serotonin reuptake inhibitors, and the tricyclics. These are all types of drugs used therapeutically for symptoms of depression (same therapeutic class), but they work differently, and there is more than one brand on the market representing each mechanism of action.

Another example is the class of cardiovascular drugs known as cholesterol and triglycerol reducers, or antilipidemics. Within this therapeutic class, there are different types of drugs with different mechanisms of action. For example, the most popular are the so-called statins or HMG-CoA reductase inhibitors. There are also the fibric acid derivatives and the bile acid sequestrants in this (antilipidemic) class, each of which has a mechanism of action that is different from the statins. Furthermore, nicotinic acid is used as an antilipidemic, and has a mechanism of action that is unique in its own right.

THERAPEUTIC PRODUCT MARKETS

A "therapeutic product-market" is a marketing concept, which is very useful in overcoming inconsistencies among references on therapeutic categories, classes, mechanisms of action, etc. A therapeutic product-market is a segment or sector of the pharmaceutical market consisting of a differentiable group of drugs that appear to be competing against each other for one or more therapeutic uses. Often, this will consist of the drugs comprising a given therapeutic class, but it can equally often consist only of those drugs within a class that have a common mechanism of action; it all depends on the market. For example, the statins are often considered to represent a distinct therapeutic product-market, and although there are other antilipidemics on the market, the *structure of the market* seems to be that the statins are a clearly differentiable group from the others.

Depending upon a number of factors that are used to conceptualize market segments, including physician prescribing practices based on off-label indications (therapeutic uses for which a particular drug has not been officially approved by the appropriate regulatory authority), a therapeutic product-market can consist of drugs representing **different** therapeutic classes within a therapeutic category or, even representing different therapeutic categories entirely, which are, nevertheless being used or are competing against each other for the same, generalized condition (therapy).

Prescribed therapies for the same condition can vary widely, and must be decided on an individual basis. As stated by Goodman and Gilman (2001, pg. 48) in their highly regarded text on pharmacology and therapeutics: "Therapists of every type have long recognized and acknowledged that individual patients show wide variability in response to the same drug or treatment method."

As an important example, the drug Neurontin (gabapentin) is an anticonvulsant, indicated as therapy in the treatment of partial, epileptic-type seizures. In addition it has been recently been approved for treating symptoms of chronic, neuropathic pain. Thus, in differentiating market segments, it could be important to include *Neurontin* in the same **therapeutic product-market** as another therapeutic "class" of drugs entirely, in a totally different therapeutic category.

Proper definition of therapeutic product-markets is important because of significant differences in the nature of competition within them. The level of market share that is attainable in any product-market is a function of many factors, including the number of competing brands. If a brand is the first to enter a particular product-market, then, obviously, it will garner 100% of the sales in that particular market segment, as a monopoly. However, if other brands are able to successfully enter this segment of the market, possibly as a result of improved, or at least different, safety and/or efficacy profiles, then the structure of the product-market will have changed. It could no longer be described as a monopoly, but possibly a duopoly or triopoly.

The relative levels of market share that each brand is able to attract will continue to be a function of many factors, but importantly it will depend upon whether a brand is first, second, third, fourth, etc., to enter a particular product-market. Very dramatic structural changes can occur when a brand with a demonstrably superior therapeutic profile enters the market. However, such brands do not exist in all therapeutic categories, and there are many cases where several competing brands co-exist for many years. Therefore, it is important not to generalize across market segments when describing the structure of the global pharmaceutical market. Each segment can have its own unique characteristics.

With all other things being equal, and 20 pharmaceutical companies representing approximately 70% of worldwide pharmaceutical sales, one would expect each of these companies to have an approximately 3.5% share of the world market (70% divided equally among 20 companies). In fact, the largest two companies in 2000 to 2001 (Pfizer and Glaxo SmithKline) have something like a 6.5% to 7.5% share each, with the next four or five companies having roughly a 4% to 4.5% share each; percentages drop steadily from there on down the list. While these figures are certainly different from the expected 3.5%, they are not in the range of say 20% to 30%, or even higher. In fact, it would require the combined shares of the top three companies to approximate anything near this range of market share. However, in some countries, and in some therapeutic product-markets, a single brand can represent this much share and much more. The top two or three brands in a particular segment can represent a combined 70% or 80% share, or even higher. It all depends on the nature of the market and how it is defined.

Example of H2-Receptor Antagonists

An excellent example of changes in market structure, yielding meaningful new market segments, or therapeutic product-markets, and the related market dynamics that can occur within a therapeutic class as new drugs enter an existing market, is described in a study by Berndt, Bui, Reiley, and Urban (1994) of the U.S. anti-ulcer market between 1977 and 1993. They examined the roles of rivalrous marketing (including the activities of sales representatives and journal advertising), product quality, order of entry, and price competition within this particular market segment during this particular time period.

SmithKline was the first company to enter the then-existing U.S. anti-ulcer market with Tagamet, a revolutionary new form of anti-ulcer drug, known as an H_2-receptor antagonist, in July 1977. Sales of Tagamet grew rapidly in what was essentially a monopoly situation until Glaxo entered the market (duopoly) in June 1983 with its own brand of H_2-receptor antagonist, Zantac. Within one year of aggressive marketing (in partnership with Hoffman-LaRoche), Zantac had captured approximately 25% of this new (Tagamet-Zantac) *therapeutic product-market*, even though Zantac was priced substantially **higher** than Tagamet. Tagamet responded (surprisingly), in the face of its own declining market share, by raising price! When Merck introduced Pepcid, a third brand of H_2-receptor antagonist to the U.S. market in October 1986, it was able to capture 8% of the market within one year, even though Zantac's share was continuing to grow steadily during the same time period.

Zantac's sales finally overtook Tagamet in January 1988, 4 ½ years after having challenged its monopoly status, and more than two years since Pepcid had entered. Then, in April 1988, Eli Lilly entered the market with a fourth brand of H2 -receptor antagonist, Axid. In its first year against the other three brands comprising the product-market, Axid captured a 4% market share.

By the end of the study, in May 1993, Zantac held about 55% of the market, Tagamet held about 21%, Pepcid 15%, and Axid 9%. Furthermore, Pepcid was priced at a low of about $1.41 per day of therapy, Tagamet was priced at about $1.44, Axid was at $1.62, and Zantac was at a high of about $1.80 per day, thus showing little relationship between price and market share.

In terms of sales force activity to promote the brands (so-called detailing minutes), Zantac considerably outpaced Tagamet in any given single year, suggesting the power of detailing to generate market share. Cumulatively, however, and considering that the brands had each been in the market for different lengths of time, the relative magnitudes of detailing minutes through the end of the study were (using Axid, the last brand to enter, as a standard of 1.00): Pepcid 0.88, Axid 1.00, Zantac 2.60, and Tagamet 3.21 cumulative minutes. Thus, Pepcid, which employed the lowest price at the conclusion of the study, also had employed the lowest level of detailing cumulatively (even though it had been in the market over two years *longer* than Axid). The relatively high level of cumulative detailing by Tagamet was entirely the result of 4 ½ years of monopoly status, when it was being actively promoted in order to create the new therapeutic market segment.

While it is important to realize that the relative sales and market share of any drug will be a function of many factors, including product quality and other characteristics of the so-called physical product itself, i.e., FDA-approved indications, relative safety and efficacy profiles, dosage frequency, interactions with other drugs, etc., the structure of a product-market is not a function of such physical characteristics alone. Nevertheless, it is important to point out that even though Tagamet pioneered with indications for duodenal ulcers (1977), prevention of the recurrence of a newly healed duodenal ulcer (1980), and gastric ulcers (1982), Zantac was the first, in 1986, to be approved for the GERD indication (gastroesophageal reflux disease). Although Tagamet was also eventually approved for GERD, it was not approved until 1991, almost five years after Zantac.

Furthermore, according to a study published in 1990, Tagamet appeared to have more side effects and drug interactions than Zantac, while both Pepcid and Axid appeared to have less than Zantac. Thus, the overall conditions dictating market structure can be complex, involving not only the characteristics of the physical product, but also the combined effects of each brand's other marketing mix elements (price, promotion, distribution, etc.)

OVER-THE-COUNTER DRUGS

While they all began as prescription drugs, Tagamet, Zantac, Pepcid, and Axid are all formulated and sold as "over-the-counter," or non-prescription drugs. As previously mentioned, the prescription and over-the-counter (OTC) drug markets are so different that most companies have separate divisions or even independent subsidiaries for their OTC products.

In fiscal 1999–2000, worldwide pharmaceutical sales totaled approximately $337 billion, while total OTC sales were approximately $41 billion. The top-selling OTC therapeutic categories were vitamins and minerals, and cough, cold and allergy remedies. Each of these categories is valued at approximately $3.7 billion in the United States alone. Other major categories include internal analgesics, gastrotherapeutics, laxatives, and antidiarrheals.

While there are significant differences around the world in the regulation of OTC drugs, in general the term is synonymous with non-prescription status and far less regulation than prescription drugs. OTC drugs are also sometimes referred to as "proprietary" drugs when they are protected against free competition by trademark, brand name, or any other means. It is far less common, although not unheard of, to refer to prescription drugs as "proprietary" when they are protected against free competition, usually by patent.

Drugs that are sold as prescription-only in some countries are sold as OTC in other countries. For example, prescription-only pharmaceuticals in the United States are sold without a prescription in Mexico. Denmark is another example where prescription pharmaceuticals elsewhere are sold as OTC. Furthermore, in some countries, such as Greece, it is illegal to sell any medicine without a prescription. So, while it is indeed possible, and useful, to generalize about the worldwide OTC market, caution should be exercised when applying such generalities to specific country-markets.

Another problem is that the distribution of OTC products differs from country to country. For example, in the United States, which is the largest market for OTC drugs in the world, OTC drugs are widely distributed through a variety of retail outlets, including pharmacies, drug stores, food stores, mass merchandise, and combination stores. It is possible to purchase such medications almost anywhere in the United States, including gasoline stations. However, in Germany, where pharmacists have a powerful trade association, OTC drugs are sold exclusively in pharmacies.

TABLE 17-5 PATENT EXPIRATION DATES
GLOBAL SALES 2000 – 2001 (IN *MILLIONS* $USD)

Expiration Date	Brand Name	Sales	Manufacturer	Therapeutic Category
Pre-2002	Premarin	2,074	Wyeth	Estrogen
	Prozac	1,990	Lilly	Antidepressant
	Allegra	1,577	Aventis	Antihistaminic
	Taxol	1,197	Bristol-Myers Squibb	Antineoplastic
	Neoral	1,084	Novartis	Immunosuppressant
	Humulin	1,061	Lilly	Antidiabetic
	Vasotec	1,050	Merck	Antihypertensive
2002	Prilosec	5,684	AstraZeneca	Antiulcerative
	Claritin	3,267	Schering-Plough	Antihistaminic
	Glucophage	2,682	Bristol-Myers Squibb	Antidiabetic
	Augmentin	2,047	GlaxoSmithKline	Antibacterial
	Intron	1,447	Schering-Plough	Antiviral/ Antineoplastic
	Prinivil	1,260	Merck	Antihypertensive
	Zestril	1,097	AstraZeneca	Antihypertensive
2003	Cipro	1,758	Bayer	Antibacterial
	Neurontin	1,751	Pfizer	Anticonvulsant
	Plavix	1,350	Sanofi-Synthelabo	Antithrombotic
	Flovent	1,318	GlaxoSmithKline	Antiallergic
	Advair	1,224	GlaxoSmithKline	Antiasthmatic
	Celexa	1,087	Forest	Antidepressant
	Levaquin	1,052	Ortho-McNeil	Antibacterial
	Rocephin	1,006	Roche	Antibacterial
2004	Procrit	3,430	Ortho Biotech	Hematinic
	Epogen	2,108	Amgen	Hematinic
	Lovenox	1,301	Aventis	Antithrombotic
	Diflucan	1,066	Pfizer	Antifungal

TABLE 17-5 PATENT EXPIRATION DATES
GLOBAL SALES 2000 – 2001 (IN *MILLIONS* $USD)

Expiration Date	Brand Name	Sales	Manufacturer	Therapeutic Category
2005	Zocor	6,670	Merck	Antihyperlipidemic
	Prevacid	2,951	TAP	Antiulcerative
	Zoloft	2,366	Pfizer	Antidepressant
	Novolin	1,829	Novo Nordisk	Antidiabetic
	Zithromax	1,506	Pfizer	Antibacterial
	Biaxin	1,159	Abbott	Antibacterial
2006	Norvasc	3,582	Pfizer	Antihypertensive
	Paxil	2,674	GlaxoSmithKline	Antidepressant
	Pravachol	2,173	Bristol-Myers Squibb	Antihyperlipidemic
	Melavotin	1,621		
	Oxycontin	1,486	Purdue	Analgesic (narcotic)
	Neupogen	1,364	Amgen	Hematopoietic Stimulant
	Imigran	1,092	GlaxoSmithKline	Antimigraine
2007	Risperdal	1,845	Janssen	Antipsychotic
	Fosamax	1,760	Merck	Bone Resorption Inhibitor
	Effexor	1,542	Wyeth	Antidepressant
TOTAL		81,588		

DIETARY SUPPLEMENTS

Table 17-6 presents the most popular dietary supplements in the United States.

TABLE 17-6 POPULAR DIETARY SUPPLEMENTS		
Acidophilus	Fish Oils	Oat Bran
Bee Pollen	5-HTP	Periwinkle Extract
Benecol	Flavonoids	Phenylalanine
Beta-Carotene/	Glocomannan	Phosphatidylserine
Carotenoids	Glucosamine Sulfate	Phytoestrogens
Beta Glucan	Glutamine	Psyllium
Brewer's Yeast	Grape Seed Extract	Pyncnogenol
Bromelain	Green Tea	Red Rice Yeast
Caffein	Kelp	(Cholestin)
Carnitine	Kombucha	SAM
Chlorophyll	Mushrooms	Shark Cartilage
Choline	L-Arginine	Soy Products
Chondroitin Sulfate	Lechithin	Spirulina
Coenzyme Q10	Lipoic Acid	
Creatine	Melatonin	
DHEA	Mushroom Extract	
DMSO and MSM		
Essential Fatty Acids		

Botanical Medicines

Table 17-7 presents the most popular medicinal botanicals in the United States.

TABLE 17-7 POPULAR MEDICINAL BOTANICALS		
Agrimony	Chaste Berry	Rosemary
Alfalfa	Chinese Cucumber	Sage
Aloe Vera	Cinnamon/Cassia	St. John's Wort
Anise and Star Anise	Cleavers	Saw Palmetto
Ashwagandha	Cloves	Seneca Root
Astragalus	Comfrey	Senna
Barberry	Coriander	Slippery Elm
Barley	Cramp Bark	Lemon Balm
Basil	Devil's Claw	Licorice
Bilberry	Dill	Marijuana
Blackberry	Dong Quai	Marshmallow
Black Cohosh	Echinacea	Milk Thistle
Black Currant	Elder	Mint/Peppermint
Black Haw	Eucalyptus	Mullein
Bloodroot	Evening Primrose	Mustard
Boneset	Fennel	Myrrh
Borage	Fenugreek	Nettle
Boswellia	Feverfew	Oak
Broom	Flax	Poppy
Bugleweed	Garlic	Red Clover
Burdock	Ginger	Red Raspberry
Butcher's Broom	Ginkgo	Rose
Calendula	Ginseng	Tea Tree
Camphor	Goldenseal	Thyme
Caraway	Gotu Kola	Tumeric
Cardamom	Guarana	Uva Ursi
Cascara Sagrada	Guggul	Valerian

Dangerous Botanicals

Table 17-8 presents a list of dangerous botanicals.

TABLE 17-8 DANGEROUS BOTANICALS	
Angelica	Mayapple
Bayberry	Mistletoe
Blue Cohosh	Pau d'arco
Calamus	Pennyroyal
Chaparral	Pokeweed
Clematis	Rue
Deadly	Sassafras
Nightshade	Tansy
Ephedra	Wormwood
Foxglove	Yohimbe
Germander	
Lobelia	

THE HISTORICAL CONTEXT

Indeed, we might even consider in a new light the power of the psyche to heal in the absence of an effective ointment, or the doshas of Ayurvedic medicine, or the Orbs, yin and yang of Chinese traditional medicine, for that matter. In the final analysis, these are all as much a matter of belief as they are a matter of empiricism; and the stubbornness with which beliefs come and go is the stuff of legend.

CHRONOLOGY OF KEY DATES

TABLE 18-1 CHRONOLOGY OF KEY DATES	
3500 B.C.	Earliest known use of bronze (Sumer, Mesopotamia).
3000 B.C.	Unification of the upper and lower valleys of the River Nile in Egypt.
2500 B.C.	Minerals containing iron oxide are being smelted, or reduced by charcoal in the Middle East.
2000 B.C.	Chinese had begun to manufacture bronze,
1800 B.C.	The Babylonian King Hammurabi's Great Code of Laws is written.
1200 B.C.	The Trojan War between Greece and Troy
450 B.C.	The Laws of the Twelve Tables are erected in the Roman forum.
460–377 B.C.	Life of Hippocrates

TABLE 18-1 CHRONOLOGY OF KEY DATES

431–404 B.C.	The Peloponnesian wars between Athens and Sparta.
427–347 B.C.	Life of Plato
384–322 B.C.	Life of Aristotle
371–287 B.C.	Life of Theophrastus
356–323 B.C.	Life of Alexander the Great
106–43 B.C.	Life of Cicero
B.C.–A.D.	Life of Jesus Christ
40 90 A.D.	Life of Dioscorides
A.D. 129–216	Life of Galen
A.D. 315	Emperor Constantine grants Christians freedom of worship within the Roman Empire.
476 A.D.	Fall of Rome to the Visigoths
A.D. 570–632	Life of Muhammad
A.D. 865–925	Life of Al-Razi (Rhazes) of Baghdad
End of the 1st Millennium	
1066	Norman invasion of Britain
1096–1099	First Crusade.
Beginning of the 12th Century	
1147–1149	Second Crusade
1189–1192	Third Crusade
Beginning of the 13th Century	
1202–1204	Fourth Crusade
1217–1221	Fifth Crusade
1228–1229	Sixth Crusade
1248–1254	Seventh Crusade
1270–1271	Eighth (Final) Crusade
Beginning of the 14th Century	
1346–1351	The Black Death (bubonic plague)
1349	Founding of Prague University, jurisdiction of the Hapsburg Emperor

TABLE 18-1 CHRONOLOGY OF KEY DATES

1365	Founding of Vienna University, jurisdiction of the Hapsburg Emperor
1386	Founding of Heidelberg University, jurisdiction of the Town Council
1388	Founding of Cologne University, jurisdiction of the Town Council
1392	Founding of Erfurt University, jurisdiction of the Elector of Mainz
Beginning of the 15th Century	
1409	Founding of Leipzig University, jurisdiction of the Elector of Saxony
1459	Founding of Basel University, jurisdiction of the Canton of Basel
1477	Founding of Mainz University, jurisdiction of the Elector of Mainz
1483–1546	Life of Martin Luther
1492	Christopher Columbus discovers the New World for Spain
1493–1554	Life of Paracelsus (Philippus von Hohenheim)
Beginning of the 16th Century	
1503	Founding of Wittenberg University, jurisdiction of the Elector of Saxony
Start of the Protestant Reformation	
1517	Martin Luther posts his Ninety-Five Theses on the Wittenberg church door. Beginning of the Protestant Reformation
1521	Edict of Worms
1530	Augsburg Confession
1534	English Parliament passes the Act of Supremacy.

TABLE 18-1 CHRONOLOGY OF KEY DATES

1536	Lutheranism becomes the state religion of Denmark.
1544	Founding of Konigsberg University, jurisdiction of the Elector of Brandenburg
1555	Peace of Augsburg
1609	First separate chemistry department created at the University of Marburg in Prussia
1643–1715	Reign of Louis XIV "The Sun King" (72 years, longest in history)
1648	Peace of Westphalia
1692	Louis XIV establishes the Manufactures Royals at Saint-Gobain (glass factory).
1733–1804	Life of Joseph Priestly
1736	Joshua Ward in Britain develops a cheap method of making sulfuric acid.
1743–1794	Life of Antoine Laurent Lavoisier
1754	Joseph Black chemically identifies carbon dioxide for the first time.
1766	Henry Cavendish discovers hydrogen.
1766	John Holker establishes first sulfuric acid plant in France at Rouen.
1766–1844	Life of John Dalton
1769	Lavoisier is admitted to the French Academy of Sciences at the age of 25.
1771–1834	Life of Irenee du Pont de Nemours
1774	Joseph Priestly discovers "dephlogisticated air" (vital air).
1776	The American Revolution
1776–1856	Life of Amedeo Avogadro
1778–1850	Life of Joseph Louis Gay-Lussac

TABLE 18-1 CHRONOLOGY OF KEY DATES

1779–1848	Life of Jons Jakob Berzelius
1789	Lavoisier publishes his **Traite Elementaire de Chimie**.
1789	The French Revolution
1791–1867	Life of Michael Faraday
1794	Convention Nationale in Paris establishes the Ecole Polytechnique.
1797	Scotsman Charles Tennant patents new process for calcium hypochlorite and builds a plant at Saint Rollox near Glasgow; adds sulfuric acid and chlorine plants.
1800	Alessandro Volta invents the electric pile.
1803–1873	Life of Justus Von Liebig
1804	Alexander Von Homboldt brings guano to Europe from islands off Peru.
1807	Humphry Davy isolates sodium and potassium through electrolysis.
1811	France is producing 20,000 tons of sulfuric acid, 10-15,000 tons of Sodium Carbonate, and 600 tons of hydrochloric acid annually.
1813	Michael Faraday becomes Humphry Davy's assistant at London's Royal Institution.
1816	William Losh establishes the first LeBlanc soda plant in Britain at Tyneside.
1822	James Muspratt establishes a LeBlanc soda plant in Liverpool.
1822–1895	Life of Louis Pasteur
1830	French merchants establish a monopoly over Sicilian Sulfur, double its price.
1840	Britain had begun importing guano.

TABLE 18-1 CHRONOLOGY OF KEY DATES	
1840	First LeBlanc soda plant in Germany is established.
1840	Most of Britain's sulfur is coming from iron and copper pyrites.
1852	France is producing 45,000 tons of soda; Britain is producing 140,000 tons.
1856	Discovery of potash at Strassfurt salt deposits in Saxony
1856	W.H. Perkin discovers mauve.
1863	Parliament passes the British Alkalai Act requiring manufacturers to absorb gaseous hydrochloric acid in towers designed by William Gossage in 1836.
1870–1871	Franco-Prussian War
1874–1940	Life of Carl Bosch
1875	Peruvian guano is exhausted and replaced by Chilean saltpeter (sodium nitrate).
1888	Founding of the Institut Pasteur in Paris.

EUROPEAN HISTORY

THE BIG PICTURE

Western Europe has a long and complex history, which begins for most intents and purposes with the formation of the Roman State sometime between about 450 B.C., and its conquest and dominion of Europe for approximately 500 years, until it finally collapsed in 476 A.D. Prior to the rise of the Roman State, various peoples had lived throughout Europe in relatively large numbers for a very long time.

Their histories are obscure, however, relative to those written records of the Roman Republican era (450 B.C.–27 B.C) and those of the era of the Roman Empire (27 B.C.–476 A.D).

Rome unified and ruled Western Europe under a common legal system that was perhaps its greatest contribution to Western history and culture, and while Roman law was based on a series of rather straightforward precepts known as the Laws of the Twelve Tables (which are still studied today), the subsequent body of recorded Roman jurisprudence grew to be large and specialized in many areas of Roman life and foreign transactions. Therefore, a very significant collection of the corpus of Roman Law, including numerous specific cases and judgments, and in some cases their attached explanations and opposing opinions by contemporary judicial scholars, was assembled and then codified by the Byzantine Emperor Justinian when he briefly occupied the region of the Western Empire in the sixth century A.D. But when his army was soon thereafter defeated, and driven back eastward, out of Western Europe, knowledge of his code went with him.

While many aspects of the Roman economy, culture, political and social structure disintegrated throughout Europe as a result of the collapse of the central government, other areas of Roman influence remained quite strong, the influence of the Roman Catholic church and codification of Roman Law being perhaps the most important, although large-scale examples of Roman engineering, architecture, roads, and aqueducts also survive.

In about A.D. 300, the Emperor Constantine mandated that Catholicism would become the official religion of the Roman Empire. This situation did not change in any significant manner until the advent of Martin Luther, John Calvin, etc., and the Protestant Revolution more than 1,000 years later.

THE HOLY ROMAN EMPIRE

In the intervening period, perhaps the most significant event in Europe to follow the fall of Rome in A.D. 476 was the rather unexpected crowning of the Frankish (German) king, Charlemagne, on Christmas day, A.D. 800, as emperor of what has come to be known as the Holy Roman Empire. The creation of the Holy Roman Empire, which covered practically all of Western Europe, greatly expanded and consolidated the power of the Roman church.

Perhaps the second-most important event in those intervening years was not the Crusades themselves, but the acquisition and dissemination of the entire body of old Roman Imperial Law (the Justinian Code) throughout Western Europe during the Crusades. NOTE: The law imposed on Europe by Napoleon, known as the Napoleonic Code is largely based on the Code of Justinian.

Without doubt, the third most important event was the Protestant Reformation, the religious wars that followed, and the persecution of the French Huguenots, especially their complete expulsion from France by Louis IV who, at the same time, consolidated French rule over what was once Upper Lotharingia, and is today better known as Alsace-Lorraine, including the all-important potassium mines located there, as well as the city of Strasbourg, now the capital city of the institutions of the European Union.

Nevertheless, Charlemagne divided his empire into three parts from west to east, what we might think of as France, Lotharingia, and

Germany. Lotharingia consisted of northern Italy (Lombardy), French Provence, Burgundy, and a wide strip across Champagne to the North Sea beyond Aix-la-Chapelle including the stronghold of Verdun. It generally followed the line of the Rhone, Saone, Meuse, and Scheldt Rivers as its eastern boundary. It included parts of Switzerland, the full length of the Rhine River, and all of the BENELUX, or "low countries" in the north. Most importantly, it included the region known as Alsace-Lorraine.

After Charlemagne's death, two of his heirs, Charles the Bald (France) and Louis the German, conspired in an agreement in A.D. 842 at Strasbourg, to make war on the third heir, Lothair, who ruled the land between them. This is the oldest known document in the forerunner of the French language. The agreement was modified somewhat by a majority of the Frankish nobility and ratified the following year as the Treaty of Verdun in August of 843 A.D. As a result, France came into existence in its initial form, and the Holy Roman Empire consisted of everything east of the Rhine including Germany, Switzerland, Austria, Hungary, and Italy, etc. Lotharingia remained the heart of the Carolingian Empire. In 870 A.D. by the Mersen Accord, Charles the Bald and Louis the German divided Lotharingia between them. Germany (the Holy Roman Empire) took control of Alsace Lorraine and kept it for the next 800 years.

There have been many Holy Roman Emperors since the time of Charlemagne. In fact, at the time of the Napoleonic Wars, which began soon after the French Revolution in 1789 and lasted until his final defeat at Waterloo in 1815, the supreme rulers of Germany, if one can properly refer to it as anything resembling "Germany" at that time, were a group of hereditary nobles known as "electors" who held the right to vote in the election of the Emperors. In fact,

Frederick the Great of Prussia, who was largely responsible for the creation, organization, and training of the Prussian Army, leading to the eventual unification of the German Empire under Prussian leadership and the humiliating defeat of France, was also sometimes referred to as the "Great Elector" for this reason.

FOREST DEVASTATION

Although individual methods probably varied widely, noted expert, Nils Anderson, Jr., cites an historical reference that he considers credible stating that thirty-five to forty cords of wood were required to make one thousand bushels of charcoal and roughly six thousand bushels of charcoal were required to make a single ton of iron.

It almost defies belief, but in Britain they had so decimated their forests by the time of Elizabeth in the 1600s that, even though it seriously jeopardized their industrial base and sea power, laws were passed regulating the taking of wood for charcoal production. Furthermore, the first official British government body established in America, the Council of Virginia, decreed that clearing forests and smelting pig iron for shipment back to British factories would be the first tasks of the colonists.

THE IRISH IRON REVOLT

When the British began taking Irish timber in trade for the purpose of making charcoal to smelt iron, the Irish people revolted. This is what is referred to as the Iron Revolt of 1641. The revolt put a stop to the trade of Irish timber with Britain. By about this time, the timber resources of Germany, Sweden, and other countries had been similarly wiped out. The moment had finally arrived to think about alternatives. Fortunately, for Britain and Germany in particular, there were vast deposits of coal lying beneath their soil, and the application of charcoal technology to coking was for the first time being seriously considered by remarkably imaginative individuals.

THE CONVERSION TO COAL

Although coal was known to ancient civilizations, definitely to the Romans, it was reported that when coal gas was first suggested as a fuel to illuminate the streets of London at night, Sir Walter Raleigh exclaimed that some fool was proposing to light the city with soot! The volatile portion of coal is much different from the volatile portion of wood, and, when burned openly results in dense smog. Coal burning for heat in London resulted in so large a pollution problem that its use also had to be regulated. Wood remained the preferred fuel for heat and charcoal for many years. Master metallurgists continued to claim that charcoal produced a higher grade metal than coke long after the American Revolution. A particular problem was the amount of sulfur that is contained in most forms of coal and not in wood.

Aside from this important relationship between metallurgy and the discovery of coal tar as a feedstock for organic synthesis, iron in its own right, as well as other metals, has long been used as a medicine. Hundreds of years ago, the Hindus of India would grind up roasted sheets of iron into a fine white powder that was mixed with milk and swallowed as a cure for anemia. Mercury has long been used in medicines such as Mercurochrome and diuretic preparations used to treat kidney disease.

BONAPARTE AND THE NEW MAP OF EUROPE

Napoleon Bonaparte finally dissolved the last vestiges of the Holy Roman Empire following his conquest of Europe, and replaced it in Germany with a loose confederation of much larger, but far less numerous independent German states that soon came to be dominated by Prussian military power. Prussia began to reassert itself following Napoleon's defeat in Russia in 1813, and delivered the final crushing blow against him after he had already committed his reserves (the infamous "Old Guard") in the late afternoon at Waterloo when von Blucher unexpectedly (for Napoleon) emerged from the forest and onto the field of battle with the entire Prussian cavalry behind him. What had been a combined French Army of over 400,000 men prior to their invasion of Russia, was now completely and utterly decimated by British troops under Lord Wellington, who had been on the field all day, and the Prussian cavalry under the old and wise von Blucher, who had waited for what must have seemed an eternity to the British for Napoleon to finally commit his Old Guard in what the French Emperor must have seen as a crushing blow for the British. Even today, von Blucher's resolve in waiting for his opponent to expend all of his resources, before expending any of his own, is considered the ultimate manifestation of a characteristic German mindset to wait patiently for an opportunity to present itself, and then only to make moderate risk investments with long-term, strategic significance.

Napoleon had consolidated French control of the Alsace-Lorraine region and it was not returned to Germany following the final defeat of the French at Waterloo. Alsace-Lorraine was, however, re-taken by Germany in 1871 during the Franco-Prussian War, and was not returned to France until 1918, by the Allies at the end of World War

I. So important is this middle region between the two countries to the national consciousness of France, that if you are ever in Paris, directly under the center arch of the enormous Arc De Triomph is a very prominent, large brass plate, which celebrates 1918 not as the end of World War I, but as the date of the return of Alsace-Lorraine (and its potassium mines) to France.

GERMAN HISTORY

At the time, when the Germans were preparing their onslaught for dominance over the world's dyestuffs trade, Germany existed as a loose confederation of 39 independent states that had been somewhat on-again, off-again for many years. Four of these states were self-governing city-states. The other 35 states were still ruled by kings or princes, with their own individual flags, armies, laws and taxes. The legal environment of Germany in this era has been called a "patent jungle," which only served to facilitate the rapid growth of the larger chemical companies.

THE FRANCO-PRUSSIAN WAR

During the 1860s, France had become alarmed over the growing power of Prussia, and following a dispute over the claim of the Royal House of Prussia (Hohenzollern) to the throne of Spain, the French foolishly declared war in 1870. The German States were immediately galvanized by their resentment of the French and all of the German states joined together with Prussia to defeat France. The combined German armies surrounded the city of Paris in 1871, and then, in the palace of Louis XIV at Versailles, crowned Wilhelm, King of Prussia, as Kaiser of the new (unified) German empire.

The Franco-Prussian War ended with the Treaty of Frankfurt, which stipulated that France would give back Alsace-Lorraine to Germany, pay Germany one billion francs, and support the German army in France until this sum was paid, which (amazingly) turned out to be only three years later. Although the government of France was completely bankrupt at the end of the Franco-Prussian War, it was able to borrow enough money from the people of France, once they had deposed their emperor, to pay off the Germans much earlier than the Germans had anticipated.

GERMAN UNIFICATION

German unification occurred in 1871 under Prussian leadership from Berlin, and the Reich established a strict imperial patent law in 1877. Thus, as the major German dyestuffs companies, all located within or near to the Prussian district, began to discover the medicinal properties of the various compounds they produced (beginning in about 1885), their discoveries were protected by patent legislation enforceable throughout Germany. By the time of World War I (1914–1918) Bayer alone held over 8,000 patents for dyestuffs, drugs, and other chemicals, including the first patent for synthetic rubber. German chemical companies and their foreign subsidiaries produced 140,000 tons of dyestuffs per year on the eve of the First World War, out of a total worldwide production of 160,000 tons. They had come to completely dominate the worldwide market for synthetic organic compounds. However, at the end of World War I, and again at the end of World War II, the victorious Allied Powers (the United

States, England, etc.) took possession of all German patents and used them to grow their own domestic industries.

It must be realized that the period of time surrounding Perkin's discovery of mauve was an era of intense nationalism, particularly in Germany leading to unification. This widespread feeling of national supremacy led directly to two world wars in the first half of the twentieth century. The formation and activities of international chemical and pharmaceutical giants like I.G. Farben (formed from AGFA, Bayer, BASF, Hoechst, etc.) and ICI (formed from British Dyestuffs, Brunner Mond, United Alkalai, etc.), which significantly influenced development of the world's pharmaceutical industry in the twentieth century, cannot be fully understood without comprehending this sense of nationalism that had spread throughout Europe, especially following the French Revolution in 1789 and the rise to power of Napoleon Bonaparte.

The French had dominated Europe for many years. The Alsace-Lorraine region that lies to the west of the Rhine River (between the Rhineland-Westphalia region of Germany and Basel, Switzerland) had remained under German rule for approximately 800 years (since the time of the Franks, Charlemagne, and the creation of the Holy Roman Empire). Then France had slowly gained control of it in the 1600s.

Besides being a center of textile manufacturing, Alsace-Lorraine was as rich in potash (Alsace) and iron ore (Lorraine) as the Ruhr Valley was in coal. Even though the Rhineland-Westphalia region was returned to Germany (specifically to Prussia) in 1815 by the treaty of the Congress of Vienna, which ended the Napoleonic period, Alsace-Lorraine remained a part of France. In addition to their historical animosities, the dispute over Alsace-Lorraine served as a focal point for German-French hostilities well into the twentieth century.

Otto von Bismarck became prime minister of Prussia in 1862 and continued Prussia's policy of promoting the interests of the growing class of German industrialists. Prussia had formed a Customs Union (Zollverein) with many other German states in the 1830s, whereby they reduced or eliminated tariffs on the goods they traded among themselves; and even though member states could continue to grant patents, after 1842 they could not prevent the sale of products in their own states that were produced in other member states, thus making the grant of patent somewhat ridiculous. These policies had helped to unite Germany economically in the period between 1830 and 1860.

JAPANESE HISTORY

Marco Polo heard stories of Japan when he visited China in the thirteenth century. When Christopher Columbus sailed from Europe in 1492 on his historic voyage, it was in hopes of reaching either the East Indies or Japan, not the New World. The Portuguese were the first Europeans to reach Japan in 1543. This was during the period that had begun in the twelfth century when powerful shoguns ruled Japan in the name of the emperor. The emperors of Japan reigned from the imperial court in Kyoto but had lost all real power to feuding daimyo or large estate holders in about the ninth century. Shortly after the arrival of the Portuguese, the Tokugawa shogunate began and lasted until the Meiji restoration of the emperor in 1867 when the daimyo forced the shogun to resign. The Meiji period began just thirteen years after an American fleet of warships under Admiral Mathew Perry sailed into Tokyo Bay and forced a series of extensive treaties with the Tokugawa government.

A BRIEF HISTORY OF MEDICINE

Acetylsalicylic Acid $c_9h_8o_4$ "Bayer Aspirin"	Sulfanilamide $c_6h_8n_2o_2s$ First of the "Sulfa" Drugs
FIGURE 19-1 EARLY SYNTHETIC MOLECULES	

FROM SUMER TO HIPPOCRATES

OPIUM

Opium was probably the first drug ever discovered. Because it is naturally occurring, its use most likely predates alcohol, which requires fermentation. The preserved remains of poppy seeds, pods, and other materials indicating cultivation, have been found in Neolithic archaeological sites dating from the fourth millennium B.C. in Switzerland. Scholars believe that the secret of opium began in the region of the Balkans or else near the Black Sea, spreading south and west from there (Booth 1996). However, because written records survive only from about 4000 B.C. at best, and even so, the earliest Sumerian forms of writing (which predate cuneiform), as well as earliest Egyptian hieroglyphics (circa 3000 B.C.) were relatively simple, having at most a few hundred word signs at the height of their development. It was not until the Chinese developed a form of writing with as many as 50,000 word signs (circa 1500 B.C.) that we are given very descriptive records of ancient medicine.

FROM HIPPOCRATES TO GALEN

Theophrastus (371–287 B.C.), a student of Aristotle's (384–322 B.C.), laid the groundwork for medicinal botany, using Aristotle's work on animals as a template. Aristotle had been a student of Plato's (428–347 B.C.), and later questioned his teacher's somewhat transcendental ideas, which were based upon the notion that some things can only be known by the intellect, not by the senses; and thereby, that the empirical world, or the world of objectivity, scientific hypotheses, and careful experimentation is, at least to some extent, deceptive. Whereas Plato did not fully trust his senses, Aristotle trusted them at the expense of all else, and provided a method of scientific inquiry that lasted for nearly 2000 years. Aristotle was hired by King Philip of Macedonia as a tutor for his young son Alexander.

ALEXANDER THE GREAT AND IMPLICATIONS FOR MEDICINE

Alexander the Great (356–323 B.C.), inherited his father's well-disciplined and large army, and proved to be one of the greatest military leaders of all time in his own right by conquering virtually the whole of the known world at that time. Alexander's conquests resulted in vast new information flowing into Greece from Persia and India. In particular, there was an enormous increase in knowledge about new animals, plants, minerals, and drugs. Theophrastus classified over 550 different species of plants, trees, shrubs, and herbs, with habitats ranging from the Atlantic to India. His work was rediscovered during the Renaissance and led to a huge revival in medical botany and botanical gardens (Porter 1999).

Alexander the Great placed the whole of Persia and Egypt under Hellenistic influence. He placed the first of the Ptolemys on the throne of Egypt. (The last of the Ptolemys was Cleopatra.) King Ptolemy I built the great library of Alexandria, which was said to contain over 700,000 manuscripts, most resulting from the campaigns of Alexander. Many great physicians and teachers of the ancient world thus came to Alexandria to study and teach because of the great library. The library was partially destroyed when Julius Caesar captured the city for the Roman Empire in 48 B.C. And its final destruction came during the Muslim conquest in the A.D. seventh century. Its destruction was a tremendous loss for humankind.

Dioscorides (A.D. 40–90) was a Greek surgeon to the Roman Emperor Nero's army. He wrote a five-volume work known in Latin as *De Materia Medica*, which deals with aromatics, like saffron, oils, salves, shrubs and trees, animals, cereals and herbs, roots, juices, herbs and seeds, wines and minerals, including salts of lead and copper (Porter 1999).

Notwithstanding these enormous contributions by Theophrastus and Dioscorides and others, however, there is no doubt that the greatest name in Roman medicine was Claudius Galen (A.D. 129–216), who founded a system of medicine that was followed for the next 1500 years, until the Renaissance and Reformation when it was questioned by Vesalius and Paracelsus.

FROM GALEN TO RHAZES AND AVICENNA

During the age of Justinian (A.D. 524–565), there began an outbreak of bubonic plague in A.D. 541 that lasted, in a series of outbreaks, for nearly two centuries. These outbreaks of the plague had a significant impact on Greek culture, travel, and the cross-cultural exchange of ideas.

RISE OF ISLAM AND IMPLICATIONS FOR MEDICINE

Arabic scholars were probably the first to translate the ancient Sumerian texts.[17] The lands conquered by Arab-Islamic warriors, during the century following the life of Muhammad (A.D. 570–632), were filled with a wide variety of new medicines, derived from plants, minerals, and animals. In this respect, new knowledge acquired during the rapid spread of Islam was similar to that obtained during the conquests of Alexander the Great, almost a thousand years earlier. By the middle of the eighth century, the adherents of Islam had conquered Arabia and the Middle East, Byzantine Asia

---

[17] The Sumerian language disappeared as Semites, probably from the Arabian Peninsula gained control of Sumer about 2500 B.C. Its disappearance is analogous to the disappearance of the ancient Hattic, Hurrian, and Elamite languages of modern day Turkey following the invasion and conquest of Asia Minor by the Hittites near the end of the Bronze Age (Mallory, p. 147). Today, Arabic and Hebrew are the only surviving Semitic languages.

and Persia, Egypt, North Africa, and major portions of Spain. The remnants of subsequent centuries of Islamic rule can still be seen in the Spanish cities of Cordova, Granada (*the Alhambra*), and Seville.

Two great Islamic physicians of the period were 1) Muhammad ibn Zakariya al-Razi (A.D. 865–925), who has come to be known simply as **Rhazes** in the West; and 2) Abu al-Husayn ibn 'Abdallah ibn Sina (A.D. 980–1037), who is known in the West as **Avicenna**.

FROM RHAZES & AVICENNA TO PARACELSUS

The period from the great physicians of Islam to the period of the rather incredible Paracelsus began at about the time of the first of the Christian Crusades to conquer the Holy Land, and ended at about the time that the Protestant Reformation was changing the face of Christianity forever. At the beginning of this period, there is no question that the Islamic World was far ahead of the West in its knowledge of medicine. This began to change during the period of the Great Crusades, but it was a slow process that occurred over hundreds of years.

Paracelsus (1493–1542) lived during the period that began the Protestant Reformation in Europe. His real name was von Hohenheim, but he took the name Paracelsus when he was in his thirties and this is the name by which he is known today because, in short, Paracelsus turned the world of medicine upside down. He was born in the year following the discovery of the New World by Christopher Columbus in 1492 and the development of social relations between two human populations that had been isolated from each other for thousands of years. The Europeans brought diseases with them that proved devastating to the natives.

The first epidemic, swine influenza, broke out in the very year of Paracelsus's birth, carried by pigs aboard Spanish ships, that severely reduced the native population of Hispaniola. Then, smallpox reached Hispaniola in 1518, killing approximately one-half of the remaining population and spreading rapidly from there to Cuba and Puerto Rico. Both Hernando Cortéz, the conqueror of Mexico, and Francisco Pizarro, the conqueror of Peru, were preceded by enormous epidemics of smallpox contracted by the natives outside the cities of Tenochtitlan in 1521, and Cuzco in 1533, respectively. Approximately one-half of the Aztec population of Tenochtitlan, including their chief, Montezuma, and his immediate successor had already died of smallpox before the city fell to Cortez.

Although a few of the Spanish conquistadors became ill, none of them died of the disease. Additional diseases brought by the Europeans exterminated vast numbers of other Native Americans: Measles attacked Santa Domingo in 1519, Guatemala in 1523, and Mexico and Honduras in 1531. These were followed by repeated epidemics of influenza and typhus, which by 1600 had killed over two million Mexican highlanders and, in total, over 90% of the indigenous population had been eradicated by the successive waves of disease. As early as 1520, the Spaniards were forced to import slaves from Africa to replace the lost, local supply of labor. The Africans, in turn, brought with them malaria and yellow fever.

Some of the men who had sailed with Columbus returned soon to Europe and were present at the siege of Naples when it fell to the French in 1494. These men had brought the venereal disease syphilis back with them from the New World and through sexual relations with women of the port of Naples, the disease lay waiting for the usual orgy of sexual intercourse and rape indulged by the conquering

French. Thus, the disease spread like wildfire throughout Europe, Russia, Siberia, Turkey, India, China, and Japan.

SYPHILIS

Although the precise epidemiology of syphilis in the great epidemic that followed is still not well understood, it should clearly be regarded as typical of new diseases and plagues that can arise in an era of social turbulence, such as an age of conquest, or international warfare, but also rising population densities within cities and industrial areas (not just port cities, although these do tend toward the worst case scenario), migrations of either enlisted or discharged military personnel, movements of merchants and traders, the widespread ebb and flow of refugees and peasants, or wholesale immigration in general—all of which tend to be accompanied by changed lifestyles and sexual behavior (Porter 1999).

During the early life of Paracelsus, there was no known treatment for syphilis; in fact no effective cure was developed until Nobel Prize winner Paul Ehrlich (1854–1915), who worked for Hoechst A.G., discovered that an arsenobenzene compound (marketed as Salvarsan) was not only effective against the trypanosomes of sleeping sickness (similar to atoxyl, another organic derivative of arsenic, which A. Béchamp had synthesized in 1863), but also against syphilis. Today, penicillin is usually the drug of choice against most forms and stages of syphilis. Erythromycin, tetracycline, and other antibiotics are also used. But what is amazing about Paracelsus is that he was the first physician to break with the almost 1400-year domination of medical thought, up until that time, by the remarkable, very prolific writings of an Imperial Roman physician (to both emperors and gladiators) named Claudius Galen (A.D. 129–216).

Paracelsus boldly employed synthetic inorganic compounds, salts, metals, and minerals in the treatment of disease, rather than the plant extracts used since ancient times. The classical view of Galen, staunchly defended by the Parisian school of medicine, was the use of medications with properties contrary to the disease. Paracelsus argued vehemently for treatments by similitude (i.e., fight poison with poison). In fact, the question of whether **antimony**, which was one of the ten elements known to the ancients (see table 19-1), was a medicine or a poison was argued for centuries until it was used as an emetic to effectively cure the French Sun King himself, Louis XIV, in 1658.

TABLE 19-1 THE 10 "ANCIENT" ELEMENTS

Number/Date	Element/ Symbol	Amount In Body	Medicinal Uses Past and Present
1. Prehistory	Carbon/C	16 kg.	Most essential element to life. Isotope C-11 is used in Positron Emission Topography (PET).
2. Prehistory	Sulfur/S	140 g.	Laxative, acne, scabies, Sulfa drugs, Penicillin, Vitamin B1, Metalloproteins.
3. Prehistory	Copper/Cu	70 mg.	Wilson's Disease, Menke's Disease. Eye diseases, anti-ulcers, anti-inflammatories, and anti-cancers.
4. c.5000 B.C.	Silver/Ag	2 mg.	Warts, Anti-microbial, Antibiotic, Anti-viral, Burn treatment.
5. c.5000 B.C.	Gold/Au	0.2 mg.	Rheumatoid arthritis Gold-198 is an Anti-cancer drug. Dentistry.
6. c.2500 B.C.	Iron/Fe	4 g.	Laxative, Anaemia, Anti-biotic, Constituent of hemoglobin, DNA synthesis, Mental development.

7. c.2100 B.C.	Tin/Sn	30 mg.	Treatment of some staphylococcal skin infections.
8. c.1600 B.C.	Antimony/Sb	2 mg.	Diaphoretic; Treatment of burns, Induces vomiting; Induces sweating.
9. c.1500 B.C.	Mercury/Mg	6 mg.	Calomel, syphilis, laxative, diuretic, disinfectant, skin treatments, induces salivation
10. c. 1000 B.C.	Lead/Pb	120 mg.	Skin treatments, Induces abortion, Deactivates certain enzymes. Shield from X-rays.

It is worth noting that modern anticancer drugs work by poisoning normal cells, but at a slower rate than they poison carcinogenic cells that multiply much more rapidly. Thus, as with the Paracelsian view, the patient is being slowly poisoned, but recovers from the disease before being poisoned to death. On the other hand, the composer Wolfgang Amadeus Mozart, who was fond of dosing himself with antimony tartrate, prescribed by his doctors, died from over poisoning in 1791 at the age of thirty-five. Nevertheless, most modern therapeutic agents are recognized by practitioners as generally toxic at higher doses than what is recommended for medicinal purposes. Paracelsus administered compounds of antimony, arsenic, copper, iron, lead, mercury and sulfur for therapeutic purposes, along with laudanum (tincture of opium) to ease the pain frequently associated with such treatments.

Metals in their own right, and as minerals, are important to the pharmaceutical industry in many ways. Several metals are essential for life, such as iron, which is involved in oxygen and electron transport within biological systems and is an essential component of hemoglobin, cytochrome, and iron-sulfur proteins. Iron deficiency is common in clinical practice throughout the world, as is zinc deficiency, even in industrialized countries. Some metals are essential for animal nutrition in relatively large quantities, i.e., grams per day (such as calcium, magnesium, potassium, sodium, etc.). Other metals are essential in trace amounts, as components of enzymes or hormones necessary for metabolism (e.g., chromium, manganese, selenium, etc.).

All trace metals are toxic at higher levels. Some forms of metal poisoning can be treated with pharmaceutical products that work as chelating agents. At the time of Paracelsus (1493–1542), which marks the beginning of the end of "a millennium of medicine according to Galen," some medicinal chemists were behaving more like metallurgists, foraging mines from Basel to the Carpathians in search of new heavy metals to cure gout, insanity, leprosy, syphilis, typhus, and a host of other maladies. Antimony, bismuth, copper, iron, lead, mercury, silver, and zinc (in addition to others) each has a legitimate use in modern medicine and was promoted, against the conventional wisdom of the early sixteenth century, by Paracelsus and his followers.

Metals, and especially metal alloys, are also important to the pharmaceutical industry as specialty catalysts, particularly in chemical reactions involving biologically selective stereoisomers, enantiomers, and diastereomers. They are also important in medical devices, such as pacemakers and hearing aids, medical and scientific instruments, radiology, radioisotopes, and radiation therapy, magnetic imaging, X-ray crystallography, nuclear magnetic resonance spectroscopy (NMR), transcranial magnetic stimulation (TMS), and positron emission tomography (PET).

Most importantly, however, is the fact that although some metals are among the most abundant elements of the earth's crust (e.g., aluminum, iron, calcium, sodium), only 8 of the known 109 naturally occurring elements exist in the earth's surface in amounts exceeding **1 percent**. All but 0.5 percent of the earth's outer crust, to a depth of approximately 10 kilometers, is made up of the following 13 elements: oxygen, silicon, aluminum, iron, calcium, sodium, potassium, magnesium, titanium, hydrogen, phosphorous, manganese, and fluorine. All of the others, including copper, gold, lead, nickel, platinum, silver, tin, uranium, zinc, and 87 more, comprise, in aggregate, only **one-half of one percent** of the earth's crust.

Furthermore, a large portion exists as mineral species that are not legally permissable, or economically viable at the present time. Economic concentrations are sparsely distributed and rapidly being exhausted. More mineral resources have been consumed since the period just prior to World War II, than in the entire preceding history of the earth. Ownership has resulted not only in innovative medical technology, health care, and sustained industrial development, but commercial and political supremacy.

Of the 30 to 35 minerals considered most important for the continuation of modern society, the United States is self-sufficient in less than 10, strategically deficient in about 20, and completely absent in 5. For example, while the United States (excluding Alaska) has virtually no deposits of tin (as a by-product of molybdenum production, tin is produced in negligible quantities), it is the world's largest consumer, at approximately 30 percent of world tin production. With potential for suspending the aging process, tin forms a superconductive alloy with niobium that is capable of generating (in liquid helium) a magnetic field powerful enough to more than counteract the force of gravity at the earth's surface (Jensen and Bateman 1981, p. 374).

Hank Laskey

TALES FROM THE CRYPT

There is no question that the Protestant Reformation begun by Martin Luther in Wittenberg, Saxony, on October 31, 1517, had an enormous impact on European civilization, far beyond his ideas concerning the authority of the Bible, God's grace, or the practice of selling indulgences. For German-speaking peoples in particular, the influence of Luther has been without equal. Luther's translation of the Bible into the German dialect of the upland east-central mining regions (*Hochdeutsch*) was the first time in history that the modern German language appeared in print. It is to the German people what the Qur'an is to Islam. Far beyond its value as a religious or moral treatise, it is a literary masterpiece, a manifestation of the beauty of the language that raptures and captivates native speakers. No human has surpassed the Arabic of Muhammad, and none have surpassed the German of Luther. In the fullest possible meaning of the word "is," the highest form of the German language today "is" the language of Luther. Goethe and Schiller stood upon his shoulders, as a child stands upon those of his father. "On the wind," as Goethe would say. If German is the language of science, then science was the language of the Reformation. As Luther's German was the language of Saxon mines, so was it the language of Saxon medicine, brought up from those mines.

European medicine before the Reformation was medicine as it had been practiced, at least since the dawn of Christianity, the chiefly naturalistic, herbal and botanical medicine of Claudius Galen (A.D. 129–216) and the four Greek humors: blood, black bile, yellow bile and phlegm. Medicine after the Reformation metamorphosed into the more chemical and inorganic medicine of salts, sulfur and mercury (minerals and metals, both neat and treated with various acids or bases and compounded), i.e., the medicine of Paracelsus (1493–1542), who not only lectured (unconventionally) in German rather than Latin, but put on public spectacles in which he burned the books of both Galen and Avicenna (980–1037), the "Galen of Islam."

FROM PARACELSUS TO PASTEUR

Louis Pasteur (1822–1896) was educated at the École Normal Supérior in Paris. This excellent education, plus his remarkable motivation and skills in the laboratory, allowed him to transform both chemistry and medicine. He is remembered chiefly for his work in fermentation because his studies were chiefly related to French agriculture; but it is really microbiology in general where he made his greatest contributions, and in the germ theory of disease.

The other great chemist/agriculturist of this general period was the incredibly influential Justus von Liebig (1803–1873). The scope and contributions of Liebig's contributions to chemistry can never be minimized. He was an extremely energetic man who traveled widely and did more for the development of chemical education in Germany than anyone else in history. However, Liebig believed that the processes of fermentation and putrefaction were chemical and not biological processes. His enormous stature resulted in a considerable debate on these issues.

FROM PASTEUR TO FLEMING

Development of modern pharmaceuticals, those with a much higher therapeutic value or potency than natural products, i.e., the first synthetics (like acetylsalicylic acid) began gradually in the late nineteenth century in Germany with companies like: (1) Farben Fabrik vormals Friedrich Bayer (a joint-stock company reorganized as such in 1881 after the death of its founder, Friedrich Bayer, who had established the company in Leverkusen in 1863); (2) Farbenwerke Hoechst (similarly restructured in 1880 after being founded as a joint venture between Wilhelm Meister and Adolf Bruning in Frankfurt in 1862); (3) AGFA (Aktien Gesellschaft fur Anilin Fabrikation, established by Carl Martius and Paul M. Bartholdy in Rummelsberg near Berlin in 1873): (4) Kalle & Co. (established by Paul W. Kalle in Biebrich in 1864); and (5) Leopold Cassella & Cie (founded in Mainkur in 1807). There were, to be sure, numerous other small to medium-sized[18] German firms in the development of the German

---

[18]   The role of small to medium-sized businesses in the industrialization of Germany is well discussed by Gary Herrigel (1996), as is their role in the industrialization of Japan by David Friedman (1988). The conceptualization of such a role as well as the considerable empirical data to support it, stands in rather sharp contrast with the dominant post World War II view of the industrialization process in both countries, particularly industrialization in Germany. The dominant view focuses on the role of the large enterprise and is essentially a large-firm-centered model. It tends to be associated with the pervasive and influential post-war writings of Alexander Gerschenkron (e.g., 1962, 1966, 1968). Gerschenkron, however, was deeply influenced by the almost superhuman Joseph Alois Schumpeter (1883-1950), who virtually dominated the faculty of the Harvard Business School for decades. Both Schumpeter and Gerschenkron argued against central tenets of classical and neoclassical economics. Both Schumpeter and Gerschenkron (as well as Jürgen Kocka and Alfred Chandler) assumed that all decisions regarding the production process

pharmaceutical industry (e.g., Böhringer, de Haen, Haarmann & Reimer, Knoll, Merck, Riedel, Schering, and Von Heyden). But these five and BASF (Badische Anilin und Soda Fabrik, originally set up by Friedrich Engelhorn in Mannheim in 1865, following his association with the two Clemm brothers in 1861, and Heinrich Caro three years later) were the major players.[19] The production of synthetic medicines accelerated greatly in the twentieth century, especially with the discovery in the 1930s of the important class of *sulfa* drugs, all of which contain a *sulfonamide* functional group. The most dramatic breakthroughs were made during the period of World War II, with the development of the first modern class of antibiotics ("super drugs"), e.g., penicillin.

The first truly modern antibiotic, penicillin (what we now call a b-lactam drug) is a fermentation product. It was first used as a treatment in 1941. The first commercially formulated antimalarial

---

occurred within the boundaries of the firm, not only because it was natural to do so, but also because it was the logical extension of specialization in the division of labor. Schumpeter never considered the situation where social or political organizations participated in the production process.

[19] Politics was the province of bureaucrats and interests groups, who used power and authority as governance mechanisms. Production was the province of firms, managers, workers, and common interest associations, who all used the markets and hierarchies as their governance mechanisms. Schumpeter is most noted for his ideas on "creative destruction," wherein creative entrepreneurs within firms orchestrate organizational innovation and sweeping change to avoid the "bureaucratic trap" of lost productivity. Thus Schumpeter made it possible for creative, large-scale organizations to **avoid** the hotly debated unitary trajectory, and through entrepreneurial activity within the firm, companies could continuously realize classical economic progress. While Gerschenkron adhered to Schumpeter's ideas, he also pointed out that political intervention in the economy was not necessarily a bad thing.

(chloroquine) was introduced in 1943. *Chloroquine* was patented in Germany in 1939, the same year that Germany invaded Poland, thus beginning World War II. Winthrop Laboratories obtained the U.S. patent in 1941. Chloroquine was followed in 1946 with the British antimalarial chlorquanide at Imperial Chemical Industries (ICI), and marketed (in its hydrochloride form) under the trade name Paludrine. The French patent for the acetate form of chloroquine went to Rhone-Poulenc in 1952.

The first antitubercular, streptomycin, an aminoglycoside (see Figure 21-2), was administered in 1944, and is, like penicillin, also a fermentation product. During the 1950s, drugs for mental illness (the monoamine oxidase inhibitors) were commercialized. For example, the monoamine oxidase inhibitor, phenelzine, which has been marketed for many years under the trade name Nardil (by companies that have now been acquired by Pfizer), was first synthesized in Europe in 1932, but was not patented in the United States until 1959.

Penicillin G	Streptomycin
$c_{16}h_{18}n_2O_4s$	$C_{21}H_{39}N_7O_{12}$

FIGURE 21-2 FERMENTED ANTIBIOTICS

The first oral contraceptives were developed in the 1950s. For example, norethindrone (progestogen) is the basic steroidal precursor for a number of human sex hormones including the first oral contraceptives, and has been marketed under many different brand names and by many different companies since the 1950s. Many derivatives are available for stimulating the gonads, treating menopause, improper menstruation, premenstrual tension, and testicular maladies. At least three U.S. patents were issued on norethindrone between 1956 and 1960. The first of these went to the Mexican company Syntex S.A. in 1956 and was derived from the extract of a variety of Mexican yam, known as barbasco (order *Liliales*, family *Dioscoreaceae*, genus *Dioscorea*, species *composita*). The patent for preparation of the acetate form of norethindrone went to the German firm Schering A.G. in 1960.

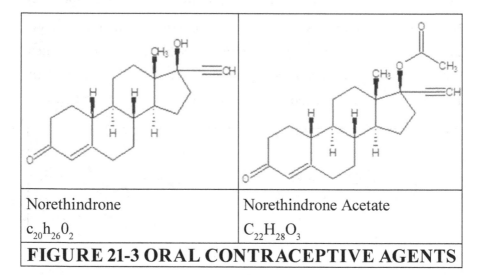

Norethindrone	Norethindrone Acetate
$c_{20}h_{26}0_2$	$C_{22}H_{28}O_3$

FIGURE 21-3 ORAL CONTRACEPTIVE AGENTS

The first drugs for diabetes were also developed in the 1950s. Metformin is an example of one of the first antidiabetics. It is a biguanide, like phenformin, which is no longer available in the United States due to associated fatalities. Metformin was first synthesized in 1922 but was not patented in the U.S. as an antidiabetic until 1965. By this time, the sulfonylureas such as tolazamide and tolbutamide were

already being used as antidiabetics. Hoechst A.G., the giant German pharmaceutical firm (now a part of Aventis), acquired both the British and German patents on tolbutamide in 1959. Upjohn (now a part of Pfizer) acquired the U.S. patent in 1961, and the British patent on tolazamide in 1962.

Biguanide	Metformin
$c_2h_7N_5$	$C_4H_{11}N_5$

FIGURE 21-4 ANTIDIABETIC BIGUANIDE

The Pharmaceutical Research and Manufacturers Association (PhARMA) has conceptualized the twentieh century of scientific evolution as follows: Prior to 1900, pharmaceuticals consisted largely of natural products and their derivatives. Then, aspirin, sulfa drugs and penicillin were discovered between about 1900 and 1950. Next, psychotropic drugs were developed largely through serendipity during the period from about 1950–1960. These were followed by the development of Receptor Theory, leading to development of the Non-Steroidal Anti-Inflammatory Drugs (NSAIDS) between about 1960 and 1970. Next came the development of Enzyme Technology and the development of H_2-Agonists and Beta-blockers between about 1970 and 1990. Genetic engineering began to bear fruit about 1990 and lipid-lowering agents (HmG CoA Reductase Inhibitors) and ACE Inhibitors (Angiotensin Converting Enzyme) came along between 1990 and 2000. Developments in cellular pharmacology and molecular biology started yielding valuable biotech drugs about 2000 and showed signs of profitability and growth in the future. Also in the future, from about 2000–2030, PHARMA sees research and development within the industry concentrating largely on chronic degenerative disease and cancer.

SCIENCE

In the West, the beginnings of science and the scientific method are usually associated with the ancient Greek philosopher, Aristotle (384–22 B.C.), who was a student in Plato's Academy in Athens and later founded his own school in Athens, the Lyceum. The differences between the thinking of Aristotle and the thinking of Plato characterize much of what we call Western culture. In a nutshell, this difference can be stated as the difference between what can be conceived and what can be observed; i.e., the difference between what we can imagine, consider, or believe and what we can measure with our five senses alone or logically infer from measurements taken by our five senses.

MEDICINE

The ancient land of Sumer was the birthplace of the world's first civilization. It was located in the fertile plain formed by the Tigris and Euphrates rivers in what is today southeastern Iraq. The Sumerians developed the world's first form of writing (called cuneiform, a system of triangular marks, or pictographic script), which was pressed into moist clay tablets with wedge-shaped tools and then dried in the sun. Tens of thousands of these clay tablets still exist. Some tablets, dating from roughly 3500 to 4000 B.C., describe the euphoric effect of the poppy, which they referred to (in rough translation) as the "joy plant," but evidence of its cultivation there appears only from about 3400 B.C.

Well-preserved Chinese medical records exist by various names, including the Ben Cao Kong Mo and the Pen Tsoa. These records catalogue the healing powers of natural substances, including plants, minerals, and animal by-products dating back to perhaps 2700 B.C., or earlier, apparently first compiled at about this time. The record known as the Pen Tsoa lists over 360 medicinal plants and their uses (Sebastian 2000).

Several famous Egyptian papyrus manuscripts exist that describe various parts of the anatomy, disease, and appropriate medicines. One of these, acquired in 1862 by Edwin Smith and bequeathed to the New York Historical Society, dates from about 1700 B.C. and is thought by some experts to have been transcribed from a much older document dating from perhaps 3000 B.C. A second manuscript, acquired in 1873 by George Ebers, dates from about 1500 B.C. and lists over 700 remedies, many of which included opium or its extracts as ingredients. The Ebers papyrus includes about one-third of the medicinal plants in use today (Lewis 1977; Booth 1996; Porter 1999; Sebastian 2000).

In India, the most ancient references to medicinal preparations are contained in the ancient Hindu Vedas, which are religious and philosophical works covering many subjects. In order of age, and beginning with the oldest, there are four ancient Vedas: Rig-Veda, Sama-Veda, Yajur-Veda, and Atharva-Veda. Following the conquest of India by the Aryans, invaders from the northwest (circa 1500 B.C.), it was forbidden to write or to hear the Vedas. Nevertheless, they were memorized and passed down orally within certain families.

SCIENCE

The language of the Vedas is very archaic and is an ancient form of what is known as classical Sanskrit. The Vedas began to appear in a written "classical form" of Sanskrit about 600 B.C. They describe a large number of plants used for their curative and therapeutic effects. Some scholars believe that portions of the Rig-Veda could date from as early as 4000 B.C. (Wheelwright 1974).

The Ayurveda, which is the basis of traditional Hindu medicine, is of more recent origin than any of the four ancient Vedas. The word "Ayurveda" is a classical Sanskrit term meaning "science of life." The Ayurveda is far more than simply a catalogue of many medicinal plants; it is a holistic system of healing that considers fundamental relationships between the individual and cosmic consciousness, spirit, energy, and matter. In this sense, it is an extension of the four ancient Vedas (Lad 1984).

About 500 B.C., the ancient Greeks were using extracts from the willow to treat pain, gout, and other diseases. Various forms of salicylic acid (e.g., salicin, methyl salicylate) exist in nature in the bark of willows, poplar trees, and in wintergreen leaves. North American Indians were also using the willow to treat pain, relieve headaches, and reduce fever prior to the arrival of the first Europeans in the western hemisphere (Lewis 1977). Opium was commonplace in Greek civilization. However, the method of incising the pod to gather the sap, which was developed by the Assyrians and is still used to this day, was apparently unknown to the Greeks, having been lost until it was rediscovered by the Romans about A.D. 40 (Booth 1996).

In general, physicians and pharmacists in ancient times tended to be secretive and fraternalistic. People were superstitious and associated health, stamina, disease and frailty with supernatural causes, esoteric rituals and spiritual practices. The great Greek physician Hippocrates (460–377 B.C.) was an historic exception and began to demonstrate openly that disease has only natural causes, thus taking treatment out of the hands of religion. Hippocrates is, therefore, regarded as the father of modern medicine. He insisted on treating patients with a proper diet, fresh air, and attention to cleanliness. In general, he objected to the use of strong drugs, without carefully testing their curative effects. He compiled a work known as the *Corpus Hippocraticum* from a variety of sources, which included treatments for allergies, asthma, fractures, ulcers, a variety of surgical procedures, and many others diseases. Hippocrates is especially remembered for his expression of medical ethics and high ideals, contained in what has come to be known as *The Oath Of Hippocrates,* or *The Hippocratic Oath*, presented below in Table 22-1.

The central concept in Hippocratic thinking was that health was equilibrium and illness was an upset of that equilibrium. In essence it was the four bodily humors that should be kept in balance: (1) phlegm (water, or a watery substance that is cold and moist); (2) blood, which is hot and moist; (3) black bile or gall, secreted from the kidneys and the spleen, cold and dry; (4) yellow bile or choler, secreted from the liver, hot and dry. Two humors in particular were associated with sickness: yellow bile and phlegm. Winter colds were due to phlegm, summer diarrhea and vomiting to yellow bile. Humoralism was widely practiced for over 2000 years following Hippocrates, up until the time of the American Civil War. It was decisively displaced only in 1858 by Rudolf Virchow.

TABLE 22-1 THE HIPPOCRATIC OATH

I swear by Apollo, the physician, and Asclepius and Health and All-Heal and all the gods and goddesses that, according to my ability and judgment, I will keep this oath and stipulation:

To reckon him who taught me this art equally dear to me as my parents, to share my substance with him and relieve his necessities if required; to regard his offspring as on the same footing with my own brothers, and to teach them this art if they should wish to learn it, without fee or stipulation, and that by precept, lecture and every other mode of instruction, I will impart a knowledge of the art to my own sons and to those of my teachers, and to disciples bound by a stipulation and oath, according to the law of medicine, but to none others.

I will follow that method of treatment which, according to my ability and judgment, I consider for the benefit of my patients, and abstain from whatever is deleterious and mischievous.

I will give no deadly medicine to anyone if asked, nor suggest any such counsel; furthermore, I will not give to a woman an instrument to produce abortion.

With purity and with holiness I will pass my life and practice my art. I will not cut a person who is suffering from a stone, but will leave this to be done by practitioners of this work. Into whatever houses I enter I will go into them for the benefit of the sick and will abstain from every voluntary act of mischief and corruption; and further from the seduction of females or males, bond or free.

Whatever, in connection with my professional practice, or not in connection with it, I may hear or see in the lives of men which ought not to be spoken abroad I will not divulge, as reckoning that all such should be kept secret.

While I continue to keep this oath inviolate may it be granted to me to enjoy life and the practice of the art, respected by all men at all times but should I trespass and violate this oath, may the reverse be my lot.

TECHNOLOGY

ANCIENT METALLURGISTS

The smelting of metal-containing ores that occur in nature requires high temperatures and evenly distributed heat in the absence of oxygen. The absence of oxygen is critical to the smelting and production of high-grade, pure, or nearly pure metals. If oxygen is present, the metals will react with it to form mainly undesirable metal oxides.

For thousands of years, human beings used charcoal as the source of intense heat that does not require oxygen in order to smelt metals from ore. Charcoal is obtained in the incomplete combustion or "charring" of wood. By driving off the moisture and other volatile materials contained in wood, a more efficient fuel is created, which is known as charcoal. It was not until the dawn of the seventeenth century, however, that people began to think about the possibility of doing the same basic thing to coal that produced coke for the first time. It would require almost two hundred more years for them to realize that the volatile components of coal, driven off when coked, might have any useful purpose whatsoever.

Ancient peoples knew how to smelt copper from the beautiful green mineral known as malachite. Malachite itself is often so pretty that it was used in its raw form in jewelry. It was also known as *soham* to the Hebrews and is one of the sacred jewels in the breastplate of high priests. Evidence shows clearly that the reduction of malachite to form copper using charcoal was known to peoples as long ago as the Neolithic age. There is evidence of considerable pollution from smelting copper on the west bank of the Jordan River, near Jericho, during this period. The Bronze Age (a synthetic metal that does not occur in nature and is a mixture of approximately 90% copper and 10% tin) began about 3500 B.C. in Mesopotamia, specifically in the land called Sumer. Bronze was the first metal alloy to be made by human beings. Tin was obtained from the mineral cassiterite, a tin oxide of brown or black color, usually having a slight metallic luster. The Chinese began to make bronze about 2000 B.C. and its use became widespread in China during the Shang dynasty about 1700 B.C.

Since the beginning, charcoal was made by forming large stacks, "cords," or piles of wood, covered over with moist earth or damp sod, leaving only small breather holes near the bottom in order to modulate the internal burn rate, and a larger opening through which hot starter coals were placed inside the pile and then this larger opening was also covered over. The internal pile of wood then burned in the absence, or mostly in the absence, of oxygen. Charcoal resulted when the pile was unearthed after a suitable amount of time had elapsed, which varied by type and conditions of the wood used, and the charcoal was free of the many impurities present in naturally occurring wood, which had been driven off, or volatilized.

A similar operation would take place in the subsequent smelting process, whereby metal-containing ore would be formed into a pile among alternating layers of charcoal. This pile of interleaved ore and charcoal was then covered as above and the charcoal inside ignited. The layered charcoal would burn at a higher, more consistent temperature than naturally occurring wood throughout the pile, again in the absence of oxygen or other impurities contained in wood, and the metal within the ore would melt, drip down inside the pile and was collected in a pool at the bottom.

THE ANCIENT HITTITE IRON MONOPOLY

The Hittites were early inhabitants of what is now Turkey, who probably immigrated from Europe or Central Asia, as suggested by the fact that their language and culture were of the Indo-European type and not indigenous to the region. The Hittites were excellent metallurgists, as well as warriors (and "business" people), who managed to retain a virtual monopoly on iron production for *hundreds of years!* They eventually lost control about 1200 B.C.

The Hittites conquered much of the Middle East, including parts of Mesopotamia and Syria, having seized the ancient stronghold of Babylon in present-day Iraq about 1600 B.C. The Hittites were the first people known to have large supplies of iron, although the oldest-surviving tools made from iron appear to have originated sometime before the Bronze Age, probably from fallen meteors about 4000 B.C. In several ancient languages the word "iron" literally means "metal from the sky." What is known today as the Iron Age began about 1500 B.C. as a, more or less, monopoly operation in the land of the Hittites, using charcoal, made from wood.

The use of iron spread slowly northward through Europe. Scandinavians did not see iron until the time of Julius Caesar, about 55 B.C., during the Roman conquest of Gaul (most of what is today modern-day France, Belgium, Luxemburg, and the Netherlands). Acquiring the knowledge and metallurgical skill necessary to manufacture effective weapons of war and bring about the demise of the Roman Empire did not occur all at once. Just as it would one day require the genius of an Antoine Lavoisier to develop the methods necessary to keep French canon under Bonaparte supplied with sufficient gunpowder to bring about the demise of the second Roman Empire, it required similar genius to wrest technology from the first. But, once they had acquired the necessary technology, Europeans began to cut down vast forests to make vast amounts of charcoal and thereby iron, in what would become enormous quantities. And, just as the space program of the 1960s and the Star Wars military spending of the 1980s led to a whole host of unanticipated spin-off technologies that revolutionized life as we knew it, and provided for the lifestyles we now enjoy; so too did the large-scale, national manufacture of charcoal, iron, coke, steel alloys, and coal tar lead to the spin-off of organic chemistry and the birth of the modern pharmaceutical industry.

ORGANIC RAW MATERIALS

NATURALLY OCCURRING SOURCES OF HYDROCARBONS

There are basically only five naturally occurring sources of hydrocarbons found in large enough quantities to be used commercially as raw materials (primary feedstocks) for the refining and chemical process industries. These very important raw materials are coal, wood, biomass, natural gas, and petroleum. They are all presented graphically in Figure 22-1, along with their major outputs, or derivatives, which become "secondary" feedstocks or inputs for so-called downstream chemical processors and, eventually, final products.

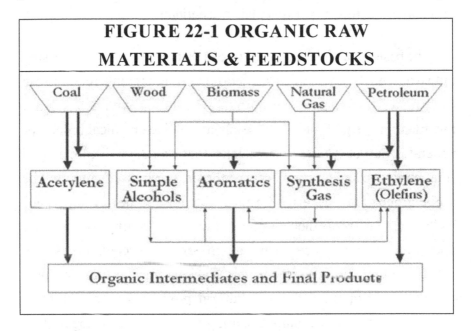

FIGURE 22-1 ORGANIC RAW MATERIALS & FEEDSTOCKS

THE ORGANIC CHEMICAL TREE

The concept of the chemical tree is extremely important to understanding the integrated structure and dynamics of the chemical and pharmaceutical industries, as well as the interactions between organic chemicals and other industries related to pharmaceuticals, such as food preservatives, disinfectants, etc. Because of the large number of chemical products and synthetic pathways involved, few people have had a comprehensive knowledge of the chemical tree or even its major components. There are literally hundreds of small, specialized branches in the tree where an individual scientist can spend his or her entire career. Even mobile professionals within the industry, that is, those who change employers every few years, usually deal with only a limited number of products and processes. We will focus here only on the organic chemical tree and discuss inorganic chemicals tangentially as they relate to specific processes in the manufacture of various pharmaceuticals.

The basic idea of the chemical tree is that the chemical-processing industries have a generally sequential and branching relationship in terms of their inputs and outputs. Beginning with a few basic raw materials (e.g., fossil fuels), each successive chemical processor generates outputs that are frequently "intermediates," rather than final products, and go on to become the next processor's inputs. The initial group of raw materials forms the "trunk" of the tree or perhaps its "roots." The *roots* then consist of the major mining and farming operations that produce such raw materials as coal, limestone, sulfur, natural gas, petroleum, and various agricultural products such as wood or cellulose. Agricultural products are important as raw materials in fermentations leading to most major categories of antibiotics, as well as medicinal botanicals themselves, their extracts, tinctures, etc.

THE SIMPLE EXAMPLE OF METHANOL

The example of methanol (see Figure 22-2) is the very simplest of the alcohols. It consists of only a single carbon atom. Historically, it has always been included as one of the most important, highest volume chemicals in the world. It is produced in volumes exceeding one billion pounds per year at each of many facilities around the world, and is used in the production of many thousands of products (see Table 22-1). In addition to being part of the chemical tree as a major reactant (or synthetic agent), it is also a common and inexpensive solvent used in the manufacture of final products. These include antibiotics (such as streptomycin), vitamins, hormones, and many other pharmaceuticals.

TABLE 22-1 DERIVATIVES OF METHANOL	
1. Formaldehyde	6. Methyl Halides
2. Methyl Tertiary Butyl Ether	7. Methyl Methacrylate
3. Acetic Acid	8. Dimethyl Terephthalate
4. Acetone	9. Methyl Amines
5. Chloromethanes	10. Methylene Chloride

Methanol reacts like other alcohols and forms similar derivatives such as (1) nitrogen derivatives and (2) methyl esters of both organic and inorganic acids. As an example of one of its methyl esters, the methyl ester of 2-aminobenzoic acid, also shown in Figure 22-2, and known more commonly as "methyl anthranilate," is easily synthesized and used as a common scenting agent (or perfume) in medicinal ointments. It also occurs naturally in bergamot, jasmine, neroli, ylang-ylang, and other essential oils, as well as in grape juice.

Methanol is sometimes referred to as "wood alcohol" because prior to the 1920s, wood was the major raw material used in its commercial production. Historically methanol was produced from wood as a by-product of charcoal manufacturing in much the same way coal tar was much later produced as a by-product of coke manufacturing.

OH | CH$_3$	(structure)
Methanol	Methyl Anthranilate

FIGURE 22-2 METHANOL AND
METHYL ANTHRANILATE

Today, methanol is obtained chiefly from natural gas, initially as methane, which is 85% of natural gas. Methane from natural gas is partially oxidized with water and carbon dioxide over a nickel catalyst to produce a mixture of carbon monoxide and hydrogen (commonly referred to as "synthesis gas"), which is then used in the manufacture of a range of other chemical products as well as methanol. Synthesis gas is "reformed" as methanol when the carbon monoxide and hydrogen are combined (in a sense "reunited"), over aluminum, chromium, manganese, or zinc oxides as catalysts at a high temperature and pressure, or a copper oxide catalyst at a lower temperature and pressure depending upon the nature of the associated processing operations. (The term "reunited" is used loosely here because in a strict sense; there is not a one-to-one correspondence between the atoms comprising the original molecules of methane and those that comprise the reformed molecules of methanol.) The process is more sophisticated than it has been historically, when methanol was distilled from wood.

In Germany, BASF began the commercial production of non-wood-based methanol through the reaction of carbon monoxide and hydrogen over a metal oxide catalyst in the early 1920s. A large number of metals, metal alloys, and metal-containing compounds are important as catalysts in the sophisticated methods employed by modern chemical technology. The copper catalyst used in most processes today is a process improvement that was developed by the British company Imperial Chemical Industries (ICI).

COAL TAR CHEMICALS

The *by-product coke oven* began about 1766 near Saarbruchen, Germany. But it was not sufficiently perfected until 1856, when an engineer in France named Knab built a battery of by-product coke ovens that could recover coal, tar, ammonia, oil, and gas. This was the same year as William Perkin's accidental discovery that led to the development of organic chemistry, rooted in a previously considered waste by-product of coal. The most important chemical by-product of coke manufacturing is benzene, whereas the largest percentage by-product in coal tar is napthalene (approximately 20% by dry weight). The chemical structure of benzene is a single-ring molecule of six carbon atoms with six hydrogen atoms strategically attached so that the ring system consists of alternating single and double chemical bonds. These chemical bonds resonate electrically around the ring across sequences of the two bond types, making benzene very stable and also providing its characteristic odor.

Benzene is used in manufacturing thousands of products throughout the chemical tree, including pharmaceuticals, dyes, lacquers, linoleum, polymers, plastics and resins, solvents, varnishes, etc. It is *the* essential component in all so-called *aromatic* molecules (hydrocarbons defined as containing one or more benzene rings; see Figure 22-3), because they frequently possess a characteristic fragrance or aroma. The aromatics are absolutely crucial in the synthesis of countless pharmaceutical products. They exist throughout nature and in a wide variety of forms and are essential for many of the mechanisms of biology that must occur in order for living things to exist. They are frequently responsible for the distinctive or unique characteristics that differentiate the various forms of life, such as color.

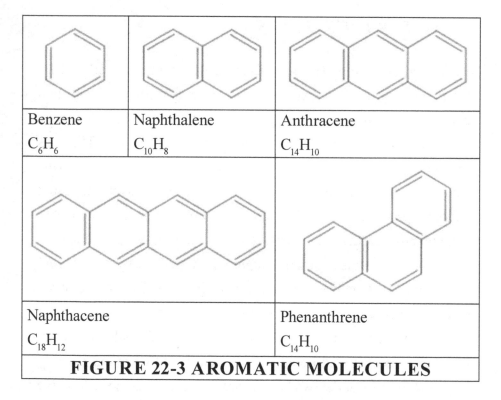

Benzene C_6H_6	Naphthalene $C_{10}H_8$	Anthracene $C_{14}H_{10}$
Naphthacene $C_{18}H_{12}$		Phenanthrene $C_{14}H_{10}$

FIGURE 22-3 AROMATIC MOLECULES

Anthracene, naphthalene, and phenanthrene are important aromatic chemicals derived from coal. Naphthalene has a two-ring molecular structure, while both anthracene and phenanthrene contain three rings. Other important chemicals derived from coal include phenol, pyridine, thiophene, toluene, and xylene. Each of these molecules has a characteristic single ring structure (see Figure 22-4, though pyridine and thiophene are not based on benzene, because one of them contains nitrogen as an integral part of its ring, and the other sulfur).

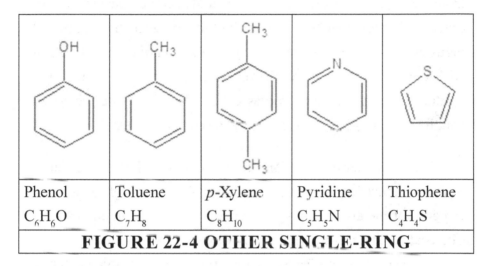

Phenol	Toluene	*p*-Xylene	Pyridine	Thiophene
C_6H_6O	C_7H_8	C_8H_{10}	C_5H_5N	C_4H_4S

FIGURE 22-4 OTHER SINGLE-RING

Phenol, toluene and xylene each contain a single benzene ring, with the respective hydroxy or methyl functional groups attached (two methyl groups in the case of xylene; the second methyl group in the xylene molecule shown in Figure 22-4 is in the para position; meta and ortho configurations, or isomers, also exist in commercial preparations of xylene). For this reason, phenol is also known as hydroxybenzene; toluene is sometimes called methylbenzene; and xylene is referred to as dimethylbenzene.

Pyridine is a single-ring molecule, but fundamentally different from the others in that like ammonia, it contains an atom of nitrogen; thus, it is a "heterocyclic compound and is an important starting material for important classes of pharmaceuticals." Remember that **all** of the alkaloids (extracted from botanicals, etc.) contain nitrogen, as do all amino acids and proteins. Finally, thiophene is a single-ring molecule, but different still in being a five-member ring structure containing four carbon atoms and an atom of sulfur.

Even though the first industrial organic chemicals were derived from wood (e.g., methanol, acetic acid, and acetone), the products of organic synthesis that led to the birth of the modern pharmaceutical industry were based almost entirely on the volatile constituents of coal, during its destructive distillation in specially designed "by-product" coke ovens in a process called "coking." (The recovered volatile materials are recovered (condensed) as coal-tar.)

Coke is the carbon portion of coal and is a vital raw material in many industries, particularly in the making of steel, which is a category of metals consisting of various alloys of iron and carbon. The coal tar that results from the by-product coking process was by far the most important feedstock material for the organic synthesis of the first modern pharmaceuticals. Coal tar is a thick, almost black, liquid or semi-solid, having a characteristic odor. Coal tar itself has been shown to be a useful anti-eczematic and is still used today as the active ingredient in several brands of dandruff shampoos such as Denorex.

In the process of making coke from coal, a number of very important substances within the coal are volatilized into gaseous vapors that, with proper equipment, can be recovered as valuable by-products. In countries like the United States, this volatile fraction was simply vented to the atmosphere as worthless for decades. In a similar fashion, when Americans first began to distill heating oil from petroleum, many distillers simply threw away the gasoline fraction as worthless——that is, until the invention of the automobile.

The use of coal tar as the major feedstock for organic synthesis began, strangely enough, with metallurgy.

PETROLEUM-BASED FEEDSTOCKS

For several decades, beginning in the United States about 1911 (the year that Standard Oil of New Jersey was outlawed by the United States Supreme Court), petroleum began to replace coal tar and became the dominant organic feedstock material in the world. Two years later, propylene (a member of the olefin-group of organic chemicals) was introduced as a by-product from petroleum through a refining process known as "cracking." The year 1920 saw the first production of isopropyl alcohol, a very important solvent to the modern pharmaceutical industry. By the time of World War II, "petrochemicals" were well developed in the United States, but not elsewhere.

A significant impact on the structure of the pharmaceutical industry was made through the transition of the chemical processing industries from raw materials and intermediates derived from coal to petroleum-based technology. It was a major factor in the subsequent rapid growth of the U.S. pharmaceutical industry. This conversion was not completed in some industrialized nations until the period of the 1960s. Then, with almost two-thirds of the world's known oil reserves existing in the Middle East, the first oil crisis of 1973–74, and the huge increase in petroleum prices that occurred during it, provided an impetus for many people to reconsider coal-based technologies. Again in 1979, oil prices doubled as a result of the revolution in Iran; however, by 1980, about 70% of the feedstock for producing olefins (e.g., ethylene, propylene, etc.) in the United

States was coming from natural gas. As might be expected, prices for natural gas significantly increased as a result and a substantial percentage return to petroleum-based feeds had occurred by the mid-1980s. This was also the general time period when a flurry of divestitures, acquisitions, and mergers (industry restructuring) began in the chemical and pharmaceutical industries that was to continue for the remainder of the century. Yet, lest we be too quick to draw overly simplified conclusions, a number of other very significant factors coincided with these fluctuations in feedstock prices.

A major difference between the coal-based and petroleum-based organic chemical industries that evolved in Germany and the United States, respectively, is that the chemical tree derived from coal was based primarily on acetylene, whereas the chemical tree derived from petroleum is still largely based on ethylene. This is a fairly general statement to make, and while there are significant, commercially relevant, and technically very important issues regarding the various chemicals that can be obtained from coal and petroleum feeds by using different methods such as destructive versus non-destructive distillation, thermal versus catalytic cracking, various reforming alternatives, etc., these complexities are beyond the scope of this book but the generality is, nevertheless, substantially true and therefore useful in describing a major divergence between the systems that evolved as a function of the two major raw materials available.

Historically, there have been certain organic chemicals that appear over and over again on lists of industrial organic chemicals with the highest sales volumes in the United States. Obviously, these particular chemicals form a portion of the trunk and major branches of the chemical tree. These recurring top 25 organic chemicals are presented in Table 22-2.

TABLE 22-2 TOP 25 ORGANIC CHEMICALS			
1	Acetic acid	14	Formaldehyde
2	Acetone	15	Isopropanol
3	Acrylonitrile	16	Methanol
4	Adipic Acid	17	Methyl tertiary-Butyl Ether
5	Benzene	18	Propylene Oxide
6	Butadiene	19	Phenol
7	Caprolactam	20	Styrene
8	Cumene	21	Terephthalic Acid
9	Cyclhexane	22	Urea
10	Dimethyl Terephthalate	23	Vinyl Acetate
11	Ethylbenzene	24	Vinyl Chloride
12	Ethylene Glycol	25	para-Xylene
13	Ethylene Oxide	--	

Every one of these top 25 organic chemicals, and countless others, can be synthesized from just seven basic feedstock chemicals. These seven very important organic feedstocks are presented in Table 22-3.

TABLE 22-3 THE SEVEN ORGANIC FEEDSTOCKS
Benzene
Butylene
Ethylene
Methane
Propylene
Toluene
Xylene

Effectively combining the information contained in Table 22-2 on the most important industrial organic chemicals (i.e., "derivatives") with that contained in Table 22-3 on the most important industrial organic feedstocks, we can create what might be thought of as the "trunk" of the organic chemical tree by listing each of the possible derivatives under each respective feedstock, as demonstrated in Table 22-4.

TABLE 22-4 THE ORGANIC CHEMICAL TREE "TRUNK"

Benzene	Butylene	Ethylene	Methane	Propylene	Toluene	Xylene
Acetone	Acetic Acid	Acetic Acid	Acetic Acid	Acetone	Benzene	Dimethyl Terephthalate
Adipic Acid	Butadiene	Ethylbenzene	Dimethyl Terephthalate	Acrylonitrile		Terephthalic Acid
Caprolactam	Methyl t-Butyl Ether	Ethylene Dichloride	Formaldehyde	Cumene		para-Xylene
Cumene	Vinyl Acetate	Ethylene Glycol	Methanol	Isopropanol		
Cyclohexane		Ethylene Oxide	Methyl t-Butyl Ether	Phenol		
Ethylbenzene		Vinyl Acetate	Vinyl Acetate	Propylene Oxide		
Phenol		Vinyl Chloride				
Styrene		Styrene				

DYESTUFFS -- THEIR IMPORTANCE TO PHARMACEUTICALS

The significance of William Perkin's discovery to the modern pharmaceutical industry was that it led to a rapid development of knowledge in organic synthesis. The subsequent production of large quantities of the new synthetic dyes led to the discovery of the first synthetic medicines. The new, profitable, and fast-growing, synthetic dyestuffs industry produced large quantities of intermediate organic compounds from coal. These intermediates also became feedstock materials for synthetic medicines, for example, the class of sedatives known as *benzodiazepines* are derived from aniline, as are the *sulfonamide* class of antibiotics and many others.

DYESTUFFS AND BACTERIOLOGY

Approximately 1675, Holland's Anton van Leeuwenhoek, using a crude microscope that he had built himself, was the first to identify bacteria. In 1796 England's Edward Jenner, based on his observation that milkmaids rarely became infected with smallpox, invented the smallpox vaccine. The year after Perkin's discovery in 1856, Louis Pasteur began to identify microorganisms that were held to be responsible for various forms of fermentation. Between 1865 and 1871, while studying a silkworm disease in southern France, he made similar discoveries regarding the linkage between microorganisms and infection. Ten years later, in 1881, he firmly established the connection between bacteria and disease when he treated a flock of sheep infected with anthrax.

PERKIN'S CONTRIBUTION TO MEDICINE

Simon Garfield's excellent book (2001) on W.H. Perkin served as an invaluable reference here. In 1956, at a celebration of the 100th anniversary of Perkin's wonderful discovery, he quoted Frank L. Rose, the research manager at ICI Pharmaceuticals, who made the point rather well concerning Perkin's contribution to the pharmaceutical industry. He had been discussing the widely recognized work of Germany's Paul Ehrlich and Gerhard Domagk in bacteriology and development of the first synthetic antibiotics (*sulfa* drugs), when he is quoted as saying that "without Perkin's observation, the progress of therapeutic medicine might have been delayed by as much as a generation." It was of course much more than simply Perkin's powers of observation. He also had an entrepreneurial spirit and work ethic of almost awesome proportions. Remember, he was only fifteen years old when he enrolled at the Royal College of Chemistry under Professor August Wilhelm von Hofmann, and only eighteen years old when he made the discovery that would change the world.

Perkin realized that the purple compound he created was an excellent, fast dye for silk cloth and quickly took out a patent in Britain, built a factory to make it in commercial quantities, and became a wealthy man from selling his product. French dye makers Renard Freres and others from Lyon attempted to acquire Perkin's synthetic process from the London patent office, prompting Perkin to hurriedly apply for a French patent. Unfortunately, because of the time that had elapsed since filing his British patent, the French statute of limitations had expired. Nevertheless, Perkin maintained a "first-mover" advantage from having been the progenitor of large-scale production and marketing of mauve.

ALIZARIN AND INDIGO

Successful as Perkin's mauve and aniline derivatives as intermediates for other specialty colors were, the big money-making dyestuffs were alizarin (red) and indigo (blue), for which there has always been an insatiable demand. Once methods of synthesizing alizarin and indigo on an industrial scale were developed, enormous quantities were manufactured in Germany, but only after the Franco-Prussian War (1870–1871).

Remarkably, it was William Perkin who developed a synthesis for alizarin and, ultimately, obtained a second important British patent on his method. This second patent was granted only after a contentious struggle with Germany's largest dye manufacturer, Badische Anilin und Soda Fabrik (BASF), who just one day earlier had filed a similar patent application in London.

Both patents were granted, however, because of technical differences in the two methods and, at Perkin's suggestion, the two competitors met in Britain and agreed to divide the world market for alizarin between them. Perkin held a monopoly in Britain, while BASF controlled the markets in Europe and the United States. Perkin began shipments of alizarin in October 1869. Production at BASF was delayed by the onset of the Franco-Prussian war. This enabled Perkin to produce and sell 40 tons of alizarin in 1870, 220 tons in 1871, 300 tons in 1872, and 435 tons in 1873.

In 1897, Perkin synthesized coumarin from coal tar, which resulted in a fragrance resembling vanilla beans, and can be found in apricots, cherries, and strawberries. This led to the development of artificial fragrances, such as jasmine, lavender, roses and violets. The reaction of acetic anhydride and sodium acetate with salicylaldehyde is still known as "the Perkins reaction." In 1904 Perkin synthesized alpha-terpineol, which, in addition to having antiseptic properties, is used in the manufacture of perfumes and the denaturing fats in soap production. He also synthesized Limonene in 1904, which occurs in lemon oil, orange, bergamot, caraway, and dill. Perkin died at the age of 69 on July 14, 1907, seven years before an assassin's bullet killed Austria's Archduke Ferdinand in Sarajevo, setting off World War I.

Indigo proved more difficult to synthesize than alizarin, but nothing like quinine, which the American Dr. Robert Woodward succeeded in synthesizing in 1944. Indigo was first described to Europeans by Marco Polo, who had first observed the blue dye derived from a plant native to India. It was expensive when it arrived in Europe and had always been for Perkin and others. Success belonged to Germany, however, and in 1890 through the use of the two-ring naphthalene molecule. It was synthesized by Karl Heumann at BASF.

FROM ANILINE TO DIAZONIUM SALTS

Like the aniline dyes mauve, alizarin, indigo, etc., the first of the so-called *azo* dyes was also synthesized in England. They are produced by first reacting aniline with nitric acid and then combining the product with various aromatic amines. They are generally superior to the aniline dyes because they are lightfast, whereas the aniline dyes are not. Unlike Perkin, J.P. Griess, inventor of the first azo dyes, did not perceive the impact his discovery would have on the world. This realization came to two German chemists, Heinrich Caro and Carl Martius, who were working at that time in the English dyestuffs industry: Caro returned to Germany and joined the giant BASF, which had been formed in 1861. Martius also returned to Germany and in 1873, following the 1871 German Empire's victory over France in the Franco-Prussian War, became the founder of another German chemical giant, Aktien Gesellschaft fur Anilin Fabrikation (AGFA), located near Berlin.

INDIVIDUAL SCIENTISTS

THE VITAL LIFE FORCE

Until 1828, it was widely believed that only living things could produce organic compounds, defined as those that contain carbon, generally in combination with hydrogen, nitrogen, and oxygen. Scientists, physicians, educated people everywhere, believed that the vital "life force" was necessary to produce all such substances. In Germany that year, Friedrich Wohler produced urea (an organic compound) by the evaporation of ammonium cyanate (an inorganic compound) and thus began the search for other raw materials and methods of synthesizing organic chemicals that have medicinal or therapeutic properties.

THE ARISTOCRAT AND THE AGRICULTURALIST

There have been a number of great French chemists, biologists, other scientists, and physicians over the years. Prior to beginning my research into the French pharmaceutical industry, I began with a study of French history in general and then its economic history, and particularly the history of the chemical industry. In the process, I had become impressed with the historical importance of Nicholas LeBlanc, who invented an inexpensive method of making commercial quantities of soda (sodium carbonate) He also built the world's first soda plant about 1791, outside Paris. LeBlanc revolutionized French industry in that country as well as in other nations at that time. He also made a lot of people very wealthy. As I spoke with the French people themselves on this matter, they would allow for no possible comparison whatsoever between any other French scientist, chemist or otherwise, and the great Antoine Lavoisier, who is generally perceived by the French to be in a class all by himself. Perhaps most important, and oddly absent from many historical records, Antoine Lavoisier was the man placed in charge of the king's arsenal, munitions, and ordnance manufacturers. It was in this capacity that he perfected his theories of oxidation and indeed, in collaboration with the British Joseph Priestly (who discovered oxygen), is credited with the more valuable discovery that oxygen and nitrogen are separable components from the air we breathe. He made these and other important discoveries while studying the "burn-rates" and explosive characteristics of various compounds, mixtures, and "charges" of gunpowder.

Lavoisier was apparently a man who loved to blow things up, especially under carefully controlled conditions. He made incredible technological improvements in France's capacity produce large volumes of high-quality explosives efficiently, and the munitions upon which Napoleon's subsequent conquest of Europe would so crucially depend. Napoleon himself made his mark before and during the French Revolution as an "artillery man," a "cannoneer," and was first and foremost an expert on the most efficacious use of field artillery (e.g., on the bluffs above Paris). He knew full well the importance of *reliable* supplies and *consistent* charges of *stable*, high-quality gunpowder, to propel his artillery shells precisely where and when he intended for them to be propelled.

Lavoisier was also a *Fermier Generale* (tax collector), one of several throughout France, who had purchased from the king the hereditary right to collect the king's taxes in various regions of France at a profit, or with the right to take out a hefty commission before turning the remainder over to the crown. It was a double-edged sword, however, because being, in essence, a tax collector for the king, the great Lavoisier eventually lost his head to the mob on the guillotine.

It was important that in his capacity as director of munitions, Lavoisier had as his assistant a young man by the name of Eleuthere Irenee duPont de Nemours, who saw for himself the unpredictable dangers inherent in the actions of a mob gone wild, and watched with his own eyes as the great chemist was led through the streets of Paris to the Place de la Concorde where stood the equally great machine of death. Irenee soon thereafter wisely slipped away and boarded a ship bound for America where, in 1802 at the age of 31, he founded, on the Brandywine Creek near Wilmington, Delaware, what would become the greatest munitions company in the history of the world: E.I. DuPont de Nemours & Co. By the time of the War of 1812, he had become America's leading munitions supplier, obtaining most of his *saltpeter* (potassium nitrate) from the natural deposits in nearby Kentucky.

Lavoisier was an undisputed science genius of the type that comes along only every few hundred years. Both he and Pasteur are considered, respectively, to be the great Aristocrat and Agriculturist.

Pasteur succeeded Lavoisier as the most respected, but not the greatest, French chemist of all time. He is remembered for his contributions to the bacteria theory of disease, his creation of a basis for modern enzyme chemistry, and his development of a vaccine against rabies. He worked for decades on fermentation products (wine, cheese, etc.) and animal diseases in the great agricultural regions of France. The Institut Pasteur, founded in Paris in 1888, once upon a time a great, world-renowned center of excellence in pharmaceutical research, became much less so under its later management by the French state. But, as we shall soon see, over and over again, such has frequently been the case with these things in France.

GENTRY AND PRIVATEERS

The industrial revolution that began in Britain had been in full swing there for well over a hundred years when Napoleon met Wellington and, later in the day, von Blucher at Waterloo. Napoleon had maintained a moderately effective naval blockade against British imports for many years and businesses on the continent had grown rich as a result of the precipitous drop in lower-priced British goods that resulted from their early industrialization. Nevertheless, British entrepreneurs grew richer still through trading with the colonies and supplying Napoleon's enemies on the continent whenever and wherever possible.

THE MOTLEY CREW

It has always been claimed that Germany had the best scientists in the world from the mid-nineteenth century onward and America had the best engineers, particularly with respect to petroleum-based hydrocarbon feeds. But it takes more than great scientists or even great engineers to conceive and undertake projects of the size and scope of the modern life sciences, pharmaceutical, chemical, and biotechnology industries.

The mindset of Germany has always differed from that of France and Britain. When a forward detachment of General Patton's Third Army arrived in Gendorf, Bavaria, in 1945, they could not help but notice most of the townspeople "protested innocence in various degrees of cunning and sophistication;" all except for this one very odd little man who seemed always to be wearing a fancy suit, and resembled "a rabbit who had come out of the nearby hills, standing alertly on its hind legs, watching with devilish friendliness these taller beings straggling warily around the town." He always seemed to be sniffing the air rather mysteriously, claimed he had no rank or serial number, and described himself as just a plain chemist.

Because the Third Army was moving so rapidly through the area, a fast succession of gradually higher-ranking U.S. officers also noted this interesting little man's extremely odd behavior, manner of dress, demeanor, and willingness to give them gifts. The G.I.s liked him immediately because he passed out bars of soap and they had not bathed in weeks. He also distributed amazingly high-quality cleansing agents and paints for their vehicles and "could tell you how to make a hundred wonderful things out of just one chemical element (*sic*): ethylene oxide."

As the months passed, higher commanding officers rolled into town and ultimately had grown suspicious by earlier reports, but especially when they learned that this man, Dr. Otto Ambrose, was apparently the manager of a factory entirely underground on the outskirts of town. It was to be many more months indeed before American intelligence was somewhat astonished to learn that, in fact, Dr. Ambrose was much more than simply a plain chemist, or even a plant manager. He was a member of the all-powerful Vorstand, or board of directors, of the largest, most powerful chemical conglomerate in the world at that time, the infamous I.G. Farben Industries. He certainly did not look the part, but he was unmistakably "odd."

A couple of years after the war, the American government decided to officially prosecute 24 leaders of I.G. Farben for high war crimes at Nuremburg, that now infamous city in central Germany where Hermann Goering and other Nazi leaders had already been convicted the prior year of crimes against humanity. The other Allied Powers would not support the Americans in this effort against the executives of I.G. Farben, however, because it was a private company and they were not military officers or high government officials. The British and French especially seemed afraid of the precedent it would set for the culpability of business leaders in the future, so the U.S. prosecuted them alone.

It took a very long time for a small team of American prosecutors with Dr. Josiah E. DuBois, Jr. in charge to uncover the actual organizational structure and methods by which I.G. Farben had operated. Dr. Otto Ambrose, for example, was not just a maker of soap and a hundred other products from ethylene oxide, but also the production chief for the awesome Buna rubber project and poison gases. He was manager of the Auschwitz plant. And he was also head of the Chemical Warfare Committee of the Ministry of Armaments and War Production. His frequently noted and incessant sniffing of the air was apparently the result of his concern for shifts in the wind that might bring traces of the smell of death from nearby crematoriums.

In sworn testimony before the judges of Military Tribunal No. 6 at Nuremburg, he described the words of his mentor, Dr. Friedrich ter Meer, who was chief of the Vorstand's technical committee, and directed all of I.G. Farben's production, and was on the boards of directors of numerous overseas corporations, including General Aniline and Film Corporation of New York (today's GAF). The quote Ambrose put into the record of ter Meer's thoughts on the natural world seem particularly illustrative of the mindset of these 24 geniuses, that Kurt Lanz (vice-chairman of Hoechst AG after the breakup of I.G. Farben) has described as "a motley group of scientists and commercial experts of varying strengths of personality," who nevertheless had come to totally dominate the world's markets for dyestuffs, organic intermediates, pharmaceuticals, and hundreds of other products worldwide. Dr. ter Meer inspired the young Otto Ambrose by describing all natural substances as "wild horses that must be broken to the reins." He quickly clarified for the court, however, that humankind was no wild horse to him.

WILLIAM PERKIN'S WONDERFUL DISCOVERY

William Henry Perkin was indefatigable, generally modest, shy, and diffident. As mentioned he was only fifteen years of age when he enrolled at the Royal College of Chemistry, under Professor August Wilhelm von Hoffman, and only eighteen years old when he made the discovery that led to a rapid development of knowledge in organic synthesis and the development of organic chemistry, rooted in a previously considered waste by-product of coal. This discovery would change the world. As also mentioned, Perkin died at the age of 69 on July 14, 1907, seven years before an assassin's bullet killed Austria's Archduke Ferdinand in Sarajevo, setting off WWI.

AUGUST WILHELM VON HOFMANN

Aniline is a single benzene ring with one of the hydrogen atoms attached to the carbon atoms that form the ring replaced by an amine group, preserving the electronic resonance of the ring structure across its alternating single and double bonds. The presence of a nitrogen atom in the amine group attached to the outside of the ring is interesting when compared to an atom of nitrogen appearing as an integral part of the ring itself, as in pyridine. August Hofmann was the first to obtain benzene from coal tar in 1845. But he was fascinated by aniline and its two-ring sister naphthalidine, which also has a single amine group attached to one of its two adjoining rings.

Hofmann had realized earlier that the amine group continues to manifest the basic character of its ammonia parent whenever attached to a number of other, though simpler, molecules, so it was natural for him to imagine that aniline and naphthalidine would react with a variety of acids, or oxidizing agents, to form entirely new chemicals with the aromatic benzene ring(s) still intact. Hofmann had been doing these kinds of experiments for over 15 years when William Perkin discovered mauve by accident.

Let us now consider the idea that in the late eighteenth century, chemistry was mostly a French science, which was subsequently stolen by the Germans. If this claim, which seems ridiculous on its face, has any semblance of truth to it, then to which men of France exactly did chemistry belong? And who exactly were the thieves who gave it (taught it) to the people of Germany? This is a wonderful question because it adds an element of intrigue to one of the most incredible eras in all of human history, and to a subject matter that to many common persons and business people alike is mundane if not outright boring. The "theft" idea seems to be rooted in the person and image of Antoine Laurent Lavoisier (1743–1794) as the "father of chemistry" (a French tax collector and scientist who lost his head on the guillotine), and the persons of Justis von Liebig (1803–1873) and his contemporary Friedrich Wohler (1800–1882).

Liebig and Wohler worked together on a large number of important projects, including work in response to demands by pharmaceutical firms for better methods of analyzing alkaloids. Together, they were responsible for freeing an emerging organic chemistry from "vitalism," or the "vital force," a concept whereby the substances and/or essences of life can be created only within living things. In so doing, it may indeed be said that they "stole" chemistry from the French. But then Liebig, who has been called "the man of nineteenth-century chemistry," also gave it to the British.

To complicate the issue of who stole what, if anything, from whom, in the final years leading up to the French Revolution, when thousands of people lost their heads on the guillotine, and the stage was set for the rise to power of Napoleon Bonaparte, the whole of the European scientific community believed in an imaginary substance called "phlogiston." They conceptualized phlogiston as a kind of pure energy, yet possessing both mass and weight, conceptualized and promulgated by the definitely boring and somewhat pompous German physician, George Ernst Stahl.

The phlogiston theory was not a bad theory. It was just a wrong theory. Theories do not have to be correct in order to be useful, and phlogiston was a very useful theory. It crystallized thinking relative to the reactions of acids and bases with metallic and non-metallic substances, and focused attention on what was truly important (the increase in mass of some reactants but not others).

If Dr. Stahl had not been so pompous, perhaps his ideas would not have been taken so seriously; but, being the royal physician to the Prussian king was no doubt a factor on both counts. And if he had not been so boring in his lectures, perhaps the eggheads would have thought he was just another fruitcake, like the alchemists of a previous generation.

In light of the claim that chemistry was a French science to begin with, it seems paradoxical that some French scientists were among phlogiston's staunchest supporters, and were accused of "stealing" that idea from the Germans![20] So we are prone to ask if it was indeed first a German science, stolen by the French, and then stolen back by the Germans? One thing is for certain, however, without some form

---

[20]   Karl Hufbauer (1982, p.1) quotes correspondence in 1790 from D. Lorenz Crell in Helmstedt, founder of the German journal of chemistry, _Chemische Annalen_ (1778), to Karl G. Hagen in Königsberg, as "our phlogiston which the French want to steal from us." Hufbauer is also much kinder to Dr. Stahl than I am here, suggesting that he opposed Lavoisier on the grounds of insufficient, sober methodological rigor with his citation of this alternative view by Kahlbaum and Hoffmann (1897) on pages 96–97. Furthermore, Hufbauer seems critical of Justus von Liebig (whom I see as one of the greatest men in the history of pharmaceutical and chemical science, education _and_ industry) when on page 150 he says "Liebig, his allies, and his successors were able to _capitalize_, _without corrosive cynicism_, on chemistry's reputation for usefulness. They harnessed the energies of _upwardly mobile youths_ who were _willing to gamble_ that a knowledge of science would prove valuable." This is his solitary reference to Liebig, other than that he succeeded Zimmerman in teaching chemistry at Giessen University (p. 243). (The italics shown above are mine and should not be attributed to Hufbauer.)

of corporate espionage, or outright patent infringement, such theft and re-theft would be difficult today.

It was Antoine Lavoisier who pointed out the inability of phlogiston to explain why metals became heavier when "calcined" (today we would say oxidized), which led to the discovery of oxygen. He proved in 1776 that it was oxygen from the air that accounted for the increase in weight of a metal when calcined (oxidized). This was after he had met with Joseph Priestly (1733–1804) in Paris in 1774 and referred to Priestly's so-called dephlogistcated air as "vital air." Later it was called oxygen. So great was Lavoisier's presence in the scientific community of his day that it would be difficult not to refer to him as "the father of chemistry."

THE YOUNG CHEMIST TURNED INDUSTRIALIST

Having a promising career as an academic, Perkin turned his back on academia (which was considered akin to blasphemy at the time) to become an industrialist and demonstrate to the world that high-volume quantities of commercially valuable products could be obtained through organic synthesis using coal tar as a feedstock material. With borrowed money, he founded a company that would eventually lead to the restructuring of the British chemical industry and formation in 1926 of chemical giant Imperial Chemical Industries. The creation of ICI was seen as essential in order for the British to compete against the German chemical behemoth, I.G. Farben, which had emerged in 1916 through a series of mergers and had expanded through an additional series of mergers in 1925.

THE ASPIRIN WARS

Acetanilide is a dye intermediate made by acetylating aniline in a reaction with acetic acid. The acetyl group from acetic acid takes the place of one of the hydrogen atoms in the amine group that is attached to the benzene ring of aniline. The presence of this acetyl group in a sense "deactivates" the aromatic ring and protects it from electrophilic attack while it participates in additional chemical reactions as part of an overall synthesis.

Acetanilide was first used as a medicine in the Alsatian city of Strasbourg, which belonged to France in 1853 but is now the capital city of the institutions of the European Union, e.g., the European Parliament, etc. Strasbourg is also the city where Charles Wurtz, August von Hofmann's classmate at the University of Giessen, went to work with the great Alsatian chemist and professor Dr. Charles Frederic Gerhardt, who was the first to synthesize acetylsalicylic acid in 1853 (Wurtz's experiments together with Hofmann's own work established the link between the reactive characteristics of the amines as bases like ammonia).

So it was that in the formerly French Strasbourg in 1886, three decades later now and belonging to the German empire, two medical interns (Cahn and Hepp) requested a supply of naphthalene to treat a case of intestinal parasites but mistakenly received a shipment of acetanilide and administered it to their patient. They found that it did not cure the patient of parasites, but it did dramatically reduce the patient's fever. Hence, the remarkable antipyretic properties (fever reduction) of acetanilide were discovered—by accident! This information reached Kalle & Co., the specialty dyestuffs manufacturer that began in 1864 across the Rhine in Biebrich, Germany, and they immediately began to market acetanilide as an antipyretic under the trade name Antifebrin. (Today, Biebrich is a heavily industrialized suburb of Wiesbaden, but it was founded in 874 as the imperial stronghold of Biburk following the Treaty of Verdun in 843 that had divided Charlemagne's empire and marks the beginning of France. Biebrich also became the principal residence of the Calvinist Counts of Nassau, related by blood to William of Orange). Kalle & Co. is today a subsidiary of Hoechst AG and thus a part of the German/ French conglomerate Aventis.

THE MODERN ERA

COSTS AND PRICING ISSUES

The global pharmaceutical industry today is dominated by about 20 companies, which together control about **70%** of worldwide pharmaceutical sales. These companies are large, integrated, research-based firms with huge sales organizations and vast resources. They include such companies as Pfizer, Glaxo SmithKline, AstraZeneca, Aventis, Merck, Novartis, and Bristol-Myers Squibb. The top companies are either American or European, with Takeda Chemical Industries, the largest Japanese pharmaceutical company, ranked fifteenth in the world in terms of 1999 to 2000 sales.

In spite of this sales dominance by so few companies, the global pharmaceutical industry is exceptionally dynamic and complex in terms of the relationships between these, and thousands of other, albeit much smaller companies. Understanding the roles played by these smaller firms is crucial to understanding the structure and dynamics of the global pharmaceutical industry.

Including the world's top 20 firms, there are approximately 50 firms with sales of over a billion dollars annually, and approximately 70 firms with sales over $500 million. This is still a lot of money in the hands of smaller companies, especially when one considers that profit margins among the smaller firms can be higher than those of the larger firms. There are many more important, but much smaller firms that do not achieve this somewhat artificial level of $500 million in sales annually. They are engaged in a wide range of discovery, development, manufacturing, and/or marketing activities that interface with the activities of the larger firms in intriguing ways.

The modern era in pharmaceutical development and marketing began during the period surrounding World War II.

On a worldwide basis, most large pharmaceutical companies maintain extensive global operations in manufacturing and marketing and much less in research and development. Major research and development activities occur in only about **10** countries of the world, with <u>limited</u> R&D going on in only about 20 more. Consequently, on a worldwide basis, pharmaceutical research and development (R&D) occurs in approximately **30** countries. The reasons for this concentration of R&D efforts are complex and range **from** the <u>educational</u> and other infrastructure requirements necessary to support research and development activities **to** a desire for <u>ownership and control</u> of the so-called fountainhead of new and improved products.

Modern research and development activities require the efforts of literally thousands of highly skilled professionals. Few companies can afford to employ so many of these people as is required, and few countries have the resources to <u>train them</u> in sufficient numbers to maintain important R&D facilities. For the most part, these highly trained professionals choose to live only in countries with a relatively high standard of living. Few countries outside of the U.S., Japan, and Western Europe are capable of supplying the abundance of consumer products and services necessary to keep such people satisfied.

Hank Laskey

Relatively few countries, therefore, have become large depots of the necessary intellectual talent and professional job skills required by the modern pharmaceutical industry.

The labor available in other countries has been suitable for some manufacturing purposes. Once the process to manufacture a particular medicine has been developed, tested, and refined, it is a relatively less complex matter to "follow the recipe" (so to speak) in the future. Much of the manufacturing process therefore can be relocated to other countries with a lower cost of labor. Of course, the decision to directly invest in foreign nations in this manner requires consideration of many other factors than simply the cost of labor. Government stability is a major factor, as are the culture and work ethic of the people. Given imported therapeutic agents, many countries have the **ability** to produce finished products (e.g., pharmaceutical compounding and tablet manufacture), and a much smaller group of countries is able to produce the therapeutic agents themselves. Most of the manufacturing that occurs in this fashion is either in generic form or branded products produced under various licenses.

Finally, what is common in the pharmaceutical industry today as well as in other industries is a form of company known as the "transnational" corporation, which is characterized by diverse, transnational patterns of ownership, transnational financing, transnational R&D, transnational manufacturing, transnational marketing, etc. Virtually every aspect of the company's existence is widely spread over many countries and not just one or a few countries, as is **currently** the case with research and development and <u>much</u> corporate ownership.

THE HIGH COST OF DRUG DISCOVERY AND DEVELOPMENT

It takes both many years and millions of dollars to discover and develop new drugs. Consensus estimates are in the neighborhood of an average 10 to 12 years and $600 million dollars to discover, develop, and bring a new drug to market. Many research and development facilities resemble the size of some universities, and they employ thousands of the most highly educated scientists and technicians in the world, along with all of the support staff necessary to maintain operations. The amount of capital invested in these facilities can be staggering. Equipment is very expensive. Some estimates put the average total cost of equipping a single scientist in an existing facility at $500,000. Others say it is higher than that, not counting annual salaries and the costs of fringe benefits. In order to attract and retain such people, the industry is forced to pay above-average wages and other forms of compensation, including ownership of intellectual property, bonuses, and stock options. The competition among pharmaceutical companies for the best people is fierce and unrelenting. It is not difficult for highly trained and experienced personnel with a strong knowledge of the industry to obtain outside offers of employment and career advancement. In fact, it happens on a regular basis.

Pharmaceutical companies employ highly advanced technologies to synthesize or otherwise create new chemical entities as candidates for new drug development. Even with the advent of combinatorial chemistry, rational drug design, and more powerful computers to resolve complex molecular structures, drug discovery is still largely a numbers game. The greater the number of chemical entities created, the greater the probability that one will possess the desired biological profile. As a result, pharmaceutical companies create thousands of new chemical entities and screen them *en masse* for biological activity. It is a repetitive, often tedious, process. It typically takes years to discover a new molecule that might represent a significant improvement over existing medications. Even after a candidate has been found, it will be many more years in development and testing in human subjects according to clinical protocols mandated by regulatory authorities. The costs associated with these clinical trials can be higher by several orders of magnitude than the entire discovery process that precedes them.

The fundamental problem seems to be that nobody really wants to buy or take medicines. In this context, pharmaceuticals are much like cemetery plots—you only have to use them when you are sick (or worse), and who wants to be sick? Pharmaceuticals can never be priced "right" because nobody really wants to buy them in the first place. There is only a price you don't want to pay, a "too-high" price, when you have little or no choice in the matter—and its either pay or be sick! People feel instinctively that this is somewhat unfair, that it is a kind of "price gouging" from the outset, companies preying upon the infirm. As a result, there is a fundamentally negative view of the pharmaceutical industry that is fairly widespread and politicians frequently seize upon this view as an opportunity to ingratiate themselves with voters by attacking the industry. For pharmaceutical companies, it is an almost constant uphill battle.

PHARMACEUTICAL PRICE CONTROLS

Most of the countries of the world exercise some form of pharmaceutical price control. In the United States, powerful managed care organizations (MCOs) and pharmacy benefit managers (PBMs) negotiate prices with manufacturers. Although the discounts they obtain are not always or fully passed on to consumers or their health insurance companies, they can refuse to list or include a particular product on their formularies because of its price and thereby exercise de-facto control over a manufacturer's ability to set price.

Formularies are approved lists of prescription pharmaceuticals that physicians, directed by managed care organizations, are allowed to select from and prescribe for member patients. Manufacturers place a very high priority on having their products listed on various formularies. No other single factor can determine the success of a particular drug in a market so much as its approval on these approved lists.

This same basic mechanism is employed in many foreign countries as part of their national health insurance or reimbursement programs. In order to qualify for reimbursement by the national insurance program, a drug must appear on the program's formulary. As a condition for placing a drug on a national formulary, an agency within the government negotiates the retail price of every drug with its manufacturer, or supplier.

PREDICTIONS FOR THE FUTURE

In aggregate, the worldwide pharmaceutical industry will continue to be characterized by a number of factors that include: (1) increased patient or consumer access to high-quality health care information; (2) a large number of complex technical factors involved in biological experiments generally, particularly in biotechnology and genomics; (3) managements, which are usually technically oriented; (4) an inability to predict the discovery of the next new drug; (5) extended time horizons necessary to discover, develop, and market new medicines; (6) a high degree of financial risk and uncertainty associated with drug discovery and development; (7) particularly high costs associated with drug testing and clinical trials; (8) predominant use of multi-stage, **batch** processing operations for drug manufacturing rather than continuous flow processes; (9) high levels of product purity under exacting standards; (10) a large number of restrictive government regulations on drug development, manufacturing, and marketing; (11) a range of increasingly complex issues associated with global regulatory compliance despite increased efforts at international harmonization; (12) high promotional costs, expanded direct-to-consumer (DTC) advertising, professional selling and sales force-related expenses; (13) increased use of generic drugs as well as brand-name pharmaceuticals and trademarks; (14) higher costs and fees associated with patent protection and enforcement litigation; (15) increased worldwide pressure to lower costs and reduce prices, especially the expanding worldwide adoption and influence of managed care and pharmacy benefit management schemes; (16) an increased attention to disease management, quality of life, and pharmacoeconomics-related issues; and (17) increased demand and trends toward expanded or nationalized health insurance coverage and socialized medicine.

Most important, it is likely that the highly charged political environment surrounding the pharmaceutical industry is likely to remain. Relative to other industries, the political environment is unusually intense for this industry. So, as we look at the external environment facing the pharmaceutical industry for the foreseeable future, we see primarily politics that are unusually intense and government regulations that are particularly extensive. Few other industries face similar circumstances.

BIBLIOGRAPHY

Aftalion, Fred (2001). *A History of the International Chemical Industry: From the "Early Days" to 2000*, 2nd edition, translated by Otto Theodor Benfry. Philadelphia: Chemical Heritage Press.

Aglietta, Michel (2000). A Theory of Capitalist Regulation: The US Experience. New York, NY. Verso.

Agrawal, Madhu(1999). Global Competitivenessinthe Pharmaceutical Industry: The Effect of National Regulatory, Economic, and Market Factors. Binghamton, NY: Pharmaceutical Products Press.

Anderson, Nils Jr. and Mark W. DeLawyer (1995). Chemicals, Metals and Men: Gas, Chemicals and Coke: A Bird's-Eye View of the Materials that Make the World Go Round. New York: Vantage Press.

Antony, Arthur (1979). *Guide to Basic Information Sources in Chemistry.* New York, NY. John Wiley & Sons Inc.

Arora, Ashish, Ralph Landau, and Nathan Rosenberg (1998). *Chemicals and Long-Term Economic Growth: Insights from the Chemical Industry.* New York: John Wiley & Sons.

Baker, Sidney MacDonald and Karen Baar (2000). *The Circadian Prescription.* New York, NY: G.D. Putnam's Sons

Bartley, W., L.M. Birt and P. Banks (1968). *The Biochemistry of the Tissues.* London, UK: John Wiley & Sons, Ltd.

Bauman, Robert P., Peter Jackson, and Joanne T. Lawrence (1997). *From Promise to Performance: A Journey of Transformation at SmithKline Beecham.* Boston, MA: Harvard Business School Press.

Benedict, Ruth (1946). *The Sword and the Chrysanthemum.* Boston, MA: Houghton Miff lin Company.

Bély, Lucien (2001). *The History of France.* Paris: Jean-Paul Gisserot, publishers.

Bian, Tonda R. (1997). *The Drug Lords: America's Pharmaceutical Cartel.* Kalamazoo, MI: No Barriers Publishing.

Biel, Timothy Levi (1997). *The Importance of Charlemagne.* San Diego, CA. Lucent Books.

Blackett, Tom and Rebecca Robins (2001). Brand Medicine: The Role of Branding in the Pharmaceutical Industry. New York: Palgrave.

Bluche, Francois (1990). *Louis XIV,* translated by Mark Greengrass. New York: Franklin Watts.

Booth, Martin (1996). *Opium: A History.* London, UK. Simon and Schuster, Ltd.

Bowden, Mary Ellen and John Kenly Smith (1994). American Chemical Enterprise: A Perspective on 100 Years of Innovation to Commemorate the Centennial of the Society of Chemical Industry (American Section). Philadelphia, PA: Chemical Heritage Foundation.

Bowden, Mary Ellen (1997). *Chemistry is Electric.* Philadelphia, PA: Chemical Heritage Foundation.

Boyer, Robert and Yves Saillard (2002). Regulation Theory: The State of the Art. London, UK. Routledge.

Brock, William H. (2000). *The Chemical Tree: A History of Chemistry.* New York: W.W. Norton & Company.

Burger, Alfred (1995). *Understanding Medications: What the Label Doesn't Tell You.* Washington, D.C.: American Chemical Society.

Burton Goldberg Group (1999). *Alternative Medicine: The Definitive Guide.* Tiburon, CA. Future Medicine Publishing Inc.

Business History Group Inc. (2001). *A Foundation for Growth: The History of American Home Products Corporation.* Madison, NJ: American Home Products Corporation.

Chandler, Alfred D. (1990). *Scale and Scope: The Dynamics of Industrial Capitalism.* Cambridge, MA: Harvard University Press.

Chemistry Looks to the Future. (1990). Ludwigshafen, FRG: BASF Aktiengesellschaft.

Chenier, Philip J. (1992). *Survey of Industrial Chemistry: 2nd Revised Edition.* Danvers, MA. John Wiley & Sons Inc.

Churchill, Winston S. (1987). Memoirs of The Second World War: An Abridgement of the six volumes of The Second World War. Boston, MA: Houghton Miff lin Company.

Code of Federal Regulations and ICH Guidelines. (April 1, 2000). Philadelphia: Barnett International.

Cody, Thomas G. (1994). *Innovating for Health: The Story of Baxter International.* Deerfield, IL. Baxter International Inc.

Commonwealth Secretariat (2001). *A Guide to the European Market for Medicinal Plants and Extracts.* London, UK: The Commonwealth Secretariat.

Compilation of Laws Enforced by the U.S. Food and Drug Administration and Related Statues: Volume One (1996). Pittsburgh, PA: U.S. Government Printing Office.

Compilation of Laws Enforced by the U.S. Food and Drug Administration and Related Statues: Volume Two (1996). Pittsburgh, PA: U.S. Government Printing Office.

Cray, William C. (1984). *Miles 1884-1984: A Centennial History.* Englewood, Cliffs, NJ. Prentice-Hall Inc.

Cussler, E. L. and G.D. Moggridge (2001). *Chemical Product Design.* Cambridge, UK: Cambridge University Press.

Danzon, Patricia M. (1997). Pharmaceutical Price Regulation: National Policies versus Global Interests. Washington, DC. AEI Press.

Davis, Natalie Zemon (1975). *Society and Culture in Early Modern France.* Stanford, CA: Stanford University Press.

Davis, Peter (1996). Contested Ground: Public Purpose and Private Interest in the Regulation of Prescription Drugs. New York: Oxford University Press.

Dogramatzis, Dimitris (2002). *Pharmaceutical Marketing: A Practical Guide.* Denver, CO. HIS Health Group.

DuBois, Josiah E. Jr. and Edward Johnson (1952). The Devil's Chemists: 24 Conspirators of the International Farben Cartel who Manufacture Wars. Boston, MA: Beacon Press.

Durant, Will and Ariel (1944). *The Story of Civilization Volume 3: Caesar and Christ:* New York, NY: Simon & Schuster.

Durant, Will and Ariel (1950). *The Story of Civilization Volume 4: The Age of Faith:* New York, NY: Simon & Schuster.

Durant, Will and Ariel (1965). *The Story of Civilization Volume 9: The Age of Voltaire:* New York, NY: Simon & Schuster.

Durant, Will and Ariel (1967). *The Story of Civilization Volume 10: Rousseau and Revolution.* New York, NY: Simon & Schuster.

Emsley, John (2001). *Nature's Building Blocks: An A-Z Guide to the Elements.* New York: Oxford University Press.

Fisher, David (2000). *In Good Company: Warner-Lambert, A Family Portrait.* Morris Plains, NJ: Warner-Lambert Press.

Foster, Lawrence G. (1999). *Robert Wood Johnson: The Gentleman Rebel.* State College, PA: Lilian Press.

Fraser, David (2000). *Frederick the Great.* New York, NY: Penguin Putnam Inc.

Friedman, David (1988). The Misunderstood Miracle: Industrial Development and Political Change in Japan. Ithaca, NY: Cornell University Press.

Gambardella, Alfonso (1995). Science and Innovation: The U.S. Pharmaceutical Industry During the 1980s. New York: Cambridge University Press.

Garfield, Simon (2001). *Mauve: How One Man Invented a Color that Changed the World.* New York: W.W. Norton & Company.

Gereffi, Gary (1983). *The Pharmaceutical Industry and Dependency in the Third World.* Princeton, NJ: Princeton University Press.

Goerlitz, Walter (1995). *History of the German General Staff: 1657-1945,* translated by Brian Battershaw. New York: Barnes and Noble Books.

Goodwin, Jason (1998). *Lords of the Horizons: A History of the Ottoman Empire.* New York, NY. Henry Holt and Company.

Greenberg, Arthur (2000). A Chemical History Tour: Picturing Chemistry from Alchemy to Modern Molecular Science. New York, NY. Wiley-Interscience.

Grubb, Philip W (1999). Patents for Chemicals, Pharmaceuticals and Biotechnology: Fundamentals of Global Law, Practice and Strategy. New York: Oxford University Press.

Hodges, Richard (2000). *Towns and Trade in the Age of Charlemagne.* London, UK. Gerald Duckworth & Co., Ltd.

Hahn, Peter A. (1968). *Chemicals from Fermentation.* Garden City, NY: Doubleday and Company Inc.

Haufbauer, Karl (1982). *The Formation of the German Chemical Community: 1720-1095.* Berkeley, CA: University of California Press.

Hardman, Joel G., Lee E. Limbird, and Alfred Goodman Gilman (2001). *Goodman & Gilman's The Pharmacological Basis of Therapeutics,* 10th edition. New York: McGraw-Hill.

Hargittai, Istvan (2002). *The Road to Stockholm.* Oxford, UK: Oxford University Press.

Heilbroner, Robert L. (1968). The Worldly Philosophers: The Lives, Times, and Ideas of the Great Economic Thinkers. New York, NY. Simon and Schuster.

Heitmann, John A. and David J. Rhees (1990). *Scaling Up: Science, Engineering, and the American Chemical Industry.* Philadelphia, PA. Beckman Center for the History of Chemistry.

Helms, Robert B. (1996). *Competitive Strategies in the Pharmaceutical Industry.* Washington, D.C.: American Enterprise Institute.

Herod, T.D. (2001). *Chemicals Used by Each Industry Group.* Toledo: OH. T.D. Herod

Herold, J. Christopher (1962). *The Horizon Book of The Age of Napoleon.* New York, NY: American Heritage Publishing Co. Inc.

Herrigel, Gary (1996). *Industrial Constructions: The Sources of German Industrial Power.* New York: Cambridge University Press.

Heywood, Colin (1992*). The Development of the French Economy: 1750-1914.* New York: Cambridge University Press.

Hounshell, David A. and John Kenly Smith, Jr. *Science and Corporate Strategy: DuPont R&D, 1902-1980.* New York: Cambridge University Press.

Howarth, David (1993). *1066 The Year of the Conquest,* New York, NY. Barnes and Noble Books.

Huf bauer, Karl (1982). *The Formation of the German Chemical Community (1720-1795).* Berkeley, California: University of California Press.

Huntington, Samuel P. (1998). *The Clash of Civilizations and the Remaking of World Order.* New York, NY: Touchstone Books.

Iizuku, Hiroshi and Atsushi Naito (1967). *Microbial Transformation of Steroids and Alkaloids.* State College, PA: University Park Press.

Information Services Manual 2002. Plymouth Meeting, PA. IMS Health.

James, Edward (1988). *The Franks.* New York, NY. Basil Blackwell Inc.

James, Robert Rhodes (1994). *Henry Wellcome.* London, UK. Hodder and Stoughton Ltd.

Jensen, Mead L. and Alan M. Bateman (1981). *Economic Mineral Deposits.* New York, NY: John Wiley & Sons.

Julien, Robert M. (1981). *A Primer of Drug Action.* San Francisco, CA: W. H. Freeman and Company.

Kelly, J. M. (1997). *A Short History of Western Legal Theory.* Oxford, NY: Clarendon Press.

Kennedy, Paul (1987). The Rise and Fall of the Great Powers: Economic Change and Military Conf lict from 1500 to 2000. New York: Random House.

Klefenz, Heinrich (2002). *Industrial Pharmaceutical Biotechnology.* Weinheim, FRG: Wiley-VCH.

Kolassa, E.M. (1997). *Elements of Pharmaceutical Pricing.* New York, NY: The Pharmaceutical Products Press.

Lad, Vasant (1984). *Ayurveda: The Science of Self-Healing.* Twin Lakes, WI. Lotus Press.

Landau, Ralph, Basil Achilladelis, and Alexander Scriabine (1999). *Pharmaceutical Innovation: Revolutionizing Human Health.* Philadelphia: Chemical Heritage Press.

Landes, David S. (1969). The Unbound Prometheus: Technological Change and Industrial Development in Western Europe from 1750 to the Present. New York: Cambridge University Press.

Lane, Christel (1995). Industry and Society in Europe: Stability and Change in Britain, Germany and France. Brookfield, VT: Edward Elgar Publishing Company.

Lanz, Kurt (1980). *Around the World with Chemistry.* New York, NY: McGraw-Hill Book Company.

Lark, Susan M. and James A. Richards (2000). *The Chemistry of Success.* San Francisco, CA: Bay Books

Lee, Stan and Graham Robinson (1995). *Process Development: Fine Chemicals from Grams to Kilograms.* Oxford, UK: Oxford University Press.

Lewis, Walter H. and Memory P.F. Elvin-Lewis (1977). *Medical Botany: Plants Affecting Man's Health.* New York, NY: John Wiley & Sons.

Lidstone, John and Janice MacLennan (1999). *Marketing Planning for the Pharmaceutical Industry.* Brookfield, VT: Gower Publishing.

Lodge, Juliet (1989). *The European Community and the Challenge of the Future.* New York, NY: St. Martins Press Inc.

Lottman, Herbert R. (1995). The French Rothschilds: The Great Banking Dynasty Through Two Turbulent Centuries. New York: Crown Publishers.

MacArthur, Brian (1999). *The Penguin Book of Twentieth-Century Speeches.* New York, NY: Penguin Books, Ltd.

Madison, James H. (1989). *Eli Lilly: A Life, 1885-1977.* Indianapolis, IN: Indiana Historical Society.

Mann, Charles C. and Mark L. Plummer (1991). *The Aspirin Wars: Money, Medicine, and 100 years of Rampant Competition.* New York, NY: Alfred A. Knopf Inc.

Mann, Golo (1968). *The History of Germany Since 1789.* London, UK: Pimlico.

Martinelli, Alberto (1991). International Markets and Global Firms: A Comparative Study of Organized Business in the Chemical Industry. London, UK. Sage Publishing Inc.

Marx, Karl (1867). *Das Kapital: A Critique of Political Economy.* Frederich Engels (editor), condensed by Serge L. Levitsky, 2000 printing. Washington, D.C.: Regnery Publishing Inc.

Merck Index. Thirteenth Edition. (2001). Whitehouse Station, NJ: Merck & Co. Inc.

Miller, Judith, Stephen Engelberg and William Broad (2001). *Germs: Biological Weapons and America's Secret War.* New York, NY. Simon & Schuster

Millonig, Marsha K., Tracy Casteuble, Susan Heffner, Heather Johnston, and Lindsay Bowen (2001). *Pharmaceutical and Healthcare Distribution: Evolving Different Capabilities to Meet New Market Needs.* Reston, VA: Healthcare Distribution Management Association.

Moulijn, Jacob A., Michiel Makkee and Annelies Van Diepen (2001). *Chemical Process Technology.* New York, NY: John Wiley & Sons, Ltd.

BIBLIOGRAPHY

Nelson, Gary L. (1988). *Pharmaceutical Company Histories: Volume One.* Bismarck, ND: Woodbine Publishing.

Newfarmer, Richard S. (1985). Profits, Progress and Poverty: Case Studies of International Industries in Latin America. Notre Dame, IN. Notre Dame Press.

Noble, David F. (1977). America by Design: Science, Technology, and the Rise of Corporate Capitalism. New York: Oxford University Press.

Ohsono, Tomokazu (1995). Charting Japanese Industry: A Graphical Guide to Corporate and Market Structures. London: Cassell.

Parker, Geoffrey (1988). *The Thirty Years' War.* New York: Military Heritage Press.

Payer, Lynn (1988). Medicine and Culture: Varieties of Treatment in the United States, England, West Germany, and France. New York: Henry Holt and Company.

Perstein, Rick (2001). Before the Storm: Barry Goldwater and the Unmaking of the American Consensus. New York, NY. Hill and Wang. Pharmaceutical and Healthcare Distribution: Evolving Different Capabilities to Meet New Market Needs. (2001) IMS Health.

Physicians' Desk Reference. (2002). 56th ed., Montvale, NJ: Medical Economics Company.

PDR for Herbal Medicines. (2000). 2nd ed., Montvale, NJ: Medical Economics Company.

Porter, Roy (1997). The Greatest Benefit to Mankind: A Medical History of Humanity. New York: W.W. Norton & Company.

Robbins-Roth, Cynthia (2000). *From Alchemy to IPO: The Business of Biotechnology*. Cambridge, Massachusetts: Perseus Publishing.

Rodengen, Jeffrey L. (1998). *The Legend of Pfizer*. Fort Lauderdale, FL: Write Stuff Syndicate.

Roussel, Philip A., Kamal N. Saad and Tamara J. Erickson (1991). *Third Generation R&D: Managing the Link to Corporate Strategy*. Boston, MA: Harvard Business School Press.

Salerni, O. LeRoy (1976). *Natural and Synthetic Organic Medicinal Compounds*. St. Louise, MO. The C.V. Mosby Company.

Scherer, F.M. (1996). *Industry Structure, Strategy, and Public Policy*. New York: HarperCollins College Publishers.

Schildhauer, Johannes (1988). *The Hansa: History and Culture*, translated by Katherine Vanovitch. New York: Dorset Press.

Schmidl, Mary K. and Theodore P. Labuza (2000). *Essentials of Functional Foods*. Gaithersburg, Maryland: Aspen Publishers Inc.

Shonfield, Andrew (1969). Modern Capitalism: The Changing Balance of Public & Private Power. London, UK: Oxford University Press.

Schumpeter, Joseph A. (1950). *Capitalism, Socialism and Democracy*. New York, NY: Harper & Brothers Inc.

Schumpeter, Joseph A. (1983). *The Theory of Economic Development.* New Brunswick, NJ: Transaction Publishers.

Schweitzer, Stuart O. (1997). *Pharmaceutical Economics and Policy.* New York, NY: Oxford University Press.

Sebastian, Anton (2000). Dates in Medicine: A Chronological Record of Medical Progress over Three Millennia. Pearl River, NY: Parthenon Publishing.

Shargel, Leon, Alan H. Mutnick, Paul F. Souney and Larry N. Swanson (2001). *Comprehensive Pharmacy Review.* Baltimore, MD: Lippincott Williams & Wilkins.

Smith, Adam (1776). *The Wealth of Nations: Books I-III.* New York: Penguin.

Smith, Emil L., Robert L. Hill, I. Robert Lehman, Robert J. Lefkowitz, Philip Handler and Abraham White (1983). *Principles of Biochemistry: Mammalian Biochemistry.* New York, NY: McGraw-Hill Book Company.

Spilker, Bert (1994). Multinational Pharmaceutical Companies: Principles and Practices, 2nd edition. New York: Raven Press.

Spilker, Bert (1991). *Guide to Clinical Trials.* Philadelphia, PA: Lippincott Williams & Wilkins.

Steiner, Richard P. (1986). *Folk Medicine: The Art and the Science.* Washington, D.C.: American Chemical Society.

Stigler, George J. (1983). *The Organization of Industry.* Chicago, IL: University of Chicago Press, Ltd.

Stipp, John L. (1955). *Devil's Diary.* Yellow Springs, OH: The Antioch Press.

Stratton, Andrew (1983). *Energy and Feedstocks in the Chemical Industry.* Chichester, UK: Ellis Horwood Limited.

Stryer, Lubert (1981). *Biochemistry.* New York, NY. W.H. Freeman and Company.

Sturchio, Jeffrey I. (1991). Values and Visions: A Merck Century.

Sturmer, Michael (2000). *The German Empire: 1870-1918.* New York: Modern Library.

Stuttard, John B. (2000). *The New Silk Road: Secrets of Business Success in China Today.* New York, NY: John Wiley and Sons Inc.

Tanner, Ogden (1996). *25 Years of Innovation: The Story of Pfizer Central Research.* Lyme, CT: Greenwich Publishing Group Inc.

Taylor, Nick (2000). Laser: The Inventor, the Nobel Laureate, and the Thirty-year Patent War. New York, NY: Simon & Schuster.

Tyson, Laura D'Andrea (1992). *Who's Bashing Whom? Trade Conf lict in High-Technology Industries.* Washington, DC. Institute for International Economics.

Volkmann, Jean-Charles (2001). *A Chronological Look at the History of France.* Paris, France. Jean-Paul Gisserot.

Waites, Michael J., Meil L. Morgan, John S. Rockey and Gary Higton (2001). *Industrial Microbiology: An Introduction.* Oxford, UK. Blackwell Science Ltd.

Wei, J., T.W. F. Russell and M.W. Swartzlander (1979). *The Structure of the Chemical Processing Industries.* New York, NY: MacGraw-Hill Book Company.

Werner, David, Carol Thuman and Jane Maxwell (1998). *Where There Is No Doctor: A Village Health Care Handbook.* Berkeley, CA: The Hesperian Foundation.

Wheen, Francis (1999). *Karl Marx.* London, UK: Fourth Estate Limited.

Zysman, John (1983). Governments, Markets, and Growth: Financial Systems and the Politics of Industrial Change. Ithaca, NY: Cornell University Press.

Zysman, John and Laura Tyson (1983). American Industry in International Competition: Government Policies and Corporate Strategies. Ithaca, NY: Cornell University Press.